The Poetry of Vision

The Poetry of Vision

Five Eighteenth-Century Poets

Patricia Meyer Spacks

Harvard University Press

Cambridge, Massachusetts

1967

For Barry

Preface

THIS STUDY examines some of the poetry of James Thomson, William Collins, Thomas Gray, Christopher Smart and William Cowper — five eighteenth-century poets of sensibility. Its purpose is not to provide a complete analysis of their work; in most cases I have made no effort to consider a man's poetic production in its entirety. Rather, my intention is to suggest some of the values this poetry holds for the twentieth-century reader by investigating the function in it of visual imagery of various kinds.

The initial research for this book was made possible by the Shirley Farr Fellowship of the American Association of University Women, which I held in 1962–63. I am most grateful for the free time and the research opportunities provided by this fellowship and by the leave simultaneously granted me by Wellesley College. Libraries I worked in at that time included the Wellesley College Library, the Widener and Houghton libraries of Harvard University, and the Cambridge University Library; my thanks are due to the staffs of all these institutions.

Parts of Chapters II, IV and V have appeared, in different form, in *Studies in Romanticism, Studies in Philology, PMLA* and *Studies in English Literature.* I am particularly appreciative of the criticism provided by scholars reading manuscripts for these publications, especially Maynard Mack, whose comments have been invaluable not only in reference to the article he read but as a general guide to critical procedure. I am also indebted to Virginia Fanger, whose fresh reading of the manuscript provided valuable perspective and critical insight; and to my students in English 228 at Wellesley College, for challenge and for illumination. My most profound and long-standing debt is acknowledged by my dedication.

P. M. S.

Wellesley, Massachusetts

Contents

I 🎋

VISION AND MEANING:
An Introduction to the Problem

THE WORK of all five poets considered in this study is extremely uneven. In the case of Christopher Smart, a romantic explanation is tempting: he wrote great poetry when liberated by madness from the restriction of contemporary convention, weaker verse when constrained by the established forms of his time. Yet this account is by no means fully satisfactory when one recalls, for example, the expert manipulation of "poetic diction" in *A Song to David*; and no explanation of even equivalent accuracy readily presents itself for Thomson, Collins, Gray and Cowper.

Whatever the causes of the great inequality of accomplishment these poets display, one of its effects has surely been to encourage critical underestimation of their capacities. The reader who remembers *The Task* or *The Seasons* as a tedious experience is unlikely to be aware of the superb passages such poems contain. An experience of Gray's extreme artifice may make it difficult to catch his note of plangency; Collins's weaker personifications may merge in the mind with Joyce Kilmer's, making it difficult to perceive the visionary energy of his best ones. To reveal the sources of both artistic strength and weakness in these five poets of sensibility, I have chosen to study them in the light of the critical theory and the poetic conventions of their time and with reference to the expectations of the modern close reader. These poets offer a complex set of aesthetic problems, solutions, partial solutions and failures which may be analyzed by concentrating on the meaning in their work of the visual and the visionary.

Samuel Johnson's *Dictionary* (1755) offers four definitions of *vision,* two having to do with perception of the visible, two with more complicated sorts of "seeing."

1. Sight; the faculty of seeing.
2. The act of seeing.
3. A supernatural appearance; a spectre; a phantom.
4. A dream; something shown in a dream. A dream happens to a sleeping, a vision may happen to a waking man. A dream is supposed natural, a vision miraculous; but they are confounded.

The last two definitions describe modes of perceptual expansion: perception of the ordinarily invisible (the supernatural) or the construction of new appearances which may be supposed miraculous, but may also be, like dreams, products of the imagination. *Visionary,* in Johnson's account of it, means, "Imaginary; not real; perceived by the imagination only."

These two notions of vision, as a power for perceiving reality or for expanding it, are both of vital importance to eighteenth-century poetry. The century's critics and poets alike believed that visual imagery was essential to effective poetry.[1] Ernest Tuveson has suggested the similarity between the poetic and the philosophic preoccupation with the imagery of sight: "From the nature of the mind as described by Locke, we could expect a new poetry to be highly visual in nature, for the faculty of sight came to monopolize the analysis of intellectual activity. Since ideas are images, since even complex ideas are multiple pictures, and since understanding itself is a form of perception, the visual and the intellectual would tend to become amalgamated."[2] Distinct visual imagery was almost a defining characteristic of successful poetry in most genres.

But what is the precise nature of "distinct visual imagery"? When Thomson and Cowper describe the same phenomena in roughly similar vocabularies, their descriptions are strikingly different. Here are two accounts of a snowfall, one first included in the second edition of "Winter" (1726; but quoted here in its slightly altered final form), the other from *The Task,* almost sixty years later:

Through the hushed air the whitening shower descends.
At first thin-wavering; till at last the flakes

Vision and Meaning

Fall broad and wide and fast, dimming the day
With a continual flow. The cherished fields
Put on their winter-robe of purest white.
'Tis brightness all; save where the new snow melts
Along the mazy current. Low the woods
Bow their hoar head; and, ere the languid sun
Faint from the west emits his evening ray,
Earth's universal face, deep-hid and chill,
Is one wild dazzling waste, that buries wide
The works of man.

("Winter," ll. 229–240)

Tomorrow brings a change, a total change!
Which even now, though silently perform'd,
And slowly, and by most unfelt, the face
Of universal nature undergoes.
Fast falls a fleecy show'r: the downy flakes,
Descending, and with never-ceasing lapse,
Softly alighting upon all below,
Assimilate all objects. Earth receives
Gladly the thick'ning mantle; and the green
And tender blade, that fear'd the chilling blast,
Escapes unhurt beneath so warm a veil.

(The Task, IV, 322–332)

Thomson's description is far more specific than Cowper's. His scene is concretely imagined: fields, river, woods; Cowper, on the other hand, describes the snow as covering generalized "earth" or even more generalized "universal nature." Thomson wishes us to "see" the process by which the snowfall gains in intensity; and he calls our attention to various modes of contrast: between the "dimming" effect of falling snow and the "brightness" of the snow fallen; similarly, between the dimness of "the languid sun" and the dazzle of the snow on which it shines. There is contrast, too, in the snow's function as adornment for the fields and as burden for the woods; visual contrast between the snow's whiteness and the blackness of its melting on the water; the contrast of paradox in "dazzling waste," with its implication of beauty in desolation.

Cowper considers contrast of a larger and simpler sort. Before the storm description, several lines (311–321) stress the variations in color perceptible in the scene before it is enveloped by snow. The significant contrast is between variety and uniformity; consequently, the emphasis of the account of the actual snowfall is necessarily on its singleness of effect. This snow does not vary its rate of fall; "never-ceasing," inexorable, it simply covers all. There is no need to specify what it envelops; the point is that it "assimilate[s] *all* objects."

Cowper, unlike Thomson, here deals directly with feeling, both sensuous and emotional. Initially, we learn that the snowfall is "by most unfelt." By the end of the passage, we know that earth receives her mantle "gladly," and that snow protects "the green/ And tender blade" which has "feared" the winter's blasts. Feeling is asserted to reside in nature rather than in man, although the reader must feel as well: the "total change" described commands his wonder. The coming of the snow testifies to the benevolence of the natural order; we imagine the "face" of an abstract "universal nature" instead of contemplating the concrete (although of course very general) "universal face" of earth. Thomson's pattern of contrasts and of kinships between the human and natural world (implied by his reference to "cherished fields" and to "the works of man" as well as by his figurative language) is more intricate than Cowper's; and the difference in the patterns, the meanings, which interest the two poets determines the differences in their visual presentations of a natural event.

In their general import, the two descriptions exemplify significant facts about the poets although these selections are by no means fully characteristic. It would be easy to find examples in which Cowper is far more specific than Thomson; such examples are probably more abundant than their opposites. Yet Thomson tends to concern himself with certain sorts of *meaning* (particularly about relations between the human and non-human aspects of nature); Cowper is interested in aesthetic patternings and in certain kinds of *feeling*. For him meaning often derives from feeling; for Thomson the process is usually reversed.

Poetic descriptions must be controlled by poetic purpose; for this reason, to analyze the significance of visual imagery, or its nature, becomes in practice a complex problem. For the modern critic, two large issues seem particularly vital: what exactly is the nature of the "poetry of vision" in the eighteenth century; and to what purposes was the reliance on imagery turned?

Vision and Meaning

The century's criticism elaborately explored the first of these questions. As Meyer Abrams has demonstrated,[3] the notion that poetry, like the other arts, was essentially imitative, offering a reflection of the real world, remained dominant throughout the eighteenth century. If the function of the poet was to imitate, to offer a "speaking picture," one test of his achievement might be the accuracy with which he rendered the world around him. The better the poet, the more exact his reproduction of external reality. "Description is the great test of a Poet's imagination," Hugh Blair pronounced; "and always distinguishes an original from a second-rate Genius." [4] His contemporary Richard Hurd, on the other hand, asserted flatly that "the poet has a world of his own, where experience has less to do, than consistent imagination," that poets, "lyars by profession," do not expect to have their lies believed, but demand imaginative participation from their readers: "a legend, a tale, a tradition, a rumour, a superstition; in short, any thing is enough to be the basis of their air-form'd *visions*." [5]

The diametrically opposed views of poetry implied by these quotations define the poles of eighteenth-century critical theory. It may be safely said that virtually all literary critics and rhetoricians agreed on the fundamental importance of imagery to poetry — although Edmund Burke had serious doubts whether it functioned as most critics supposed, to create images in the mind of the reader. But about the nature of the good poetic image there were divergent views. Many critics assumed that the mark of the good image is its precise, accurate, vivid rendering of actuality.[6] They were pleased to find the accuracy of the naturalist or of the close observer of human nature made part of verse; they admired Thomson for the quality of his recorded observation. The vision they valued was almost scientific in its precision; they might praise a poet by saying that he showed the reader nature as if through a microscope.

Some, on the other hand, valued Hurd's "air-form'd *visions*" far more highly than any rendition of actuality. Although they might agree that precision and vividness of imagery were admirable, they would define the poetic gift as the power to bring such precision and vividness to the creation of compelling fictions. To them images could seem the very *substance* of poetry, not its decoration; they might admire Collins. And they could even — like Hurd — suggest an actual divorce between the world of the poet and that of normal human experience.

Both these views are stated or implied by critics writing throughout the century, all of whom admired the "visual" in poetry, many of whom felt that the "visual" included a great deal. A single critic might praise accuracy in the rendition of images and extravagance in their conception. The vision which records actuality and the visions which can hardly be distinguished from dreams alike provided material for the images which were widely agreed to be a distinguishing mark of poetry. As early as 1757, Robert Andrews rejected the distinction between kinds of images, explaining that the mere existence of images was far more important than their nature, and that imagery is improperly called "one constituent of Poetry . . . ; for it is rather its essence, its soul and body: so that the more or less any composition has of it, it has the more or less of Poetry." [7]

Ideas about the value of different kinds of imagery reflected psychological as well as aesthetic theory. John Locke's description of perception, which of course stresses the importance of the visual, also emphasizes that only a few primary qualities actually reside in the perceived object; the more numerous secondary qualities, such as color, are products of the perceiver's mind.[8] Physical vision, then, cannot offer a precise picture of objective reality; poetic records of that vision are one degree farther removed from reality. Memory and selection have intervened even before the translation of sense impression into language; no matter how "objective" the poet, how concerned to convey the actual appearance of an object, he must offer in his images an impression of his own imaginative processes. So the kind of poetic vision which perceives and describes a tree and the kind which perceives and describes a centaur, or a figure of Revenge, are at opposite ends of a single continuum: the difference between them is one of degree of imaginative activity — more importantly than of kind.

The poet, then, must necessarily alter actuality in his very attempts to render it. But to what extent are his alterations valuable in themselves? For Locke, the specifically poetic resource of "wit" ("lying most in the assemblage of ideas, and putting them together with quickness and variety, wherein can be found any resemblance or congruity, thereby to make up pleasant pictures and agreeable visions in the fancy") was inferior in value to "judgment," the discriminating power which separates ideas on the basis of even the most minute difference, in order "to avoid being misled by similitude." The procedures of judgment, Locke points out, are quite opposed to "metaphor and allusion; wherein for the most part lies that entertainment and pleasantry of wit, which strikes so lively on the fancy, and therefore is so acceptable to all people, because its beauty appears at first sight, and there is required no labour of thought to examine what truth or reason there is in it." [9] Although the "agreeable visions" that wit produces combine ideas gained from experience, they bear little essential relation to actuality; figurative language should be scorned because the reader's response to it, instantaneous and nonintellectual, is likely to mislead him.

But the Lockean psychology did not necessarily imply Locke's value judgments. Joseph Addison quoted approvingly the entire passage from Locke on wit, judgment and metaphor,[10] but his own emphasis in dealing with such matters was far less dominated by the assumption that intellectual activity is the most significant mode of human endeavor.[11] Indeed, he suggested that the poet's deviations from actuality are not only inevitable but valuable, that the poet's selectivity or heightening is vital to the achieved aesthetic effect.[12] It is an easy step from this view to the notion of the poet as maker, his achievements analogous to God's, and Addison took that step, thus placing himself in a long and eloquent critical tradition.[13] The talent of affecting the imagination, he wrote, "has something in it like creation; it bestows a kind of existence, and draws up to the reader's view several objects which are not to be found in being. It makes additions to nature, and gives a greater variety to God's works." [14] Earlier, he had supplied a longer statement of the same arguments:

But because the mind of man requires something more perfect in matter, than what it finds there, and can never meet with any sight in Nature which sufficiently answers its highest ideas of pleasantness; or, in other words, because the imagination can fancy to itself things more great, strange, or beautiful, than the eye ever saw, and is still sensible of some defect in what it has seen; on this account it is the part of the poet to humour the imagination in its own notions, by mending and perfecting Nature where he describes a reality, and by adding greater beauties than are put together in Nature, where he describes a fiction.[15]

According to Addison's own statement, all pleasures of the imagination are based on the sight; no image can be created which does not originate in the physical faculty of vision. But here he points out explicitly the limitations of the eye in comparison with the creative imagination, which can produce visions "more great, strange, or beautiful than the eye ever saw." If the power of sight is in one sense the poet's most important resource, it can also be his limitation if he fails to go beyond it. The poet must, Addison clearly states, exceed verisimilitude even when he describes reality; he must also be willing to deal in fictions.

The progression of ideas which led Addison to his exalted sense of the poet's function was highly characteristic of his contemporaries and even of much later eighteenth-century critics. A mass of the century's literary criticism appears to rest on the assumption that poetic excellence in the creation of images consists in the accuracy with which the external world is reproduced, but such a view was formulated most often in some limited context of concentration on a particular poet, a specific rhetorical device, a special sort of imagery. Critics who concerned themselves with broader aesthetic issues more characteristically echoed Addison in expressing their awareness that the best poet was not the photographer — to use a modern metaphor — but the creative painter. "The mind of man possesses a sort of creative power of its own," wrote Burke,[16] and the fact was widely recognized. William Duff's *Essay on Original Genius* (1767) declares, "That Imagination is the quality of all others most essentially requisite to the existence of Genius, will universally be acknowledged," [17] before offering a detailed account of the activities of imagination. The power of the poet's imagination, Duff explains, is directly associated with the intensity of his feeling, yet poetic images are finally self-justifying, through their beauty, their variety, or their wonder; they prove the presence of imagination and nothing more is required of them.[18] The most impassioned defences of imagination in the eighteenth century tend to resolve themselves in this way. Although they may explore the processes through which images are created — concluding, characteristically, that the poet's emotions are the vital source of his fictions [19] — they most frequently demand of an image only that it vividly exist. Yet one may also note some tendency to assume that the most "creative" images, the ones based on imaginative visions far removed from actuality, must be the best.

The eighteenth-century emphasis on the value of imagery — whatever, precisely, *imagery* might mean — seems in some ways singularly modern: our own era has its exponents of image-making as the supreme poetic skill. "It is better to present one Image in a lifetime than to produce voluminous works," wrote Ezra Pound.[20] "Imagist" poetry, to be sure, is radically different from that of Thomson and Gray, contemporaries admired by the earlier glorifiers of imagery. The discursive elements in the work of the eighteenth-century poets seem now at least as conspicuous as the images, which can no longer excite rapturous praise. Something in the structure and texture of much eighteenth-century verse obscures the vividness and clarity of imagery which it may actually possess; if the value placed on imagery accords with certain modern theories, the *use* made of it bears little relation to twentieth-century theory or practice.

This brings us back to the second fundamental critical problem about the eighteenth-century poetry of vision, a question never fully raised by eighteenth-century critics: to what purposes was the reliance on imagery turned? The question was not asked, clearly, because in general terms its answer was assumed: imagery was instrumental in fulfilling the functions of poetry, to please and to instruct. Perhaps the most eloquent statement of this general view comes from Thomas Sprat, who provides a strong defense of "the Ornaments of speaking" in the very act of rejecting them. He explains the original function of such ornaments: "to describe *Goodness, Honesty, Obedience*; in larger, fairer, and more moving Images: to represent *Truth,* cloth'd with Bodies; and to bring *Knowledg* back again to our very senses, from whence it was at first deriv'd to our understandings." [21] Now, however, Sprat continues, language, like men, is grown corrupt, and figurative language no longer serves its proper purpose; for this reason it must be abandoned. Fénelon, on the other hand, with a similar conviction of "the Degeneracy of human Nature," believes that imagery provides

9

the only feasible means for keeping a reader's attention on abstract truth.[22] The end of poetry was agreed to be moral instruction; imagery provided a method for achieving this end.

This large and vague assumption about the place of imagery, however, is hardly adequate to explain its various functions in the actual poetry of the eighteenth century, or its various sorts of success and failure. In 1817, some appropriate questions about function were finally asked — fully answered, rather, without being asked. Samuel Taylor Coleridge, in *Biographia Literaria,* wrote, that images, however beautiful or accurate, "do not of themselves characterize the poet. They become proofs of original genius only as far as they are modified by a predominant passion; or by associated thoughts or images awakened by that passion; or when they have the effect of reducing multitude to unity, or succession to an instant; or lastly, when a human and intellectual life is transferred to them from the poet's own spirit." [23]

In an obvious sense, Coleridge's remarks seem a logical development of ideas articulated from the mid-eighteenth century on, not a departure from them. Bishop Lowth and William Duff had both recognized the connection between the poet's passions and the nature of the images he creates. Yet the shift of emphasis in Coleridge's view exemplifies a real imaginative leap. There is a vast gap between the idea that interesting images are the product of passion and the idea that they are interesting *only as far as* they manifest passion or otherwise reveal the poet's mental and emotional processes. The specific functions here accorded to imagery are all aspects of the poet's self-revelation; the new specificity about the meaning of images is part of a new interest in the individual poet and the way in which his essential being is exposed by his utterance. It is, in short, a single manifestation of the general shift Professor Abrams has documented from the imitative to the expressive theory of poetry.

Yet it would be a mistake to assume the poetry waited upon criticism before becoming, in fact, "expressive." When one examines the poetry of the eighteenth century, after its opening two decades, that poetry which Coleridge, on the whole, patronized or actively scorned, it seems surprising that the view Coleridge articulated had to wait so long to find statement: it is implied by a good deal of the verse written between 1726 and 1800, which manipulates imagery in elaborate ways to express emotion or to stimulate "associated thoughts" or to sum up and emblemize multiplicity or to convey the "spirit" of its author. Nor does this paraphrase of Coleridge fully sum up the variety of purposes for which imagery was actually employed, the ways in which it was used. Of course poetic practice is characteristically in advance of theory. Wordsworth, Coleridge, Pound or Wallace Stevens may define, explain and justify his own experimentation, but less theoretically oriented poets have frequently created a quiet revolution long before the critics realized it had taken place. The eighteenth century was, in some respects, a period of such revolution; its nature, and its relation to contemporary critical theory, are well worth examining.

We know a good deal already about the language of eighteenth-century poetry. It has long been recognized that the poets of the 1700's did not, after all, rely solely on an artificial diction which they suddenly discarded in 1798. Pope's varied vocabulary has been analyzed and admired, his use of classic rhetorical devices examined; the philosophical implications of periphrasis have been explored; we know about the rhetoric of the heroic couplet; we have statistical records of the proportions of nouns, verbs and adjectives and of the most frequently used words in the major poetry of the age. But the "sublime" poets, the poets of sensibility, have been less thoroughly examined than their predecessors in the "line of wit," and many questions about poetic language in use remain yet unanswered. What is the relation between critical theory and poetic practice in regard to imagery? "Judgment begets the strength and structure, and Fancy begets the ornaments of a Poem," wrote Thomas Hobbes, in 1650.[24] A hundred years later, "fancy" had assumed a far more important place in critical theory; but what was its place in the actual writing of poetry? Why, when rhetorical theory insisted so emphatically on the poetic value of conciseness, was the actual poetry determinedly diffuse? (One recalls Dr. Johnson's account of reading aloud only every other line of *The Seasons,* to the admiration of the listeners.) To what extent could the poetic language of the eighteenth century be individualized? Such questions can only be answered by close examination of the century's poetry, in conjunction with its theory.

As subjects for such examination Thomson, Collins, Gray, Smart and Cowper seem obvious choices. All wrote the poetry of sensibility; although all except Collins made at least brief excursions into satire, their main poetic achievement is verse of feeling and description. They span three-quarters of the century, from 1726 (when "Winter," the first part of *The Seasons,* was published) to 1799, when Cowper wrote "The Castaway." All rely heavily on visual imagery of one sort or another: cursory examination of their work suggests that Thomson and Cowper depend more on recorded visions of reality; Collins and Smart are "visionary" in a fashion which may take them far from actuality; Gray occupies a middle position, employing both kinds of vision. Through analysis of these poets' work, and of the theoretical commentary which surrounded it, we may hope to discover a good deal of what, precisely, comprised the "visual" in eighteenth-century poetry; how vision was expressed and used; how adequate the poetic resources of the period were to its poetic aims.

II 🌺

JAMES THOMSON:
The Dominance of Meaning

THE IMMEDIATE aesthetic rationale for such a poem as *The Seasons* was described by Addison, in one of his papers on the pleasures of the imagination, fourteen years before James Thomson published "Winter." "If we consider the works of Nature and art, as they are qualified to entertain the imagination," wrote Addison,

we shall find the last very defective, in comparison of the former; for though they may sometimes appear as beautiful or strange, they can have nothing in them of the vastness and immensity which afford so great an entertainment to the mind of the beholder. The one may be as polite and delicate as the other, but can never show herself so august and magnificent in the design. There is something more bold and masterly in the rough, careless strokes of Nature, than in the nice touches and embellishments of art. . . . For this reason we always find the poet in love with a country life, where Nature appears in the greatest perfection, and furnishes out all those scenes that are most apt to delight the imagination.[1]

Thomson's well-known self-justification for "Winter" has similar implications:

I know no subject more elevating, more amusing; more ready to awake the poetical enthusiasm, the philosophical reflection, and the moral sentiment, than the works of Nature. Where can we meet with such variety, such beauty, such magnificence? All that enlarges and transports the soul! What more inspiring than a calm, wide survey of them? . . . How gay looks the Spring! how glorious the Summer! how pleasing the Autumn! and how venerable the Winter! — But there is no thinking of these things without breaking out into poetry; which is, by-the-by, a plain and undeniable argument of their superior excellence.[2]

Although *The Seasons* was early admired for its fine sentiments, it clearly exercised its greatest influence as a work of natural description.[3] Thomson himself, however, soon became aware of the essential impossibility of recording actuality in poetry. "Spring" (1728) contains a revealing passage (quoted here in its slightly altered final form):

> But who can paint
> Like Nature? Can imagination boast,
> Amid its gay creation, hues like hers?
> Or can it mix them with that matchless skill,
> And lose them in each other, as appears
> In every bud that blows? If fancy then
> Unequal fails beneath the pleasing task,
> Ah, what shall language do?
>
> (ll. 468–475)

That the eye can discriminate more colors than language can define was an eighteenth-century truism. Thomson, however, here goes further, to suggest that the limitation exists in the imagination — the human re-creative power — as well as in language. The task of accurate poetic description is by definition impossible. Yet this is the task Thomson set himself, and for its accomplishment he was widely praised; indeed, John Aikin, late in the eighteenth century, asserted that the success of *The Seasons* proves the value of description as "the sole object of a poem." [4] Early in the century Fénelon, after insisting that "The Perfection of Poetry itself . . . depends on a full and lively Description of Things in all their Circumstances," had added that this truth does not imply that reality should be described in all its individual circumstances. "We shou'd represent nothing to the Hearers but what deserves their Attention; and help's [*sic*] to give a clear and just Idea of the Things we describe." [5] But before 1800 particularity of description had become a poetic ideal (although obviously other qualities were also demanded of description), and for this shift in taste Thomson was at least partly responsible. "Some Criticks have supposed, that poetry can only deal in generals," wrote John Scott of Amwell, "or in other words, that it cannot subsist with any very minute specification of particulars. To such, this passage [the description of birds building their nests, from "Spring"] might well be produced as a proof, that their opinion is erroneous." [6] Joseph Warton, another admirer of Thomson, is yet more emphatic: "A minute and particular enumeration of circumstances judiciously selected, is what chiefly discriminates poetry from history, and renders the former, for that reason, a more close and faithful representation of nature than the latter." [7] Thomson repeatedly figures as the supporting example for such a point of view. He is praised because, in a passage of landscape description, "It is as if the range of the eye were, at once enlarged by the aid of the telescope, and every object magnified by the microscope." [8] As early as 1739, a rhetoric intended for school boys defines the figure of "vision" as "a Representation of Things distant and past as if seen and present," and advises its readers to see *The Seasons* for the best examples of the figure.[9]

If there was little disagreement in Thomson's own century about his skill at detailed, accurate description (only more recently has it been argued that his skill is really the evocation of general scenes rather than the delineation of particularity [10]), there was yet room for dissatisfaction with Thomson specifically as a descriptive poet. The case against him is eloquently put by John Pinkerton: "The objects which he exhibits appear in those lights exactly in which their forms and colours have the most pleasing effect which they can produce to the eye. *But, to say the truth, I do not see that he has improved their beauties with too much of that magic colouring with which the fancy of the impassioned inamorato often gives to the object of his fondness, a perfection of beauty which none but himself can discover.* Yet, the power of doing this, is that which above all other qualities, constitutes the poet." [11] The critic's italics emphasize how grave is his indictment; it amounts to an accusation that Thomson possesses clear physical vision, and the ability to reproduce its perceptions, but that he lacks the vital gift of transforming imaginative vision. The charge has been echoed in modern times; [12] it raises fundamental questions about the poetic value of Thomsonian description — and the even more basic question: what, exactly, does such description consist of?

In a letter written in 1730 Thomson remarked, "Travelling has been long my fondest wish for the very purpose you recommend: the storing one's Imagination with Ideas of all-beautiful, all-great, and all-perfect Nature. These are the true materia poetica, the light and colours with which Fancy kindles up her whole creation, paints a sentiment, and even embodies an abstracted thought." [13] If these comments suggest the poet's conviction that perception and the memory of perception must be the source of his art, they also imply that he proposes to move, somehow, from perception to "sentiment" and even to "abstracted thought" and that both sentiment and thought can be "embodied," "painted," given physical form. Semi-philosophical ideas, and emotions derived from them, typically dominate his descriptions in *The Seasons*. If the "insight" they offer is not the sort we usually desire from nature poetry, still they provide far more than mere "sight."

A characteristic descriptive passage in "Spring" begins, "And see"; ends, "shuts the scene" (l. 47): it is presented as a visual panorama. It opens, characteristically, with a personification:

> And see where surly Winter passes off
> Far to the north, and calls his ruffian blasts:
> His blasts obey, and quit the howling hill,
> The shattered forest, and the ravaged vale;
> While softer gales succeed, at whose kind touch,
> Dissolving snows in livid torrents lost,
> The mountains lift their green heads to the sky.
>
> (ll. 11–17)

Despite the command to "see," only the last of the seven lines is predominantly visual. Stress is rather on "character" than appearance. The passage creates an impression of Winter as fierce, disagreeable, "surly" criminal, attended by "ruffian blasts," as a cosmic highwayman victimizing the natural world; it does not, on the whole, evoke physical images. Nature is personalized without being quite personified, through such modifiers as *howling, ravaged, kind*. To treat inanimate nature thus as closely akin to sentient beings is vital for Thomson, as for most writers in the pastoral or georgic tradition. In the lines quoted above, the reader must be made aware of nature's insistent vibrancy in order to understand the passage's philosophic underpinnings.

With "green" introduced in the description of mountains, the tone is set for the remainder of the passage, its emphasis on the "bright," "light," "white," "shining" quality of spring. As typical of Thomson as his introduction of the personification is his quick abandonment of it.

As yet the trembling year is unconfirmed,
And Winter oft at eve resumes the breeze,
Chills the pale morn, and bids his driving sleets
Deform the day delightless; so that scarce
The bittern knows his time with bill engulfed
To shake the sounding marsh; or from the shore
The plovers when to scatter o'er the heath,
And sing their wild notes to the listening waste.
    At last from Aries rolls the bounteous sun,
And the bright Bull receives him. Then no more
The expansive atmosphere is cramped with cold;
But, full of life and vivifying soul,
Lifts the light clouds sublime, and spreads them thin,
Fleecy, and white o'er all-surrounding heaven.

(ll. 18–31)

The loose metaphoric foundation of the description begins to emerge, based on the antithesis between the "expansive atmosphere," "full of life and vivifying soul," and the state of being "cramped with cold." Martin Price has pointed out that all Thomson's "best landscapes involve tension and movement," adding that such tensions, "like an abstract form — musical or pictorial — . . . articulate patterns of tension that underlie or are embedded in much of our experience." [14] In this instance, the sense of tension helps to focus the details of the scene and to suggest their significance. While the year trembles, "unconfirmed" ("Not fortified by resolution; not strengthened; raw; weak," as Dr. Johnson defines the word), Winter, vaguely personified once more, takes control of natural energies ("resumes the breeze") in order to remove vitality and warmth from the scene, to "Deform" (literally destroy the form of) the day. Opposed to winter are the forces of movement and of life. The bittern tries to "shake the sounding marsh"; the plovers, which "scatter o'er the heath," sing to a "waste" which is none the less, in this time of approaching vitality, "listening."

Now man appears, as part of the natural scene:

    Forth fly the tepid airs; and unconfined,
Unbinding earth, the moving softness strays.
Joyous the impatient husbandman perceives
Relenting Nature, and his lusty steers
Drives from their stalls to where the well-used plough
Lies in the furrow loosened from the frost.

There, unrefusing, to the harnessed yoke
They lend their shoulder, and begin their toil,
Cheered by the simple song and soaring lark.
Meanwhile incumbent o'er the shining share
The master leans, removes the obstructing clay,
Winds the whole work, and sidelong lays the glebe.
   White through the neighbouring fields the sower stalks
With measured step, and liberal throws the grain
Into the faithful bosom of the ground:
The harrow follows harsh, and shuts the scene.

(ll. 32–47)

The heavy stress, towards the beginning of the section, on participles which recall their opposites emphasizes the theme of winter's
rigidity versus spring's energy. *Unconfined, unbinding, relenting,
loosened, unrefusing*: such modifiers insist on the antithesis,
heighten the impression of spring's vitality by reminding one of
winter's confinement. The pattern Thomson outlines is clear. Man
"Winds [*Wind*: "To regulate in action" (Johnson)] the whole
work," controls the agricultural activity which fulfills spring's
fertility, but master, sower and lusty steers also participate in the
simple assertion of life which is spring's triumph: cheered by the
lark, cattle affirm as importantly as birds the essentially celebratory
activity which defies and destroys the binding force of winter.
The passivity of earth suggested at the outset in such phrases as
"howling hill" and "ravaged vale," when earth is the victim of
winter, becomes ultimately the source of fruition, as "the faithful
bosom of the ground" — a metaphor faintly ludicrous in the context, but clearly intended to enforce the thematic statement of the
entire passage — receives the sower's grain. Thomson's real subject is the total pattern of nature.

Be gracious, Heaven, for now laborious man
Has done his part. Ye fostering breezes, blow;
Ye softening dews, ye tender showers, descend;
And temper all, thou world-reviving sun,
Into the perfect year.

(ll. 48–52)

This in turn leads to moral generalization about the value of
rural poetry and rural virtue — "morals" which the poet appears
to find implicit in his view of natural pattern.

18

Thomson: Dominance of Meaning

In spite of his insistence that he is offering us something to "see," then, Thomson controls his descriptive passage through idea, a sense of pattern, rather than through visual detail. Not only are the actual "scenes" highly generalized, much of the presentation is not visual at all, hardly even sensuous. We may be reminded of a curious fact revealed by Josephine Miles's tabulation of the words Thomson uses more than ten times in a thousand lines: *eye* and *scene* are among the most frequently used nouns (although *man* and *soul* occur twice as often, and *life* three times as frequently); *see* is one of the eight favorite verbs; but of the twelve adjectives listed, only four are at all visual, and even they are very general (*deep, fair, long, wide*). The more characteristic Thomsonian adjective, these statistics suggest, points to the emotional or spiritual: *fierce, gay, great, happy, mighty, pure, sad, wild.*[15]

Even the passages of *The Seasons* most famed as descriptive set-pieces reveal the same preoccupation with emotional and intellectual significance rather than mere appearance. The well-known description of a garden is a case in point, although it is misleading to isolate it from its context. (A persistent problem in examining *The Seasons* is that its effects usually depend on units about a hundred lines long: too long for quotation or detailed analysis.) The passage begins, in the final version of the poem, with an invocation to "Amanda" and an appeal that she join the poet in his walk ("Spring," ll. 480–493). Then she is invited to "see" how the vale is irrigated, the lily watered; to appreciate "The negligence of nature wide and wild" (l. 505); to contemplate "the busy nations" (bees; l. 510) at "their delicious task" (l. 508).

> At length the finished garden to the view
> Its vistas opens and its alleys green.
> Snatched through the verdant maze, the hurried eye
> Distracted wanders; now the bowery walk
> Of covert close, where scarce a speck of day
> Falls on the lengthened gloom, protracted sweeps;
> Now meets the bending sky, the river now
> Dimpling along, the breezy ruffled lake,
> The forest darkening round, the glittering spire,
> The ethereal mountain, and the distant main.
>   (ll. 516–525)

The Poetry of Vision

This is all introductory to the famous description of garden flowers, part of the same verse paragraph. Its emphasis is double: on the viewer, and on the curious power of nature. Thomson does not offer this scene simply as a description of what he himself has seen; he presents it, rather, as something *to be* seen. His use of the definite article ("the view," "the hurried eye") depersonalizes and universalizes the presentation, but that presentation depends upon the context of the broad appeal to Amanda to see and understand what nature has to offer. "The hurried eye" is the grammatical subject of the sentence which extends from line 518 to line 525; the eye sweeps the bowery walk, meets the bending sky, the lake, the forest and the main. Yet the eye is not the active agent here. It is "snatched" through the maze, as though the scene itself had power and energy. The eye itself, "distracted," can only wander. Energy resides in the river which dimples, the forest which darkens, the breezy lake; the eye is led, without volition, from one object to another. The poet must recall the abstracted viewer to the immediate scene:

> But why so far excursive? when at hand,
> Along these blushing borders bright with dew,
> And in yon mingled wilderness of flowers,
> Fair-handed Spring unbosoms every grace —
> Throws out the snow-drop and the crocus first,
> The daisy, primrose, violet darkly blue,
> And polyanthus of unnumbered dyes;
> The yellow wall-flower, stained with iron brown,
> And lavish stock, that scents the garden round:
> From the soft wing of vernal breezes shed,
> Anemones; auriculas, enriched
> With shining meal o'er all their velvet leaves;
> And full ranunculus of glowing red.
> Then comes the tulip-race, where beauty plays
> Her idle freaks: from family diffused
> To family, as flies the father-dust,
> The varied colours run; and, while they break
> On the charmed eye, the exulting florist marks
> With secret pride the wonders of his hand.
> No gradual bloom is wanting — from the bud
> First-born of Spring to Summer's musky tribes;
> Nor hyacinths, of purest virgin white,
> Low bent and blushing inward; nor jonquils,

Of potent fragrance; nor narcissus fair,
As o'er the fabled fountain hanging still;
Nor broad carnations, nor gay-spotted pinks;
Nor, showered from every bush, the damask-rose:
Infinite numbers, delicacies, smells,
With hues on hues expression cannot paint,
The breath of Nature, and her endless bloom.

(ll. 526–555)

Nature, in this near-at-hand view, seems far more passive than in the prospect which precedes it. Yet its power remains, conceived now in more abstract terms, recalled to the reader every few lines. Reuben Brower has pointed out that these lines "loosely compose a metaphor — of Spring, and beyond that of the vaguely benign Thomsonian Nature." [16] The presented pattern alternates between what is visible to the eye and what is only imaginable, or perceptible by what Thomson frequently terms "the eye of reason." There is the mass of flowers, which the observer may even perceive as a "wilderness"; there is also the *source* of these flowers, consciousness of which turns wilderness to order. The aesthetically satisfying vision of colorful flowers and the emotionally satisfying awareness of meaning in those flowers together create the image of Spring and of Nature.

"Fair-handed Spring unbosoms every grace": this first reminder that the garden is significant primarily as the product of Spring recalls the personification with which Thomson opens the poem (see ll. 1–4). There are subsequent, subsidiary hints that Spring is the presiding deity: anemones are shed from the "wing" of spring breezes (ll. 335–336); auriculas are "enriched" with their "shining meal" (ll. 336–337): the participle (as opposed to the obvious adjective *rich*) defines the flowers as passive recipients of Spring's bounty. In the description of "the tulip-race" (ll. 339–344), where the vocabulary insists upon the connection between the animate and inanimate worlds, emphasis on the sources of visual effects virtually excludes actual description: personalized beauty herself is a cause of the tulips' colors; so is "the father-dust"; so, the exulting florist believes, is he. But the ultimate cause, as the total context makes clear, is Spring, and beyond Spring, the natural order.

The Poetry of Vision

"The charmed eye" now has replaced "the hurried eye" with which the sequence began; Nature exerts her power over the observer, to hurry or to charm. But visual perception is by no means the most significant kind, as two lines added only in 1744 clearly suggest ("No gradual bloom is wanting — from the bud/ First-born of Spring to Summer's musky tribes"). Crocuses and carnations do not actually bloom together, but the summary lines quoted above suggest the irrelevance of such an objection to Thomson's grouping of flowers. The poet wishes to present not an actual scene but an imagined panorama of the garden's progress from early spring to summer. Léon Morel has said of Thomson, "Les objets . . . se montrent surtout au poète comme partie d'un vaste tableau, et lors même qu'il les observe séparément, ils lui apparaissent toujours comme animés, mobiles et changeants; c'est là une condition qui exclut la notation précise de formes arrêtées." [17] The garden passage strongly supports this thesis. In it the "vast tableau," the pattern, is above all important, and description supplies only a metaphor for the pattern. In the concluding section of the garden passage, Thomson recapitulates briefly the possible modes of flower description: by color (the hyacinths), fragrance (jonquils), mythological association (narcissus), form (carnations and pinks). Then he reminds us once more that description is, paradoxically, impossible: there remain "hues on hues expression cannot paint." This fact, however, matters little, since the importance of flowers is not their indescribable colors but the fact that they are "The breath of Nature, and her endless bloom." In even so "descriptive" a passage as this, Thomson clearly values insight more than sight.

His realization that observation of nature could be used to express nature's grand significance marks an important step toward true romantic nature imagery, which has been well defined by W. K. Wimsatt: "The common feat of the romantic nature poets was to read meanings into the landscape. . . . characteristically . . . concerning the spirit or soul of things. . . . And that meaning especially was summoned out of the very surface of nature itself. It was embodied imaginatively and without the explicit religious or philosophic statement which one will find in classical or Christian instances." [18] In Thomson's imagery, meaning does not really inhere in the landscape; it is felt as the product of human imagination or intelligence contemplating the natural scene. And the eighteenth-century poet felt obliged to make his meanings explicit. The passage immediately following the garden scene begins, "Hail, Source of Being! Universal Soul/ Of heaven and earth!" (ll. 556–557), and elaborates the relation between the Deity and natural process, stating directly the meanings implicit in the earlier description. Yet one's sense that the immediate prospect of nature is genuinely important to Thomson remains despite his insistent didacticism; his ability to convey the sense of importance directly through imagery is perhaps his most vital poetic gift.

Mark Akenside's *The Pleasures of Imagination* was published in 1744, the year that *The Seasons* received its final major revision. Much of it is merely ponderous versification of Addison's essays on the imagination, with some broadening of Addison's principles. Even more completely than Addison's aesthetics, however, Akenside's theory of beauty, as defined in the poem, conforms precisely with that implied by *The Seasons*. Beauty, asserts *The Pleasures of Imagination*, resides first in color alone, then in shape, then in color and shape combined. The addition of growth produces an object yet more aesthetically satisfying (the flowers of a garden, for example); sentient life is more appealing still, and the greatest beauty is in beings combining life and mind.[19] "In nature's fairest forms, is aught so fair/ As virtuous friendship?"[20] enquires Akenside rhetorically. The implications of this position are important in understanding *The Seasons*, where similar assumptions seem to be made. A modern reader can easily feel that its long sections praising famous men or glorifying some such human activity as plowing or prison reform are excrescences on a poem which would do far better to concentrate entirely on nature, its true subject. But if Thomson believed that description of peasants (or for that matter, of city folk) almost by definition offered aesthetic pleasure of a higher order than description of nature, and that the presentation of such themes as "virtuous friendship" was necessarily superior to either kind of description, superior in beauty and in power over the imagination, he would conceive it a necessary part of his poetic responsibility to record, for the sake of aesthetic effect, his impressions of humanity as well as of the natural world, to use description of nature as a method for approaching discussion of man.

The Poetry of Vision

The most successful descriptions of human activities in *The Seasons* are much like the poem's typical nature passages in technique and in apparent purpose.

> Now swarms the village o'er the jovial mead —
> The rustic youth, brown with meridian toil,
> Healthful and strong; full as the summer rose
> Blown by prevailing suns, the ruddy maid,
> Half naked, swelling on the sight, and all
> Her kindled graces burning o'er her cheek.
> Even stooping age is here; and infant hands
> Trail the long rake, or, with the fragrant load
> O'ercharged, amid the kind oppression roll.
> Wide flies the tedded grain; all in a row
> Advancing broad, or wheeling round the field,
> They spread their breathing harvest to the sun,
> That throws refreshful round a rural smell;
> Or, as they rake the green-appearing ground,
> And drive the dusky wave along the mead,
> The russet hay-cock rises thick behind
> In order gay: while heard from dale to dale,
> Waking the breeze, resounds the blended voice
> Of happy labour, love, and social glee.
>
> ("Summer," ll. 352–370)

Here, as in the garden scene, one is reminded by such a phrase as "swelling on the sight," however unfortunate its faint prurience, of the actual presence of an observer. Here, as in the nature descriptions, the diction hints some essential identity between man and nature: the mead is "jovial"; the "ruddy maid" resembles a summer rose; the voices of the workers are heard "Waking the breeze." If the garden provides a metaphor for natural order, the haying scene supplies an image of man in nature, a functioning part of the universal pattern. The poet's use of the metonymy of abstract for concrete ("stooping age," "kind oppression") and of the generalizing, unrealized personifications at the very end suggest his greater concern with function than with scene. The activity of the haymakers provides a visual pattern of order, as they advance, wheel, "drive the dusky wave along the mead," and leave behind them haycocks "In order gay." But the visual pattern, like the aural one suggested by "the blended voice/ Of happy labour, love, and social glee," is primarily important in reflecting a vital philosophic pattern. Here again, scenic yields to conceptual in what purports to be a descriptive passage; the poet's "vision" is more significantly internal than external.

The view that human activity must be aesthetically interesting of course encouraged descriptive presentation of human affairs. But Akenside also justifies on aesthetic grounds the inclusion of non-descriptive material, by the principle — an outgrowth of the Lockean concept of association of ideas — that the imagination receives greater pleasure according to the perceiver's specific situation. Akenside offers these examples: spring is more delightful to one who has been ill; the rainbow is more beautiful to one who understands its nature; consciousness of divine wisdom makes the spectacle of nature more compelling.[21] They are very Thomsonian instances. "Spring" discusses the beauty of the rainbow to the educated observer (ll. 203–217); "Summer" contains a similar treatment of the joy which the sight of a comet gives "the enlightened few" (l. 1714). And the rôle of divine wisdom in relation to the beauties of nature is a recurrent — *the* recurrent — theme of *The Seasons*. Akenside provides an important aesthetic rationalization for Thomson's characteristic pattern of alternating description and commentary, which does not come merely, as Jean Hagstrum suggests, from the fact that Thomson's material forced him to "the picture-gallery method of 'see and respond.' "[22] Akenside also suggests why, throughout *The Seasons*, commentary is typically embedded in description. The richest aesthetic satisfaction can be achieved by a presentation which suggests not only visual actuality but the importance of that actuality in some larger context. To establish contexts appears to be one of Thomson's principal purposes in virtually all his descriptions; this is one reason why their visual detail frequently evaporates under close examination.

Thomson's frequent use of perceptual metaphors for intellectual activity suggests the persistence of his attempts to unite sensuous and intellectual response. He repeatedly associates both reason and imagination with vision. Early in "Spring," for example, at the end of a description of rainfall, the poet points out that the falling rain is the bounty of heaven, producing fruits and flowers.

> Swift fancy fired anticipates their growth;
> And, while the milky nutriment distils,
> Beholds the kindling country colour round.
>
> (ll. 183–185)

The Poetry of Vision

Fancy can "behold" a scene which does not yet exist, "see" simultaneously the reality of the present and that of the future. This capacity of fancy justifies the adjective *milky*, which is not necessarily visual in its reference: "milky nutriment" may denote the rain itself, understood as analogous to milk in its capacity to nourish; or it may suggest the conversion of the rain into the unseen sap which would appear "milky." Thomson frequently presents perceptions which can only be products of imagination as though they were visual. Thus, contemplating a mass of flowers,

> the raptured eye
> Hurries from joy to joy, and, hid beneath
> The fair profusion, yellow Autumn spies.
>   ("Spring," ll. 111–113)

Again, Amanda is invited to

> See how the lily drinks
> The latent rill, scarce oozing through the grass
>   ("Spring," ll. 495–496)

The eye, asserted able to see the unseeable, is identical with the imagination.

The capacity of imagination to enlarge the bounds of physical perception appears to be its chief value for Thomson. In a rhapsodic passage on the sources of water, he relies heavily on the analogy between imagination and sight.

> Oh! lay the mountains bare, and wide display
> Their hidden structure to the astonished view,
>   ("Autumn," ll. 779–780)

[he begs:]

> Give opening Hemus to my searching eye, . . .
>   Unveil
> The miny caverns. . . .
> Amazing scene! Behold! the glooms disclose!
> I see the rivers in their infant beds!
> Deep, deep I hear them labouring to get free!
> I see the leaning strata. . . .
>   (ll. 785, 799–800, 807–810)

The poet thus gives tacit assent to the view that reality can only be grasped in images. He asks his fancy to "view the wonders of the

torrid zone" ("Summer," l. 632), begs his readers to "see" what
goes on there (l. 635), reminds them repeatedly throughout his
travel-book descriptions that he is offering "scenes," something to
"behold." "To every purer eye," Thomson maintains, "The inform-
ing Author in his works appears" ("Spring," ll. 895–860). That
"purer eye" is presumably the eye of fancy, which in association
with reason, can lead the soul, under the guidance of Philosophy,
to God. Fancy's eye

> receives
> The whole magnificence of heaven and earth,
> And every beauty, delicate or bold,
> Obvious or more remote, with livelier sense,
> Diffusive painted on the rapid mind.
> ("Summer," ll. 1748–1752)

With livelier sense than what? The phrase suggests the poet's conviction that the impressions of fancy are more vivid, more intense,
than literal sense impressions. "The mind's creative eye" ("Autumn," l. 1016) has mysterious powers; it can exalt thought "Beyond dim earth" (l. 1013), can even "anticipate those scenes/ Of
happiness and wonder" ("Winter," ll. 605–6) which the afterlife
will provide.

Thomson recognizes that the eye of imagination can even control physical vision. His description of human love stresses the
extent to which the lover exists in an imaginative world, "Wrapt
in gay visions of unreal bliss" ("Spring," l. 988). When the youth
despairs,

> the darkened sun
> Loses his light. The rosy-bosomed Spring
> To weeping fancy pines; and yon bright arch,
> Contracted, bends into a dusky vault.
> All Nature fades extinct.
> (ll. 1009–1013)

Under the influence of jealousy, "internal vision" is "tainted" (l.
1084), and imaginary perceptions dominate love's victim. The
visions of imagination can be dangerously as well as rewardingly
compelling.

The peroration of "Winter," which in effect resolves *The Seasons*
as a whole, depends heavily on a visual metaphor. The reader is

invited to "see" with his mind's eye the glories of the future, as "The great eternal scheme . . . / To reason's eye refined clears up apace" ("Winter," ll. 1046, 1049). As Thomson asserts triumphantly the supremacy of good in the universe, the ultimate benignity of the universal scheme, he relies on the antithesis between the unlimited vision which reason may, in some future dispensation, provide, and the "bounded view" which sees only "A little part" of the universe (ll. 1066–1067). The same antithesis has operated throughout the poem, with emphasis sometimes on the limitations of human vision, metaphorically or literally conceived, and sometimes on the infinite possibilities of reason's view. The "sage-instructed eye" can see the colors of the prism in the rainbow ("Spring," ll. 210–211), but the botanist, even when he tries to number the kinds of herbage, only "Bursts his blind way" through the forest (l. 228). Neither the power of education nor that of reason can enable human beings to see fully what nature offers. Even the smallest part of Creative Wisdom's works exceeds the narrow vision of the mind of Ignorance ("Summer," ll. 321–323), but not the wisest of men possesses the "universal eye" which can sweep "at once the unbounded scheme of things" (ll. 329–330). No one has seen the Great Chain of Being; man can only draw analogies from the evidence of his senses, recognize that God's "wisdom shines as lovely on our minds/ As on our smiling eyes his servant-sun" (ll. 340–341). Yet the philosophic mind has its advantages; Thomson imagines friends,

> Attuned to happy unison of soul —
> To whose exulting eye a fairer world,
> Of which the vulgar never had a glimpse,
> Displays its charms.
>
> ("Summer," ll. 1385–1388)

If fancy's eye provides the panorama of heaven and earth which leads man to awareness of his Creator, reason's eye is capable of

> up-tracing, from the dreary void,
> The chain of causes and effects to Him,
> The world-producing Essence, who alone
> Possesses being.
>
> ("Summer," ll. 1745–1748)

Thomson: Dominance of Meaning

Reason, like imagination, provides a capacity analogous to sight. The philosophic man is "intent to gaze/ Creation through" ("Summer," ll. 1784–1785); the "inward view" (l. 1788) of Philosophy provides visions even of "the ideal kingdom" (l. 1789), although it cannot penetrate where God has set obscuring cloud (ll. 1798–1799). The poet begs Nature to "show" her workings, to allow him to "scan" her laws, to light his "blind way" through the deep and upward, to open all the universe to his "ravished eye" ("Autumn," ll. 1357–1366).

The eye provides for Thomson an image for man's pettiness and for his greatness. The significance of sight is, characteristically, at least as important to him as the actual revelations the sense provides; those revelations, to be really meaningful, must, Thomson clearly feels, be immediately commented upon by the reason as an organizing or an analytical faculty. At the beginning of "Winter," the poet expresses his desire to fill the "judging ear/ With bold description and with manly thought!" (ll. 28–29). His attempts to unite the two, to express his sense of how necessarily they relate to one another, to a large extent controls both the structure and the selectivity of *The Seasons*.

If Thomson criticism has frequently praised the poet for his descriptive powers, it has typically damned him for his style. Johnson set the tone for generations of critics when he pointed out that Thomson's diction had defects inseparable from its virtues. That diction, according to Johnson, "is to the highest degree florid [in the positive eighteenth-century sense: splendid] and luxuriant, such as may be said to be to his images and thoughts 'both their lustre and their shade'; such as invests them with splendour, through which they are not always easily discerned. It is too exuberant, and sometimes may be charged with filling the ear more than the mind." [23] The Thomsonian style was, critics agreed, turgid. Even such an enthusiast for *The Seasons* as Joseph Warton admitted that "the diction of the Seasons is sometimes harsh and inharmonious, and sometimes turgid and obscure." [24] John Aikin, attempting a balanced view, suggested that Thomson's "language . . . is best suited to themes of dignity: it is expressive and energetic, abounding in compound epithets and glowing metaphors, but inclining to turgidity, and too stiff and stately for familiar topics." [25] John Scott of Amwell added that Thomson "is often turgid, often obscure, and often redundant" because of his constant effort to elevate his diction.[26] A more detailed analysis, published in 1816, suggests that the poet's "genius" is his ability to conceal lack of meaning through the splendor of his language. Thomson's style, says the anonymous critic, "is indeed learned and ornate. But Burke has shown that words may the most powerfully affect the mind when their meaning is indefinite. Where Thomson's language is the most inflated, his expressions have generally a specious grandeur of meaning derived from the felicity with which they are selected. His genius is in this respect conspicuous: like the evening sun, which imparts pomp and brightness to the unsubstantial clouds with which it is enveloped, it changes the very character of the faults which it appropriates." [27]

One of the few critics who made any attempt to defend Thomson's style in its own right — as opposed to explaining its sources [28] — was Percival Stockdale, a late eighteenth-century apologist for Thomson who only grudgingly granted any defects at all in the author of *The Seasons*. He asserts flatly that "there is not a feeble, not a superfluous word, in the Seasons; not a word which does not contribute to inform the mind; to enrich the fancy, or to improve the heart." [29] The basis for this enthusiasm is rather more complex than its apparent naivete would suggest. "Style is the copy of thought," Stockdale points out; "therefore, as our substance, and manner of thinking *are*, such will our words, and such will their order *be*. The language, like the sentiments of Thomson, has an essence, and a structure, by which it is prominently discriminated from the style of other poets. The style of *his* poetry is almost constantly impressive; and his epithets are often as happily applied to their objects as they are new" (II, 96).

It is manifestly impossible to "rescue" Thomson's diction for the modern reader: its remoteness, its air of contrivance, its frequently unjustified portentousness are all profound obstacles. Only in isolated passages is Thomson a readable poet for a twentieth-century audience. Yet the very peculiarity of his diction presents a challenging critical problem. That diction *is*, I think, in large part defensible; and the grounds for defense reveal some interesting elements in Thomson's poetic techniques and purposes.

Stockdale's apology for Thomson, despite its obvious lack of critical sophistication, suggests by its insistence on the relation of the poet's language to his manner of thinking a valuable approach to analysis of Thomson's diction. It has been long recognized that Thomson's "originality" in language is largely the product of borrowings: from John Milton, importantly, from Virgil and from the physico-theological philosophers. These three sources also suggest three major areas of concern in *The Seasons*: religious, humanistic and scientific. All three, of course, relate directly to the primary concern with nature which was the starting point for "Winter" and thus for *The Seasons* as a whole. But the special effect of Thomson's style has to do largely with the quality achieved by the mixture of divergent dictions, and the uses to which he puts them.

A passage in "Autumn," for example, purports to discuss the sources of water on earth, with reference, as Professor McKillop has fully demonstrated, to contemporary scientific theory. It begins with one of the most Miltonic passages in *The Seasons*:

> Oh! lay the mountains bare, and wide display
> Their hidden structure to the astonished view;
> Strip from the branching Alps their piny load,
> The huge incumbrance of horrific woods
> From Asian Taurus, from Imaus stretched
> Athwart the roving Tartar's sullen bounds;
> Give opening Hemus to my searching eye,
> And high Olympus pouring many a stream!
> Oh, from the sounding summits of the north,
> The Dofrine Hills, through Scandinavia rolled
> To farthest Lapland and the frozen main . . .
>
> ("Autumn," ll. 779–789)

The invocation of resounding names, the exalted tone and language continue for seventeen lines more, modulating then into a more exclusively "scientific" section.

The lines quoted are Miltonic not only in tone and in their reliance on the rhetorical value of resonant names; they include a specific echo of two lines in *Paradise Lost*: "As when a vulture on

Imaus bred,/ Whose snowy ridge the roving Tartar bounds" (*P.L* III, 431–432).[30] Like Milton, too, Thomson here relies on the Latinate force of such words as *incumbrance*, carrying its original overtones of "heap" as well as weight, and *horrific*, with the Latin sense of "bristling" as well as the more modern meaning; even *sullen* hints its original sense, "lonely." (Professor Havens, incidentally, although obviously an admirer of Milton, finds this characteristic device of Thomson's irritating. "The fact is," he remarks, "that, if there is a pompous, contorted way of saying a thing, Thomson is likely to hit upon it; that of two words he prefers the one of Latin origin and of two Latin words that which is less common. Calling things by their right names and speaking simply, directly, and naturally, as in conversation, seems to have been his abhorrence." [31]) The extended, convoluted sentence is also obviously an attempt at Miltonic technique.

The total effect of this passage, though, is not Miltonic at all, but peculiarly Thomsonian. The desire to "see" which dominates the invocation is of course characteristic, as the tone of excitement through which Thomson emphasizes his concern with "hidden structure." As the poet begs to be shown that structure, promising to be astonished by it, he simultaneously perceives another sort of pattern, a relationship among the most widely separated of geographical phenomena; the diction and syntax of the passage particularly stress this fact. The section addresses "thou pervading genius, given to man/ To trace the secrets of the dark abyss" (ll. 777–778); this genius may be some external being (like the muse, say), but, like the muse, it can also be imagined as an internal power which the poet, and potentially all men, possess. The very invocation of this power demonstrates its workings. The Alps, for example, are "branching"; their metaphoric similarity to the trees which cover them thus emerges. *Load* and *huge incumbrance*, applied to the woods, stress the similarity: such language might as easily describe mountains. Moreover, the entire passage insists on geographical relationships, the fact that even the most widely separated portions of the earth share in a single great enterprise: providing the world's water. Repeated references to limitations of vision emphasize the poet's imaginative range. There is the "roving Tartar," confined to his "sullen bounds"; a few lines later we learn that the Caucasus is "seen by those/ Who in the Caspian and black Euxine toil" (ll. 790–791); then that "the wild Russ" believes the "cold Riphaean rocks" to be "the stony girdle of the world" (ll. 792–793). Such perceivers see only a small part; the poet, imaginatively swept away, glimpses the great whole. The long, elaborate sentences insist on the scope of his vision; the heavy stress on participles makes the natural world itself seem to partake in some vast action.

The most specifically "Thomsonian" aspect of this passage is its function in the poem as a whole: as an introduction to a section of scientific explication. There is nothing particularly "scientific" about the language of the passage so far, except possibly for the single word "piny," formed, as John Arthos has demonstrated, by analogy with contemporary scientific practice in constructing English equivalents for Latin terminology.[32] But this Miltonic section moves directly, with little change of tone (although considerable change in diction), into the more technical treatment of the sources of rivers. The scientific portion initially concentrates on the excitement of the ideas here to be expounded:

> Amazing scene! Behold! the glooms disclose!
> I see the rivers in their infant beds!
> Deep, deep I hear them labouring to get free!
> I see the leaning strata, artful ranged;
> The gaping fissures, to receive the rains,
> The melting snows, and ever-dripping fogs.
> Strowed bibulous above I see the sands,
> The pebbly gravel next, the layers then
> Of mingled moulds, of more retentive earths,
> The guttered rocks and mazy-running clefts,
> That, while the stealing moisture they transmit,
> Retard its motion, and forbid its waste.
> Beneath the incessant weeping of these drains,
> I see the rocky siphons stretched immense,
> The mighty reservoirs, of hardened chalk
> Or stiff compacted clay capacious formed:
> O'erflowing thence, the congregated stores,
> The crystal treasures of the liquid world . . .
>   ("Autumn," ll. 807–824)

Such terms as *guttered* and *strata*, and all the ideas of this treatment, come, Professor McKillop shows, directly from *Spectacle de* la Nature by the Abbé Noël Antoine Pluche.[33] But it is Thomson who introduces into the language and structure of the geological description the emphasis on order which dominates and justifies the passage. This order, the "artfulness" of the arrangements he describes, accounts for the exalted tone, the atmosphere of what may seem to a modern reader somewhat factitious excitement. The "leaning strata" are "artful ranged"; so, too, are fissures, sand, gravel, clay and rocks, all components of the pattern. For a spatially extended vision the poet now substitutes one in depth, a vertical rather than horizontal view of the world. As the geographical panorama insisted that the farthest corners of the earth contribute to gather the waters, so this geological one reveals how many kinds of matter help to purify and transmit "The crystal treasures of the liquid world." As so often in *The Seasons*, the syntax here reveals relationships: the ordering of layers, one above another; the parallels of rains, snows and fogs; rocks and clefts; chalk and "stiff compacted clay." With few exceptions, the adjectives of the passage precisely define functions: *melting* snows and *ever-dripping* fogs remind us that snow and fog are alike forms of water; *retentive* earths recall the rôle the earth plays, as do *guttered* and *mazy-running*; the importance of the "rocky siphons" comes specifically from the fact that, being rocky, they stop the slow seepage of water. This precise "scientific" language mingles with such words as *infant, bibulous, weeping*, which suggest the pervasive analogies between the human and the inanimate in Thomson's world. By the time one reaches *crystal treasures*, the extravagant periphrasis seems justified. The poet has described the intricacy of the plan through which these treasures are preserved and conveyed to man; their value depends on their sources. When, finally, Thomson sums up the entire passage with reference to "The full-adjusted harmony of things" (1. 835), his explanation merely reasserts what has been implied through the successive presentation of geographic and geologic visions and through the mixture of Miltonic and scientific language. The diversity of subject and language reveals alternative ways for perceiving the same phenomena and insists that the poet can unite different ways of perceiving through his awareness of universal pattern.

Of course to produce a lengthy description in blank verse of the origins of rivers would be at best a poetic tour de force, and one can hardly claim that Thomson has created moving poetry from such material. He has not the tact, sensitivity or clarity of a Virgil; the multiplication of exclamation points toward the beginning of the scientific section, a superficial index of excitement, suggests the poet's awareness that his subject matter did not integrally justify the intensity with which he treats it. His excitement seems theoretical, not deeply felt; one can see — theoretically — why such a vision might excite someone, without believing that anyone has actually been moved by it. Thomson's "science" is of course discredited by now, and so are his assertions of emotion. Yet the emotion is undoubtedly real; its intensity corresponds to that perceptible in many other portions of *The Seasons*. It derives from that vision of nature which dominates the entire poem: nature as passive, receptive, divinely ordered but subject also to the ordering power of man, who plows and gardens, enriches and arranges the world around him. The earth which receives and preserves the water has here no explicit relation to man, yet this conception of natural structure is a typical Thomsonian image of organized passivity, here contrasting with the energy of the struggling waters.

When the language of science merges with that of direct observation, the result is sometimes more immediately appealing poetry. Passages characterized by this sort of mixture, like those we have just investigated, suggest how significant to Thomson was the fusion of ideas, the amalgam of different points of view which has justified attacks on *The Seasons* for its lack of intellectual unity. The unity of the poem is obviously exceedingly complex, and its complexity is reflected in its individual sections.

The account of the sources of frost, for example, like the lines on the origin of rivers, begins in the tone of rhetorical exaltation, but there is a marked shift in tone later:

> What art thou, frost? and whence are thy keen stores
> Derived, thou secret all-invading power,
> Whom even the illusive fluid cannot fly?
> Is not thy potent energy, unseen,
> Myriads of little salts, or hooked, or shaped
> Like double wedges, and diffused immense
> Through water, earth, and ether? Hence at eve,
> Steamed eager from the red horizon round,

The Poetry of Vision

With the fierce rage of Winter deep suffused,
An icy gale, oft shifting, o'er the pool
Breathes a blue film and in its mid-career
Arrests the bickering stream. The loosened ice,
Let down the flood and half dissolved by day,
Rustles no more; but to the sedgy bank
Fast grows, or gathers round the pointed stone,
A crystal pavement, by the breath of heaven
Cemented firm; till, seized from shore to shore,
The whole imprisoned river growls below.

("Winter," ll. 714–731)

The naivete of the theory it advances creates much of the charm of the passage's opening for a modern reader, but of course Thomson's suggestions about the nature of frost represented up-to-date theorizing in his own time,[34] and they are straightforwardly presented: the anticlimax when the "explanation" follows the resounding beginning is presumably inadvertent. The personal address to frost as "thou," the series of rhetorical questions, the use of such honorific adjectives as *potent* and *all-invading*: these are invitations to take this material seriously. If the theory about frost no longer seems worth attention, the succeeding description in its precision and point continues to invite close examination — and although its rhetoric is less pretentious than that of the opening section, the ideas dominating it are precisely the same. The description is in some sense a gloss on the generalizing questions that precede it; through a characteristic combination of the language of scientific precision with that of personal observation Thomson evokes the mystery and meaning of a commonplace winter scene.

Mystery and meaning alike derive from the contrast between the power of the "secret all-invading" frost and that of the "illusive [deceptive, but also, in Thomson's time, elusive] fluid" it captures. The poet fully recognizes the potency of both forces; he dwells on the paradoxical relation between them. His perception of paradox, however, extends further still. The "icy gale" which "Arrests" the stream has all the appearance of heat: it is "Steamed" from the horizon, that horizon is "red," a color traditionally associated with heat; it is suffused with "fierce rage," often symbolically expressed as heat. Moreover, a "gale" is by definition a force of movement; it passes over the pool "oft shifting," manifesting a potent energy.

36

Thomson: Dominance of Meaning

The power of the gale, and of the frost it diffuses, is energy which stops motion; that of the river is energy which creates motion. The conventional description of the stream as "bickering" here serves a precise function. In the first place, throughout the passage sound is systematically associated with the water, which bickers, causes rustling, finally growls. Moreover, the participle *bickering* expresses activity as well as sound, evokes the ceaseless motion of the water now about to be arrested "in its mid-career." The force of the water — "illusive" — is more insidious even than that of the frost. It loosens the ice, half dissolves it, lets it down the flood; yet the power of the frost is far greater, fully conveyed in the contrast between the "bickering stream" and the "crystal pavement" [35] it becomes. The reason for its greater force becomes clear as the implications of *pavement* are emphasized by the verb *Cemented*: the gale which carries the frost is "the breath of heaven" (both literally and metaphorically), and this is one more in the endless series of exempla about how heaven's power works. Ultimately it hardly matters to Thomson — much less to the reader, of course — whether his little salts are hooked or shaped like double wedges: the final and most important point is that, however they are shaped, they function as agents of heaven's will.

The pattern of contrast through which the poem arrives at this revelation is characteristic of *The Seasons*, and an important part of its meaning. Many sections of the poem, dealing with many phenomena, depend on the same principle: contrasts between motion and stasis, between light and dark, sound and silence, fertility and sterility often provide the structural basis for extended treatments of animal life, of storms, of minerals — of all the manifestations of natural order. The implicit point is, of course, the familiar eighteenth-century one: "order in variety we see,/And here though all things differ, all agree." It is the lesson of the physico-theologians, a commonplace of the time; yet the intensity with which Thomson perceives it, the extent to which it permeates his individual sensuous impressions and dictates his language makes it seem in his work something peculiarly individual. In the frost passage, the questions which at the outset seem merely rhetorical receive finally an unexpected answer. The third of those questions ("Is not thy potent energy . . .") appears at the outset to supply at least a tentative answer to the preceding two. But by the end of the succeeding description, the poet has made a new point, leading one to feel that, after all, no man can really hope to answer questions about the origin of frost; there is mystery at the heart of all natural process. The elevation of the opening, which seems at first an artificial attempt to dignify, is ultimately justified; the repeated rhetorical questions have more than rhetorical meaning.[36]

In the frost passage, as in the one in "Summer" which refers to the botanist's way as "blind," Thomson does not reject the necessity or value of scientific exploration and analysis. Although the descriptive lines are not strictly "scientific" in their language — at least not in the technical sense — they do attempt to be precise, to contribute to the explanation of what frost really is. They help to reveal a central paradox of *The Seasons*: man is at his best in attempting to understand the workings of the world around him; yet the workings of that world are such that man can never fully comprehend them. "I always accounted as extraordinary foolish those who would make human comprehension the measure of what Nature has a power or knowledge to effect," observes one participant in Galileo's *Dialogue on the Great World Systems*, "whereas on the contrary there is not any least effect in Nature which can be fully understood by the most speculative minds in the world." [37] This is Thomson's spirit throughout *The Seasons*: scientific in its desire to "see" and understand the workings of natural force, reverent in its recognition that it is finally impossible to understand — and that this fact itself affirms the greatness of God.

The lines on frost, like all the best nature passages in the poem, demonstrate simultaneously Thomson's capacity simply to appreciate the natural world and his yearning to "see" it completely. The nature of his constant perception of pattern is richly revealed here. Each of the two sentences which compose the description conveys a slightly different point of view about the described phenomena. The first, characteristically concerned with relationships, its syntactical complexity entirely the product of that concern, uses the Thomsonian language of personalization: *eager, fierce rage, Breathes, bickering*. This diction is not, of course, emphasized to the extent that it conveys any coherent view of the natural world as participating in characteristics of the human one, but it hints once more the pervasively perceived connections between the animate and inanimate realms. The first sentence deals with more general perceptions than the second, in which the adjectives are precise and specific; the language of personalization (except for "the breath of heaven") has now disappeared. Emphasis on the contrast between the energy which produces stasis and that which maintains motion continues; the final clause provides the strongest contrasting impressions of the two forces, in the juxtaposition of the energetic participle *seized*, which dramatizes the potency of the frost, and the verb *growls*, describing the river's most forceful sound, a sound which is the product of its very imprisonment.

Thomson's special diction and syntax, then, derive from his constant, almost obsessive effort to reveal the patterns he perceives as he "sees" the world. His dependence on varied sorts of language, used often in conjunction with one another, is itself another representation of the "order in variety" theme. Each kind of language points to a distinct way of perceiving; the juxtaposition of varied dictions insists that many different modes of perception must merge to express even approximate truths about nature.

The poet deals always with the revelation of pattern. The visual presentation of the storm in "Winter" (see above, pp. 2–3) of course parallels the presentation of storms in the other seasons, but no explicit "philosophic" or "scientific" commentary accompanies it. Still, the language itself points to the poet's constant preoccupation with certain sorts of meaning in his visions.

The first part of the description deals with the physical phenomena of the tempest, without reference to its human or animal victims:

> The keener tempests come: and, fuming dun
> From all the livid east or piercing north,
> Thick clouds ascend, in whose capacious womb
> A vapoury deluge lies, to snow congealed.
> Heavy they roll their fleecy world along,
> And the sky saddens with the gathered storm.
> Through the hushed air the whitening shower descends,
> At first thin-wavering; till at last the flakes
> Fall broad and wide and fast, dimming the day
> With a continual flow. The cherished fields
> Put on their winter-robe of purest white.

'Tis brightness all; save where the new snow melts
Along the mazy current. Low the woods
Bow their hoar head; and, ere the languid sun
Faint from the west emits his evening ray,
Earth's universal face, deep-hid and chill,
Is one wild dazzling waste, that buries wide
The works of man.

("Winter," ll. 223–240)

The storms of spring, summer and autumn have been carefully differentiated from one another; the winter storm is dramatically different from them all. The other storms are relatively noisy; in this one the air is "hushed" and nothing suggests the presence of sound in the falling snow. As the world awaits the storm in "Spring," " 'Tis silence all" (l. 161); after the winter storm, " 'Tis brightness all." The alternation of darkness and brightness has the importance in "Winter" of the pattern of silence and sound in "Spring." When the sun shines on a landscape cleansed by rainfall, it produces brilliance; in the winter storm, brilliance comes from the landscape rather than from the sun, which itself is "languid" and produces only a "Faint" ray. The source of brightness is darkness: the tempests come "fuming dun," emitting a dark vapor, derived from the "livid" east or piercing north, laden with thick clouds, saddening the sky (*i.e.*, making it gloomy). The snow, as it falls, *dims* the day with its flow. Yet the result of that flow is universal whiteness, brightness, dazzle, in which "The works of man" seem unimportant.

Many commentators have noted the precision of visual detail here, the exactness with which Thomson observes, for example, the visual effect of the gradual change in the intensity of the snowfall. Details are, indeed, carefully observed and exactly conveyed, even to the accent of blackness in the pure white scene "where the new snow melts/Along the mazy current." (Earlier editions had made this point explicit by using the word *blackening*. But Thomson's later, subtler technique is more effective: the word *save* directs the reader's attention to the contrast created by the blackness of the stream's surface as the snow melts on it; to underline the point is needless.) The very rhythms of the lines often suggest the rhythms of the storm, which is conceived vividly as a process, an almost melodic series of movements.

As usual, though, Thomson is not merely concerned with visual exactitude. His language here is directed toward the suggesting of far-ranging connections. The term *deluge* applied to the snow as it exists potentially in the clouds, for example, insists on the relation between this kind of storm and the others that have preceded it: not simply a relation of contrast, but one of similarity as well. The "fleecy world" of the next line is a particularly interesting phrase. The early part of the line, which has the clouds "rolling along" their burden, suggests that it is a manageable one, its weight analogous to, say, that of cannon balls. *World* involves a radical shift of perspective. Suddenly the significance and scope of the clouds have expanded; the effect is something like that of the word *universal* later in the passage. *Fleecy* connects the world of the clouds metaphorically with that of men and of those animals whom Thomson elsewhere calls man's "fleecy care." And the phrase "fleecy world" suggests that the clouds themselves represent, or contain, an entire world of snow; it reminds us that those clouds also contain the potential of a "fleecy world" for men, contain the power to transform a familiar world into one totally robed in white.

The idea of the snow as a "winter-robe" emerges only later in the passage, after the fields have been described as "cherished." This, too, is an adjective of complex force, suggesting simultaneously two opposed yet related points of view. By whom are the fields cherished? The obvious answer would be, "by man," although man has so far not appeared in the passage at all. These are the fields that man has cultivated, that bear him sustenance, that provide the source of rural wealth; the snow which decks and buries them is part of the natural process through which they come to fruition — for man. But another possibility is suggested by the conjunction of "cherished fields" and "Put on their winter-robe of purest white." Perhaps these fields are "cherished" also for their place in the total arrangement of the universe; the power that provides for them a beautiful winter robe may be also the power that cherishes. The conjunction of these two possibilities of course reiterates a point which Thomson often makes more directly: that the scheme which concerns him is total, all-enveloping, including man along with less dignified natural phenomena.

The Poetry of Vision

A final example of the complexity of Thomson's diction here is the phrase "one wild dazzling waste," which may recall the beautiful line, "all This waste of music is the voice of love" ("Spring," ll. 614–615). The meaning of *waste* is different in each case: in "Winter" it connotes "wasteland," in "Spring" it seems to mean something closer to "useless expenditure." Both meanings, however, have primarily negative connotations; in both cases Thomson exploits such connotations in order to deny them. What appears to be "waste" is also love, or beauty; the ordering power of ideological perspective emerges once more.

The tempest passage continues to its most famous section, the one which presents the redbreast in human company. The robin, however, is shown to us primarily in association with other forms of animal life facing the rigors of winter.

> Drooping, the labourer-ox
> Stands covered o'er with snow, and then demands
> The fruit of all his toil. The fowls of heaven,
> Tamed by the cruel season, crowd around
> The winnowing store, and claim the little boon
> Which Providence assigns them. One alone,
> The redbreast, sacred to the household gods,
> Wisely regardful of the embroiling sky,
> In joyless fields and thorny thickets leaves
> His shivering mates, and pays to trusted man
> His annual visit. Half afraid, he first
> Against the window beats; then brisk alights
> On the warm hearth; then, hopping o'er the floor,
> Eyes all the smiling family askance,
> And pecks, and starts, and wonders where he is —
> Till, more familiar grown, the table-crumbs
> Attract his slender feet. The foodless wilds
> Pour forth their brown inhabitants. The hare,
> Though timorous of heart, and hard beset
> By death in various forms, dark snares, and dogs,
> And more unpitying men, the garden seeks,
> Urged on by fearless want. The bleating kind
> Eye the bleak heaven, and next the glistening earth,
> With looks of dumb despair; then, sad-dispersed,
> Dig for the withered herb through heaps of snow.
>   (ll. 240–264)

The organization of this passage is particularly indicative of the way in which Thomson's mind works, the nature of his preoccupations. The careful and significant progression of animals depends not so much on distinctions of kind as on the differences in the animals' relation to heaven and to man. The "labourer-ox," because he is a labourer, can demand the reward to which his toil entitles him; his being covered with snow is significant primarily because it establishes that this is the proper time to make such demands. The "fowls of heaven" are distinguished from domestic fowl, but also associated with them by the locution. They are wild birds, yet a long tradition tells us that they are the special care of heaven, and although they toil not, they too have a boon assigned them in the face of winter. The robin, among them, is in a special position; his "boon" comes not from the "winnowing store" which men have accumulated, but more directly from men, in the form of "table-crumbs." Other inhabitants of the wilds are less fortunate — less directly, it would seem, under the care of heaven. The hare, although man is his enemy, is, under the pressure of "fearless want," forced to seek sustenance from that enemy. Finally, the "bleating kind," the sheep, find heaven "bleak" — metaphorically as well as literally — and the beauty of the earth equally bleak; receiving no help from heaven or from men, they have to find nourishment where they can. The progression has taken us from an animal especially protected by man, because of his labor, through forms of wild life especially protected by heaven, to the hare which, although it has no special protection, can still profit from the works of men, to the helpless sheep who profit neither from God nor from men, except minimally through "the withered herb." There is no special reason, except in the case of the labourer-ox, why one animal should receive more favor than another; the poet's perception is merely that apparent differences in the degree of favor do exist, and that they form a rough scale of being in themselves.

The close attention given to the robin represents an interesting shift of perspective. If the wild birds appear to be the special care of heaven, the robin is "sacred to the *household* gods," thus in the nature of things more intimately connected with man than his fellows. As the poet considers the redbreast's approach to men, his attitude toward the other birds changes: they become the robin's "shivering mates," condemned to "joyless fields and thorny thickets," although only a few lines before they had seemed particularly blessed by Providence. The change in perspective is a deliberate change to the limited human point of view; most of the passage attempts something closer to a cosmic viewpoint. The narrower view concentrates on appearance rather than meaning; the various movements of the robin suddenly seem enormously interesting simply as a spectacle in themselves. The security and comfort of the "smiling family" who watch the bird, who cluster round their "warm hearth," eating and able to afford to scatter crumbs, contrast strongly with the precarious sustenance and security which animals in the wilds can find in winter. Immediately after "the table-crumbs" comes a reference to "The foodless wilds"; this contrast prepares dramatically and pictorially for the moral adjurations which follow the description, the poet's injunction, "Now, shepherds, to your helpless charge be kind" (l. 265). The description, in other words, has moral as well as metaphysical meaning.

Although — or because — it is so much concerned with precise description, this passage contains three interesting periphrases: "The fowls of heaven," for wild birds; "brown inhabitants," for the small animals of the forest; "The bleating kind," for sheep. They are characteristic in their precision of Thomson's skill at handling this device. Elsewhere in *The Seasons* he refers to sheep as "gentle tribes," "peaceful people," "fleecy care"; each different periphrasis reflects a specific and immediately significant point of view. In the passage at hand, the important aspect of the sheep is their plaintiveness, their helplessness in the face of natural forces; their plaintive bleating suggests these aspects of their nature. They are here defined as the "kind" of animal which can only bleat in the face of adversity. On the other hand, the forest animals here are not a "kind," but "inhabitants," residents for whom wild nature provides a normal habitat: a fact which makes it the more poignant when nature suddenly refuses them nourishment. Their brownness. at this juncture, emphasizes their temporary apparent lack of harmony with the natural world: their color does not blend with that of the snow any more than their lives can now blend with that of the forest. "The fowls of heaven" has precisely the opposite emphasis: the birds, unlike the animals, *are* in a harmonious state in the winter because they are the domestic creatures of heaven, cared for and comparatively safe, however cruel the season, however little the boon which Providence assigns them.

The point by now should be clear, without more of the analysis which Thomson's diction repays and indeed constantly invites. The variety of the poet's language, like the occasional contortions of his sentence structure, derives from his constant attempt to convey metaphysical meaning in direct observation or in recital of the observations of others or even in entirely imagined panoramas. Scientific language, Virgilian language, Miltonic language, the diction which seems more personal and direct — all reveal a single effort, and their diversity is in itself a partial statement of what Thomson is constantly trying to say. The large structural patterns of *The Seasons* have to do mainly with the poet's metaphysical meaning, his perception of order in the universe. And it is perhaps because moral and metaphysical meanings emerge so successfully from the indirect presentations that many of the directly moralistic passages of *The Seasons* remain unsatisfactory even to the sympathetic reader. As Thomson recites his lists of great men, or glorifies the plow, or sings the praises of industry, he seems to reduce rather than enlarge the import of what he has to say. At his best, he controls his diction and syntax so skillfully that they partake directly in his "message"; a message strongest, on the whole, when least explicit.

III ❧

JAMES THOMSON:
The Retreat from Vision

If *The Seasons* was taken from the beginning to be a triumph of vision in the literal sense, a poem whose excellences were importantly descriptive, the metaphorical meaning of "vision" has always seemed relevant to discussion of *The Castle of Indolence*. The "vision" it offers, commentators have largely agreed, is that of a dream. Alan D. McKillop points out that the landscape of the poem is simultaneously objective and subjective: "The dreamer dreams for himself an appropriate land to dream in. The poet is in the vision which he sustains and elaborates, though the time is to come when he must break the spell and get outside the vision." [1] Léon Morel long ago made a similar point, with emphasis on the curious atmosphere created by this technique: "paysage et personnages sont baignés d'une atmosphère vaporeuse qui estompe les contours et fond les silhouettes, si bien qu'ils sont à la fois vrais de la réalité de la nature et imaginaires comme les visions d'un rêve." [2]

The method of suggesting simultaneously a world of reality and a dream landscape does not demand, obviously, the sort of meticulous observation one finds sometimes in *The Seasons*; accurate recording of the artistry of nature is not fundamentally necessary. It is the more surprising, therefore, that in *The Castle of Indolence* Thomson admits his inability to depict "fair Illusions" in terms strikingly similar to those he had used in "Spring" to explain that the beauties of nature must exceed the poet's capacity to describe them:

> No, fair Illusions! artful Phantoms, no!
> My Muse will not attempt your Fairy-Land:
> She has no Colours that like you can glow;
> To catch your vivid Scenes too gross her Hand.

(I, xlv)

Thomson: Retreat from Vision

In *The Seasons,* Thomson solved the problem of the imagination's inadequacy to depict reality partly by his insistent reference to the meaning of the scenes he presented. *The Castle of Indolence* adopts a similar method, referring its visions constantly to their import. But it also retreats from reliance on the visual. Imagery of sight is rarely crucial; the sense of hearing becomes increasingly important. And Thomson elevates the technique of negative suggestion, which he had employed with notable success in isolated passages of *The Seasons,* into a vital structural principle.

A three-stanza passage early in Canto I, depicting the realm of Indolence, is one of the most extended pieces of description in *The Castle*; examination of it may clarify Thomson's technique here and indicate the descriptive ideal of the poem: not vividness, but vagueness made suggestive:

iii
Was nought around but Images of Rest;
Sleep-soothing Groves, and quiet Lawns between;
And flowery Beds that slumbrous Influence kest,
From Poppies breath'd; and Beds of pleasant Green,
Where never yet was creeping Creature seen.
Mean time unnumber'd glittering Streamlets play'd,
And hurled every-where their Waters sheen;
That, as they bicker'd through the sunny Glade,
Though restless still themselves, a lulling Murmur made.

iv
Join'd to the Prattle of the purling Rills,
Were heard the lowing Herds along the Vale,
And Flocks loud-bleating from the distant Hills,
And vacant Shepherds piping in the Dale;
And now and then sweet Philomel would wail,
Or Stock-Doves plain amid the Forest deep,
That drowsy rustled to the sighing Gale;
And still a Coil the Grashopper did keep:
Yet all these Sounds yblent inclined all to Sleep.

v
Full in the Passage of the Vale, above,
A sable, silent, solemn Forest stood;
Where nought but shadowy Forms were seen to move,
As *Idless* fancy'd in her dreaming Mood.

47

And up the Hills, on either Side, a Wood
Of blackening Pines, ay waving to and fro,
Sent forth a sleepy Horror through the Blood;
And where this Valley winded out, below,
The murmuring Main was heard, and scarcely heard, to flow.

The last of these stanzas is, as Professor McKillop points out, a particularly good example of Thomson's trick of suggesting that the landscape is simultaneously "the setting and the substance of a reverie." [3] The opening line of stanza iii establishes the meaning of the images that follow, all primarily justified as "Images of Rest." This is nature made for man in a more literal sense than anywhere in *The Seasons*. The repeated pun on "beds" exemplifies this fact: both "flowery Beds" and "Beds of pleasant Green" are on one level simply garden beds of flowers or of greenery, but the reader is never far from consciousness of the other meaning, the beds as settings for human repose. (Awareness of this second sense may be intensified by the reference later in the poem [st. xliv] to "flowery Beds" displaying "melting Forms" who lie on them "languishingly.") The human participant is always implicitly in the scene: only in relation to him can the groves be "Sleep-soothing," the flowery beds cast their "slumbrous Influence," the creeping creatures be seen or not seen, the streams provide a *lulling* murmur, the lowing herds be heard. Effects are more important than causes here — in marked contrast to the emphasis of *The Seasons,* which is most often concerned at least subterraneously with the great Cause of all effects.

The frequent repetition of *and* in this passage creates intense syntactical stress on linkages, particularly on connections in time. Only the last of the three stanzas deals intensively with physical relations of the scene's various components. We know that the quiet lawns are between the groves, that the streams are in the glade, that the hills are distant; but we know more emphatically that the landscape's effects are simultaneous. Such modifiers as *Mean time, Join'd, still,* insist that everything is happening at the same time; the repeated *and* suggests the scene's lack of subordination. Even when, in the last stanza, the physical relations of various elements in the landscape emerge, all seem of precisely equal importance. Groves and lawns and flowery beds receive equivalent stress, all alike "Images of Rest"; they are thus justified, thus meaningful, but one is no more significant than another. The playing of the streamlets, the lowing of the herds, the bleating of the flocks and piping of the shepherds occupy the same moment in time; their blended effect is the center of interest; no one phenomenon is sufficiently striking to justify special attention. An important thematic point thus emerges simply through repetition of a single coordinate conjunction almost to the point of tedium: the lack of hierarchy, of value system, of any real order in the realm of Indolence. There is, of course, a strong *appearance* of the order in variety that Alexander Pope so valued. This is a land "Half prankt with Spring, with Summer half imbrown'd" (si. ii), illuminated by "a Kind of checker'd Day and Night" (st. vii); the description alternates images of brightness and of darkness: there is perfect balance of a sort. But that balance is ultimately meaningless, and the first canto hints, by its structural principles, much that becomes fully explicit only in the second.

Like so many portions of *The Castle of Indolence,* this one is largely dominated by a pattern of negative suggestion which hints the dangers of the beauty here described. The very form of the opening line ("Was nought around but . . .") reminds us initially that something is left out of this scene; the "sleepy Horror" (reminiscent of the "cogenial horrors" of "Winter") sent "through the Blood" by the pine grove may make us aware of sinister possibility, even though this particular horror seems merely titillating. Similarly, the "never yet" in "Where never yet was creeping Creature seen" suggests ominous possibilities for the future, as if we were in a sleeper's parody of Eden. Philomel's song is a "wail," the stock doves "plain"; the poem insists that such sounds blend into a sleep-producing atmosphere, yet the nature of the sounds hints some danger or melancholy implicit in the scene but not yet realized.

Except for its occasional archaisms, the language of these stanzas is straightforward and effective. Its vividness is rarely visual: *glittering* and *blackening* are the only modifiers which evoke even momentarily a strong visual impression, although the line "And hurled every-where their Waters sheen" creates a brief, vigorous image. The strongest words allude to the emotional rather than the visual: *Sleep-soothing, slumbrous, vacant, dreaming, sleepy Horror.*

49

To be sure, the emotional emphasis of this language is to some extent created by the context: the action of the poem insists on the association between the languorous and the pleasant, so that a word like *slumbrous* gradually takes on increasing richness. Individual lines or phrases could be part of *The Seasons*: "bicker'd through the sunny Glade," "the Prattle of the purling Rills," "the lowing Herds along the Vale,/ And Flocks loud-bleating from the distant Hills"; and such compounds as *Sleep-soothing* and *loud-bleating* remind us of the dictional peculiarities of the earlier poem. Yet the effect of the diction is strikingly different here, and not only because of the intermixture of Spenserian language or the peculiar demands of the Spenserian stanza; the difference derives most importantly from the new purposes to which the language is put.

A passage in "Spring" describing the wanderings of George, Lord Lyttelton, through his estate of Hagley Park contains many descriptive elements which appear also in the first two stanzas of the *Castle of Indolence* selection:

> There along the dale
> With woods o'erhung, and shagged with mossy rocks
> Whence on each hand the gushing waters play,
> And down the rough cascade white-dashing fall
> Or gleam in lengthened vista through the trees,
> You silent steal; or sit beneath the shade
> Of solemn oaks, that tuft the swelling mounts
> Thrown graceful round by Nature's careless hand,
> And pensive listen to the various voice
> Of rural peace — the herds, the flocks, the birds,
> The hollow-whispering breeze, the plaint of rills,
> That, purling down amid the twisted roots
> Which creep around, their dewy murmurs shake
> On the soothed ear.
>
> ("Spring," ll. 909–922)

Here, too, we find two of Thomson's peculiar compounds: *white-dashing* and *hollow-whispering*. Apart from these, only one word, *shagged*, seems characteristically his own: the language of this passage, like that of the one from *The Castle of Indolence,* is on the whole not strikingly individual. It is more visual than the other selection: the opening lines approximate the ideal of an image for

50

every word. On the other hand, the last six lines stress sound almost as heavily as those from the later poem.

Although the elements of scene and of sound are virtually identical in the two passages, their effects are vividly different; the difference resides more in structure than in language. The thirteen lines from *The Seasons* comprise a single sentence; no sentence in *The Castle of Indolence* — such, obviously, is the influence of the Spenserian stanza — is more than nine lines long. But the contrasting effects depend not so much on the length of the sentences as on the way in which they are formed. The passage from *The Seasons* is almost obsessively concerned with relationships: the dale is adorned with wood and with rocks; it is the source of the cascade; the oaks are specifically related to the mounts, and the mounts to the work of Nature; the various sounds all derive from "rural peace"; the rills purl amid the roots, the roots "creep around," and the murmur of the rills has a specific effect on the ear. This concentration on relationships produces a certain structural awkwardness which makes one acutely conscious of the length of the sentence: Thomson is so much concerned to subordinate accurately, to suggest precisely the intricacies he perceives, that he seems about to founder in the complexities of his own syntax. Yet these complexities give the passage its interest; through them we sense the poet's control, his awareness of the exact meaning of every natural detail. The peculiarly Thomsonian irony of "Nature's *careless* hand" dominates the description; as all the sounds of the environment compose together the "voice/ Of rural peace," so all its sights display the subtle patternings of Nature, which provides rough cascades and gleaming vistas as different aspects of a single stream: "All Nature is but Art, unknown to thee."

The contrast in the effects created by the two passages may be partly suggested by the use of the word *solemn* in each. In both cases, the adjective refers to a group of trees; the "sable, silent, solemn Forest" of *The Castle of Indolence* parallels the "solemn oaks" of "Spring." But the multiplication of adjectives in the one case is significant. An adjective of sight is followed by one of sound, then one of emotion. Alliteration links the three, but so does meaning: each has similar emotional overtones. And the tripling of emotional impact forces the reader's attention to the connection of landscape with feeling. The solemn oaks, on the other hand, are no more emphatically described than the "swelling mounts" which fill out the line, and *solemn* seems, like *swelling*, most importantly a descriptive adjective, with overtones of its early, specific meaning, "somber, dark." The emotional implications of the word are here subordinated to the descriptive ones; and the emotional import itself is primarily meaningful as an element in a complex pattern. Even the language of *The Castle of Indolence* which duplicates characteristic language of *The Seasons* occurs in the later poem with strikingly different effect.

Although no single passage can fully represent the techniques or preoccupations of *The Seasons*, specific comparisons do suggest significant contrasts between the two poems. Professor McKillop points out, for example, another analogue for this descriptive section of *The Castle of Indolence* in "Spring," ll. 197–202, a passage describing the "music" of nature after rainfall. Two lines in it almost duplicate two from the later poem:

> the distant bleatings of the hills,
> The hollow lows responsive from the vales.

But the single emphatic word that distinguishes the "Spring" passage exemplifies the difference between the two: the lows are here "responsive"; in *The Castle of Indolence* they merely coexist with the other sounds of indolence. The sounds of the landscape in the environs of the castle blend to incline the listener to sleep; in "Spring," the zephyr sweetened by the rain blends the music of nature. Again, *The Seasons* emphasizes the relationships which the other passage avoids; the meaning which dominates the description in "Spring" has to do with total pattern rather than with emotional effect.

In *The Castle of Indolence* Thomson relies heavily on aural and tactile appeals; his "images" are frequently impressionistic. Many of his similes stress the impressionistic aspects of his technique. One adapted, as Professor McKillop points out, from Milton, is exemplary:

> Heaps pour'd on Heaps, and yet they slip'd along
> In silent Ease: as when beneath the Beam
> Of Summer-Moons, the distant Woods among,

Thomson: Retreat from Vision

Or by some Flood all silver'd with the Gleam,
The soft-embodied Fays through airy Portal stream.

(I, xx)

The corresponding passage from *Paradise Lost* compares the devils entering Pandemonium to

Fairy Elves,
Whose midnight Revels, by a Forest side
Or Fountain some belated Peasant sees,
Or dreams he sees, while over-head the Moon
Sits Arbitress, and nearer to the Earth
Wheels her pale course.

(*pl* I, 781–786)

The possible truth or fiction of the vision, an issue suggested by Milton's passage, interests Thomson not at all. The later poet adds one new visual detail: his "Flood" (corresponding to Milton's "Fountain") is "silver'd" by the moon's gleam. But the main shift of emphasis is atmospheric; no more than Milton does Thomson provide a precise picture. For Milton the person on the scene, the peasant-perceiver, is important, and the personified moon supplies another acting participant in addition to stressing the supernatural aspects of the occasion. For Thomson, on the other hand, the *glamor* of the image is all-important. The fact that the fays are supernatural beings is significant mainly because it makes them more mysteriously attractive; the change from "Fairy Elves" to "soft-embodied Fays" heightens the immediate emotional appeal — the appeal, largely, of luxurious ease — of Thomson's personages. The silvery gleam of the moonlight, the fact that it is a *summer* moon, that the woods are *distant*, the portal *airy*: these details also add to the ease, the delicacy, the glamor of the scene. The immediate emotional effect of the simile is one of a series of similar effects which contribute importantly to the "atmosphere" of *The Castle* but directly contradict the poem's explicit moral, that effort is superior to indolence. Morally, of course, the superiority of effort is readily apparent; emotionally, as this poem fully demonstrates, indolence has far richer appeal. Perhaps the most brilliant achievement of *The Castle of Indolence* is to document intensively in poetic terms the irreconcilable conflict between emotion and conscience.

The Poetry of Vision

The concern with emotional effect in *The Castle of Indolence* is one of the most striking aspects of the poem. Josephine Miles has pointed out that throughout the eighteenth century it was assumed that emotions were the proper concern of poetry, that any judgment of valid poetic technique must depend upon the extent to which such technique moved the reader. The conflict between those who believed in the value of generalization and the champions of particularity was not a divergence about the value of emotion. "Both schools, all the critics, based every argument upon emotion, its workings, its powers, its connection with objects." [4] Critical dispute centered, rather, on the method by which emotional power could best be achieved. In this dispute, *The Seasons* was, as we have seen, frequently used as an example by believers in the value of particularity, of detailed description as a technique for moving the reader. Yet Thomson's own position is not perfectly clear, and *The Castle of Indolence* suggests that he was beginning, finally, to experiment extensively with more subtle modes of emotional suggestion. The poem is most obviously a jeu d'esprit, a playful exercise in a mode not on the whole taken seriously in the eighteenth century. But Professor McKillop has demonstrated how deeply it is concerned with genuine questions about the ambiguous value of indolence as a mode of existence, and it should not be surprising to find it also seriously concerned with nice emotional discriminations.

Indolence as a state implies a special emotional condition, as the enchanter's song explains:

> here . . . soft Gales of Passion play,
> And gently stir the Heart, thereby to form
> A quicker Sense of Joy.
>
> (I, xvi)

But it also implies the rejection of a range of emotions: the same stanza reminds one that the accepter of indolence is "Above those Passions that this World deform." The root sense of *indolence* is negative: the absence of pain, freedom from pain. But the poem reveals with considerable subtlety the extent of the *other* rejections implied by indolence; in this sense most profoundly the logic of the first canto necessitates the second.

An insistent pattern of negative suggestion conveys the inexorability of choice, the extent to which every acceptance implies a corollary rejection. The opening stanza places the pattern in the broadest possible context, reminding the reader of the Fall of Man and its relevance to the constant invocation of the negative. The initial imperative, which summarizes the moral implications of the entire poem, is formulated in negative terms:

> O Mortal Man, who livest here by Toil,
> Do not complain of this thy hard Estate;
> That like an Emmet thou must ever moil,
> Is a sad Sentence of an ancient Date.

But the reason one is not to complain, it turns out, is that the state opposed to man's doom of work, given that "sad Sentence," is worse than the one it replaces:

> Withouten That would come an heavier Bale,
> Loose Life, unruly Passions, and Diseases pale.

This is the authoritative voice of the poet, and its utterance is particularly interesting in the light of the wizard's later assertion that indolence creates "soft Gales of Passion" as opposed to "those Passions that the World deform." The enchanter's "soft Gales" conceal the poet's "unruly Passion": a metaphor may obscure the reality of emotion's dangers.

As the poem begins to describe the realm of Indolence, it continues to rely on negative statement. The wizard is one "Than whom a Fiend more fell is no-where found" (st. ii); in his domain "No living Wight could work, ne cared even for Play." But the important lack in his realm is emotional, although its chief temptations are likewise emotional. We learn, in stanza vi, that "whate'er smack'd of Noyance, or Unrest,/ Was far far off expell'd from this delicious Nest," and the point is gradually amplified. In the enchanter's song, the birds are invoked as models for men because "They neither plough, nor sow" (st. x), yet they receive the benefit of the harvest. Two full stanzas (xii–xiv) subsequently describe what in human life the choice of indolence avoids. Various human activities are made to seem superficially undesirable, and depicted always as negatives of the "positive" values of indolence. "With me," says the tempter, "you need not rise at early Dawn,/ To pass the joyless Day in various Stounds." The joylessness to be avoided includes emotional and physical difficulties. To engage in business or law or politics involves compromises, necessary evil; one can sidestep evil by simply refusing the engagement. To live a human life involves troublesome contact with other people; the enchanter promises, on the other hand, "No Dogs, no Babes, no Wives, to stun your Ear," no "Sounds that are a Misery to hear." In place of misery he offers, explicitly, calm, calm composed of "all Nature, and all Art," calm which turns out, in stanza xvi, to be completely identified with virtue; the emotional and the moral spheres have become one:

> What, what, is Virtue, but Repose of Mind?
> A pure ethereal Calm! that knows no Storm;
> Above the Reach of wild Ambition's Wind,
> Above those Passions that this World deform.

From the enchanter's point of view only a limited emotional range is acceptable: if he values, on aesthetic grounds, the pleasures of calm and the emotions associated with it, he is at least equally emphatic in his rejection of the fiercer, more dangerous, "deforming" emotions. Stanza xv outlines the process by which he justifies his association of calm with morality, with heavy dependence on negative statement of alternatives:

> Here nought but Candour reigns, indulgent Ease,
> Good-natur'd Lounging, Sauntering up and down:
> They who are pleas'd themselves must always please;
> On Others' Ways they never squint a Frown,
> Nor heed what haps in Hamlet or in Town.
> Thus, from the Source of tender Indolence,
> With milky Blood the Heart is overflown,
> Is sooth'd and sweeten'd by the social Sense;
> For Interest, Envy, Pride, and Strife are banish'd hence.

The technique of this stanza reveals the poet's precise awareness of the values of Augustan terminology. Such positive terms as *Good-natur'd, tender, social Sense* are reinforced by the banishment of the conventional personified villains of much eighteenth-century verse: Interest, Envy, Pride, Strife. "They who are pleas'd themselves must always please" qualifies the "bad" word *indulgent*, offering an invitation to realign one's values, to see hedonism as a source of social virtue. But on the whole little realignment seems called for — such is the enchanter's skill, and Thomson's. The value of indolence is to some extent genuine (stanza xvii, beginning "The Best of Men have ever lov'd Repose," identifies it with the ideal of classical retirement); simple semantic manipulation can make it seem entirely so.

By banishing all emotional stress, then, indolence offers, it can be argued, a state of repose which makes possible maximum purity. This is a fugitive and cloistered virtue, justified by constant implicit reference to the impossibility, or extreme difficulty, of achieving any more active state of goodness. To remove oneself from "deforming" passions is to avoid the possibility of certain sorts of vice; but such a choice involves vice, too, vice whose nature has so far only been hinted. The enchanter's manipulation of language to create meanings with little ultimate validity provides a significant hint, if one is aware of the disparity between the appearance he creates and the reality which underlies it. Such manipulation is the central technique of his song, which establishes a crucial tension between the yearning that life should be so easy and ease so rewarding, and the knowledge that real experience requires strenuousness. When the song finally suggests that the lack of toil in the realm of indolence produces results as satisfactory as those gained by exertion in the outside world, with fewer penalties, the reader may be uneasy: this sort of uneasiness is vital to the poem's ultimate emotional effect.

Emphasis on negative statement diminishes for a time after the enchanter's song. The first canto has already made its central point: absence of the evils of life seems temporarily equivalent to the presence of virtue; emotional ease and moral serenity are apparently identical. The succeeding description uses negative terms for even trivial observations, although with no special emphasis. A negative comparison defines the enchanter's great power: "Not stronger were of old the Giant-Crew,/ Who sought to pull high *Jove* from regal State" (st. xxii); the analogue once more hints some theological meaning to this tale of indolence. When this villain seizes his victims, "Their Joints unknit" (st. xxiii): the formulation suggests the unnaturalness of the realm which has been labeled "all Nature." The porter cannot prevent himself from yawning; the page minds nought but sleep and play; the poet praises the state of "Undress." These modes of presentation, reminding the reader constantly of alternative possibilities, continue to evoke the pervasive sense of uneasiness.

After the poet discusses his own problem of indolence and invokes his muse (st. xxxi–xxxii), he describes in more detail the luxuries provided in the enchanter's realm. Now stress on the negative increases, to insist on the superiority of the castle's offerings to those of the real world. The normal phenomena here rejected range from the "shrill alarming" doorbell to the "Gossip's Tale" and "saintly Spleen." Tapestries hung throughout the castle's rooms remind one that in the "Patriarchal Age" of Abraham, "Toil was not then": the rejection of unpleasant necessities seems to have Biblical as well as classical sanctions. Listening to the music of the castle, the heart forgets "all Duties and all Cares"; the demons of the tempest find no entrance; Titian could not equal the beauty of the dreams here provided. There is nothing ominous about this group of negatives, except possibly their number: certainly a great many things are being rejected. But this is a siren song: one can hardly wish to accept these earthly phenomena, and when the magic globe reveals the "Ant-Hill Earth," the real world, one sees that there, too, choice necessitates rejection. The negatives in the description of the castle intensify awareness of the emotional serenity provided by the realm of indolence; the negatives of the world outside add up to emotional poverty. The businessman dominated by the maxim "A Penny saved is a Penny got" will not "bate a Jot" in his effort to get and preserve money — "Till it has quench'd his Fire, and banished his Pot." His spendthrift heir is his opposite: "of Nothing takes he Care." By their rejections, of carefulness or of all besides, they severely limit and ultimately destroy themselves. Similarly, the "Race of learned Men," like Dr. Johnson's "Young Author," "lose the present" to "gain the future Age,/ Praised to be when [they] can hear no more." The rejections of the world are vividly self-destructive; those of the castle seem merely self-indulgent.

As the poet begins to characterize the castle's residents, he continues to employ negative statement. The "Man of special grave Remark" is "Pensive not sad, in Thought involv'd not dark." His talents are buried: "Of the fine Stores he Nothing would impart,/ Which or boon Nature gave, or Nature-painting Art" (st. lvii).

The alternatives in his case are rather subtly conceived. He does not pass his days in thoughtless slumber (st. lix), but builds glorious systems, allows great ideas to fill his mind: "But with the Clouds they fled, and left no Tract behind" (st. lix). His companion is one "who quite detested Talk," whose rejection is of language and consequently almost of life itself: his only speech is at evening: "Thank Heaven! the Day is done." The next stanza depicts the "Wretch" who rejects human contact and cleanliness, in contrast to the "joyous Youth" who demonstrates that "not even Pleasure to Excess is good" (st. lxiii). The succeeding characterizations, including the one of Thomson himself written by Lyttelton, employ similar verbal techniques; only the concluding stanzas by Dr. John Armstrong (author of *The Art of Preserving Health*) abandon such modes.

The first canto, then, makes extensive use of a rhetorical device which Thomson had used before to good effect in isolated sections of *The Seasons*. The multiplicity of examples, however, makes it seem of central significance to this particular canto. Through it the poem underlines important points: the fact that indolence is a state almost entirely defined by its refusals of many aspects of ordinary life; the fact that such refusals are both tempting and dangerous; the possible range of rejections; the important truth that ordinary life, too, involves denials, that choice always implies rejection. The chief temptation of indolence is emotional; its chief rejection the rejection of care, in a double sense. The enchanter's equation of indolence with virtue seems temporarily plausible; nothing clearly contradicts it in the first canto, although a strong opposed literary and theological tradition presumably makes the reader wary of giving it full credence, and the infirmities of the castle's inhabitants make the wizard's thesis seem dubious. It is the function of the second canto to undermine that thesis more fully.

Although its purpose and its general mode are very different, the second canto, too, makes extensive use of negative statement, both to comment on the first and to establish new truths. Selvaggio, father of the Knight of Arts and Industry, "neither sow'd nor reap'd": in this respect, but in no other, he is like the birds in the enchanter's song. The reminiscence is significant, for this canto reveals that the wizard's exclusions are not all necessary ones. Selvaggio, appropriately for the quasi-historical allegory, spends his time in hunting; he sires a boy who knows "no Beverage but the flowing Stream," who passes a youth as "void of Care" (st. viii) as any resident of the castle, without the annoyance of parents, but with help from Minerva and the rural deities. The canto details his various pursuits both in negative and in positive terms, describes the savage state of the world he was born to save with heavy reliance on the negative (st. xiv–xv); he rescues mankind, then retires into his own version of the classic choice. From his retirement "Th'amusing Cares of Rural Industry" (st. xxvii) are not banished; his notion of pleasure is richer than that implicit in the realm of indolence. He polishes "Nature with a finer Hand: / Yet on her Beauties durst not Art incroach" (st. xxviii). The rejection of art here serves a higher purpose: nature, "polished" by man, transcends any conceivable achievement of man alone.

This version of man's relation to nature, much like the ideal frequently embodied in *The Seasons*, may call to the reader's attention how strikingly different the image of nature in the first canto of *The Castle* is from that in *The Seasons*. The realm of Indolence is, of course, deliberately falsified and glamorized. But it is also a land of wish-fulfilment. In it, nature is not, as in the longer poem, the field for man's activity; it is the encourager of his passivity. The excitement over order and the capacity to order which dominates *The Seasons* here gives place to excitement over the possibilities of anti-order, total freedom from structure. Although the hero-knight reveals forcefully in the second canto the fallacies of the values of indolence, he never demonstrates at all fully the positive values that might replace them. For a complete statement of these values, one must turn to Thomson's own earlier work: in a real sense *The Seasons* and *The Castle of Indolence* are complementary poems; but the emotional power of the later poem implies a rejection of that of the earlier one.

When the Knight and his bard begin their journey to overthrow the enchanter's power, they discover, looking down at his realm, an environment where "without Hurry all seem'd glad" (st. xxxvii). Philomelus, the bard, "half-enraptur'd" suddenly perceives that vice and virtue always mingle inextricably, so that no process of exclusion can be entirely successful (st. xxxviii); the Knight, however, rejects this insight, insisting that one must discriminate between those determined to maintain their choice of vice and those willing to repent. Then the Knight's bard sings a song opposed to that of the enchanter in the first canto, its burden that the truth of God's dominion needs no proof; this song establishes a new series of alternatives directly opposed to the tempting ones earlier offered. The essence of its argument — which emerges only through many detailed examples — is that "vile Loitering in Ease" (st. l) must be rejected because if mankind, "unambitious" (st. li), had indulged in it, "None e'er had soar'd to Fame, None honour'd been, None prais'd." (The enchanter, it should be remembered, through his reference to "wild Ambition's Wind" [I, xvi], has suggested that ambition is among the world's horrors which the choice of indolence avoids.) A stronger argument appeals not to the desire for fame but to the thirst for emotional fulfilment: the Bard's weapons are surprisingly like the enchanter's. "Toil, and be glad!" adjures the bard; "Who does not act is dead" [II, liv]. No true joy can come from self-indulgence, he insists, and he outlines the various rejections which the true worker can make to achieve self-fulfilment. Then, he appeals to the victims of indolence not to "spill" their talents, but to follow him to "Where Pleasure's Roses, void of Serpents, grow" (st. lix); we may recall the early description of indolence's domain, where never *yet* was creeping creature seen. The argument of moral strenuousness appeals to the same desires as the argument of indolence; like the enchanter of indolence, the bard of effort threatens various ills as penalties for the alternate choice; like him, too, he promises emotional delights as concomitants of virtue. To be sure, the final appeal of Arts and Industry is one for which the enchanter can offer no equivalent: this time the bard's negative formulation reveals the most substantial flaw in the opposed argument:

> Heirs of Eternity! yborn to rise
> Through endless States of Being, still more near
> To Bliss approaching, and Perfection clear,
> Can you renounce a Fortune so sublime,
> Such glorious Hopes, your backward Steps to steer,
> And roll, with vilest Brutes, through Mud and Slime?
> No! No! — Your Heaven-touch'd Hearts disdain the piteous Crime!
>
> (st. lxiii)

The Poetry of Vision

"Enough! enough!" cry "The better Sort," in a moment of inadvertent comedy; and it *is* enough: the stanza expands the ominous
theological hints at the beginning of the poem to reveal the ultimate
weakness of indolence. Most of the remainder of the second canto
objectifies other hints offered earlier, as the Knight waves his wand
of "anti-magic Power" to turn falsehood into truth, reveal the landscape's true horror and that of indolence. In the desert where the
indolent finally find themselves, "nor trim Field, nor lively Culture
smil'd;/ Nor waving Shade was seen, nor Fountain fair" (st.
lxxvii): the scenery dramatizes the rejection of labor and reveals
the meaning of earlier exclusions.

The argument of the poem as a whole has dealt directly with
moral, social and artistic truths, as Professor McKillop perceptively
demonstrates. But the extensive pattern of negative statement also
shows that the moral, the social and the artistic for Thomson essentially — not merely rhetorically — involve positive or negative emotional experience. The Enchanter and the Bard alike use the
emotional appeals of their respective programs as bases for argument, but the richness of the first canto suggests that in emotional
force the Enchanter must triumph; the domain of the Knight of
Arts and Industry is more theoretical, less attractive, than that of
the wizard. In this respect particularly the poem cannot resolve its
conflict of values: the Knight can win full assent only if one
rejects (as Thomson does not) the felt emotional riches of the Enchanter. But although Thomson was fully aware of the compelling
emotional power of indolence, he combated it in the poem by his
discussion of the proper function of poetry.

Professor McKillop suggests that in the first canto we are really
most interested in the history of the poet in the castle, the "I" who
emerges suddenly at stanza xxxi. This poet is one focus throughout
The Castle of Indolence of major discussions of the proper function of poetry, but poetry's function is a recurrent issue in other
contexts as well. Poetry is one of the amusements which the castle
offers its habitués. The wizard's song praises the birds who "Hymn
their good God, and carol sweet of Love./ Such grateful kindly
Raptures them emove" (st. x). Spontaneously moved to song, the
birds sing indiscriminately of love or of God; they provide an ideal
for the poet in the castle. "Amid the Groves you may indulge the

Muse," the enchanter points out later (st. xvii), "Or tend the Blooms, and deck the vernal Year." The juxtaposition of puttering in the garden with writing poetry suggests their equivalent value — or lack of value — as activities; the writing of poetry, in this context, is mere indulgence, permissible as a form of emotional release. Similarly, the description of the joys of the castle emphasizes the great rule "That each should work his own Desire"; it is consequently permissible to "melt the Time in Love, or wake the Lyre,/ And carol what, unbid, the Muses might inspire" (st. xxxv). *Unbid* is, of course, the operative word: poetry is acceptable if it involves no particular effort. "The Rural Poets" long ago sang of love (st. xxxvi), and "Dan HOMER" of Nepenthe (st. xxvii). Such authority supports the case for merely "pleasant" poetry; but the kind of poetry appropriate to the realm of Indolence has also a certain utility. The poet compares the splendor of the castle with that of Bagdad, where "'Verse, Love, Music still the Garland wore," where "When Sleep was coy, the Bard, in Waiting there,/ Chear'd the lone Midnight with the Muse's Lore" (st. xlii). This is poetry reduced to a substitute for the sleeping pill. On the other hand, the Mirror of Vanity, which reflects the "real world," reveals to the castle's inhabitants the futility of literary effort directed toward the achievement of fame, which involves genuine work; so the indolent relegate poetry to a subsidiary place. The portrait of Thomson himself as resident of the castle depicts him as pouring forth "his *unpremeditated* Strain" (st. lxviii); we catch glimpses of those whose "only Labour was to kill the Time," and who do so as "They sit, they loll, turn o'er some idle Rhyme" (st. lxxii). The first canto repeatedly alludes to poetry as a mode of hedonism; it is an emblem both of the evil of the castle and of its allurement.

The latter point, hinted several times in the first canto, becomes more explicit in the second, through the voice of the first-person narrator:

> Come then, my Muse, and raise a bolder Song:
> Come, lig no more upon the Bed of Sloth,
> Dragging the lazy languid Line along,
> Fond to begin, but still to finish loth.
>
> (II, iv)

The Poetry of Vision

But awareness of the evil involved in this temptation has been explicit much earlier. The poet-speaker asks in the first canto how he can "attempt such arduous String" — how he can sing of this realm since he has spent his time in it, "In this Soul-deadening Place, loose-loitering" (I, xxxi). He then urges his muse to sing warlike and heroic themes, "Dashing Corruption down through every worthless Age" (I, xxxii). The contrast between the poetry of indulgence and that of morality reveals more sharply than anything else in the first canto the essential flaw of the wizard's domain; Thomson, on the side of morality as poetry's chief aim, rejects as mere self-indulgence the idea of an easier sort of poetry. But he fully understands the temptation he rejects, and its power.

The eighteenth-century poet's conventional plaint about the difficulty of finding a patron occurs early in the second canto; the writing of poetry, in this context, becomes the "noblest Toil" (II, ii). After explaining that poets receive no earthly reward, the speaker continues that he doesn't care, after all, about wealth, since Fortune cannot rob him "of free Nature's Grace," or of health; and "Of Fancy, Reason, Virtue, nought can me bereave" (II, iii). The sequence is interesting. These are presumably the vital items of equipment for the poet: perception of the beauties of nature, good health to write about them, fancy, reason, virtue. As in *The Seasons*, Thomson here seems convinced that observation of nature can lead ultimately to morality, that the imagination is — or should be — a means of inculcating virtue. The Knight of Arts and Industry himself is a poet among his other accomplishments, but he gives less attention to the fine arts than to other concerns, because, Thomson points out, the arts, "the Quintessence of All," must be "The Growth of labouring Time, and slow increast" (II, xxii). The poet needs unencumbered time to work; but the ultimate patron of poetry is Liberty, which "inspires the noblest Strains" (II, xxiii): once more, poetry is assumed to be ultimately concerned with virtue. The Bard's inspirational song reminds us of Homer in a new context: now he is important as having fired the breast "To Thirst of Glory, and heroic Deeds" (II, lii). The Bard outlines possible occupations open to those who repent their indolence; some, he says, will go to the muses, "who raise the Heart" (II, lx). And the view of the Bard is that of Thomson himself. It contrasts at all points with that of the enchanter, who uses poetry for seductive rather than constructive purposes.

A large proportion of each canto offers dramatic representation of contrasting kinds of poetry, in the song of the enchanter and that of the Bard. The enchanter can make the worse appear the better reason:

> With magic Dust their Eyne he tries to blind,
> And Virtue's tender Airs o'er Weakness flings.
> What pity base his Song who so divinely sings!
>
> (II, xli)

The listeners marvel that he can "with such sweet Art, unite/ The Lights and Shades of Manners, Wrong and Right" (II, xlii). His mode of confusion is through delight: by enchanting his hearers metaphorically, he enchants them literally. The Bard, on the other hand, is less concerned to please than to inspire. The Knight urges him, "thy heavenly Fire impart;/ Touch Soul with Soul, till forth the latent Spirit start" (II, xlv); the Bard, when he begins to sing, is "raptur'd," (II, xlvi), "ardent" (xlvii), his primary concern is to clarify, not to glorify.

Yet the two contrasted songs, the song of the first canto and that of the second, are in many respects alike. The Bard cannot sing successfully without invoking emotional appeals; poetry of emotion is the only persuasive poetry possible. For the Bard, emotion is a means to a moral end; for the Enchanter, creation of the emotion is more nearly itself the end. And the same seems to be true of much of the poetry of the first canto. Description, meaning are subordinated to emotional effect; Thomson shows himself master of an impressionistic sort of verse with powerful direct appeal. It is unquestionably true, as several critics have maintained, that the first canto requires the second to complete its logic. Yet the logic of the second canto unfortunately also implies the rejection of the poetry of sensuous enchantment that Thomson had just demonstrated his ability to write: his capacity to create it made him no less vividly aware of its dangers. The approved function of emotion in eighteenth-century poetry was to move readers toward some great end. If one abandons awareness of the end, *The Castle of Indolence* argues, emotion becomes far too dangerous a poetic resource.

65

IV 🌬

WILLIAM COLLINS:
The Controlling Image

IN THE POETRY of William Collins, as in that of Thomson, the power and the danger of emotion are vital issues. The frenzy and obscurity of the poet's images raise immediate questions about the importance of emotion to his work. Thomas Gray's judgment of Collins's *Odes on Several Descriptive and Allegoric Subjects* was, "a fine Fancy, model'd upon the Antique, a bad Ear, great Variety of Words, & Images with no Choice at all." [1] The problem of Collins's imagery has seemed crucial ever since. The intellectual discipline which dominates, sometimes excessively, Gray's own images is obviously absent in Collins; and eighteenth-century and modern critics have tended to agree that Collins's unique imagery is the main source of his poetic power. "*His* originality consists in his manner," wrote Mrs. Barbauld, with surprising acuteness; "in the highly figurative garb in which he clothes abstract ideas; in the felicity of his expressions; and his skill in embodying ideal creations. He had much of the mysticism of Poetry, and sometimes became obscure, by aiming at impressions stronger than he had clear and well-defined ideas to support." [2] A century and a half later, Marcel Delamare echoed her, pointing out that Collins's special personal gift was "le don de la vision. Ce n'est pas certes la vision hallucinatoire de Coleridge ou de Poe, mais la faculté d'évoquer de vivantes images et d'animer, suivant un mode foncièrement identique, les allégories ou les êtres merveilleux qui, à défaut de thèmes lyriques proprement dits, donnent à l'oeuvre sa substance propre." [3]

In his "Ode on the Poetical Character," Collins outlines a view of poetry which implies the paramount importance of imagery.[4]

Collins: The Controlling Image

As explicitly stated in the poem it is a vague and by no means revolutionary theory, its tenets held in common by many of Collins's contemporaries. Yet in combination with the poetic practice which the ode exemplifies, the theory implies an approach to poetry which was not to be fully explored in English, after Collins, until the twentieth century. I will touch on it here, and consider other implications of Collins's theory in the concluding chapter.

Fancy, the image-making faculty, and God are the presiding — and "kindred" — powers of this ode. Judgment is conspicuously absent. Inspiration, which Collins believes the most important element in the creation of poetry, helps to devise the images which record the poet's vision. Poetry, founded on the power of vision (metaphysical, not merely physical vision), is closely associated with the divine: this is the chief point Collins's ode makes, relying heavily on religious language (*Angel, Divinest, God-like, blest, hallow'd*). Poetry is connected not only with God, but also with wonder, truth and intellect. The poet's glory has nothing to do with his rôle in the world, nothing to do even specifically with his accomplishment; it is the product simply of his visionary power and of his feeling:

> Young *Fancy* thus, to me Divinest Name, . . .
> To few the God-like Gift assigns,
> To gird their blest prophetic Loins,
> And gaze her Visions wild, and feel unmix'd her Flame!
> (ll. 17, 20–22)

The triumph of poetry is its potentiality for expressing vision, and the poet's vision is self-justifying. A poem need simply *be*.

A. S. P. Woodhouse long ago demonstrated the extent to which Collins's ideas about imagination were in tune with those of his contemporaries;[5] Norman Maclean, more recently, has documented and analyzed the development of the eighteenth-century ode from emphasis on action (human achievement) to stress on the image in the new allegorical and descriptive odes of the mid-century.[6] Awareness of the importance of imagery had manifested itself from the beginning of the century, although it was, as we have seen, sometimes accompanied by the sense that to rely on the image as a mode of communication was an unfortunate weakness of poetry — or of human nature.[7] The shift in outlook toward the middle of the century, the "new movement" with which Collins is often associated, is perhaps best represented by Joseph Warton: "The use, the force, and the excellence of language, certainly consists in raising, *clear*, *complete*, and *circumstantial* images, and in turning *readers* into *spectators*. . . . This excellence [is] of all others the most essential in poetry." [8] The difference between this and Fénelon's definition of poetry as "the lively painting of Things" [9] is simply a matter of emphasis: for Warton imagery seems more nearly an end in itself, not a technique for achieving other ends. But in his idea of readers as spectators he echoes — like so many other critics of the period — Lord Kames, and Lord Kames is perfectly clear that the reason for turning readers into spectators is that "the eye is the best avenue to the heart." [10] When Burke, in 1757, had the temerity to challenge the supremacy of imagery, insisting that even descriptive poetry does not actually create images in the reader's mind and that it would be less powerful if it did so,[11] Goldsmith could retort, in the *Monthly Review*, that "Distinctness of imagery has ever been held productive of the sublime." [12] Burke had questioned a truism.

Collins, then, in assuming that poetry is the product of the image-making power and of divine inspiration, participated in a critical tradition lively both before and after the publication of his odes. But if the theory explicitly articulated in the "Ode on the Poetical Character" contributed nothing particularly new, when considered in the light of the poetic practice the ode exemplifies it acquires new significance. Collins's concept of the poet as literally a seer — one who sees deep into the heart of things, and who also sees surfaces meaningfully — gains new importance from the way he uses imagery: as a mode of achieving insight as well as of recording it. Imagery provides not only the substance of the poem, but its principle of organization. The "Ode on the Poetical Character" is in this respect characteristic of all Collins's best work, and it helps to explain both his curious power and his weaknesses.

The structure of this ode, dictated by a sequence of visions, is imaginative rather than intellectual. Each of the three visions which compose the poem seems less the product than the creator of an idea. None of them has much to do with logic, common sense, or "judgment." Collins distorts Spenser to his own purposes, meanwhile protesting that he read that poet "not with light Regard" (l. 1); he creates his own highly improbable mythology, making God embrace first Thought, then Fancy in order to produce the physical and the imaginative universe ("His allegory here is neither luminous nor decent," complained Mrs. Barbauld [13]); he contradicts himself by asserting first that there are few poets (l. 20), later that there are none (ll. 72–73). Yet the poem is imaginatively compelling. Its visions are revealed in layers, each more penetrating than the preceding one. First there is the leisurely, at the outset almost playful, fantasy about the analogy between Spenser's "unrival'd Fair" and the poet. This deepens in tone as it produces the realization that the gift of poetry must, by its "God-like" nature, be offered to few. The elaborate allegory which succeeds the statement of this idea seems from the outset more serious and more economical than the strophe; it is the heart of the poem. It amplifies and justifies the vital epithet, *God-like*, by creating a complex, if somewhat confused, mythological genealogy for Poetry (the "rich-hair'd Youth of Morn," l. 39).[14] The mythology implies a total vision, in which mental, moral and spiritual powers all have vivid physical embodiment; on the basis of its inclusiveness Collins arrives at the questions which end the epode:

> Where is the Bard, whose Soul can now
> Its high presuming Hopes avow?
> Where He who thinks, with Rapture blind,
> This hallow'd Work for Him design'd?
>
> (ll. 51–54)

More than a simple reference to the decadence of the age, the *now* of the first line means, in context, "now that this vision of the universe has been offered." In the light of the mythological panorama, the facile assumption that Fancy distributes so sacred a gift even to "few" seems presumptuous. It remains for the antistrophe to resolve the issue: if poetry is a divine power, who is worthy to be a poet? What is the nature of the true poet? The antistrophe answers these questions somewhat deviously, through its creation of another "vision" in the symbolic evocation of Milton. And the conclusion is imaginatively if not logically inevitable:

69

The Poetry of Vision

Such Bliss to One alone,
Of all the Sons of Soul was known,
And Heav'n, and *Fancy*, kindred Pow'rs,
Have now o'erturned th'inspiring Bow'rs,
Or curtain'd close such Scene from ev'ry future View.

(ll. 72–76)

Imagination, indeed, has conspicuously substituted for logic throughout: one's movement through the poem is a movement through its author's emotional states. Each symbolic vision provides a concrete equivalent for an emotional situation of the poet, a situation resolved, in effect, by the very creation of the vision. The logic of Collins's misreading of Spenser demands prompt realization that there can, by analogy, be only one poet (as there is, he asserts, but one wearer of the girdle). But the whole initial conceit is obviously the product of the poet's awe at the grandeur of poethood; that sense of awe seizes on the magic girdle itself as correlative, rejecting irrelevant details of the legend, and finds in the image, by a circular process, confirmation of the emotion, which is strengthened and amplified by the strophe's conclusion. The process of selection, and of illumination through selection, goes on, as it were, before the reader's eyes. One may complain about the sloppiness of such a method, but it produces real energy and excitement by the concluding lines.

As the strophe develops from Collins's attempts to find a substantial image for an emotional state, the epode continues the effort to clarify and intensify an objective correlative for his feeling about poetry. Again there is a good deal of floundering; again the images pile up in rich profusion; again the process is of gradual illumination, the ultimate result of the vision being the focusing of the questions at the end. The process is yet clearer in the antistrophe, where the Eden image, single and richly perceived from the beginning, produces by its implications the conclusion that the bliss of poetic achievement has been fully known to one alone. This conclusion clearly derives from no logical process of thought. As the mythologizing of the epode leads Collins to fuller realization of the challenge of being a poet, the allegory of the antistrophe leads to a sense of its impossibility: an Eden is unlikely to have successive inhabitants. Imagery has dictated thought — if thought it can be called.

The ode's imagery concentrates in detail on ideas of height and of divinity, the two closely related — one sometimes a metaphor for the other — and combined in the notion of heaven, which appears in every section of the poem. In the strophe, the magic girdle is "hung on high" (l. 8); an angel-hand hovers in the air to burst it if it is illegitimately worn. The girdle of poetry is "prepar'd and bath'd in Heav'n" (l. 18); this is the sign of its authenticity and of its value. The action of the epode, which concentrates heavily on the "divine," takes place entirely in heaven; the antistrophe emphasizes most intensely the idea of physical height in its cliff-situated paradise. Both height and divinity emblemize aspiration; when Collins's imagery forces upon him a sense of how great is the height, how tremendous the divinity, he recognizes that his hopes are not only "high" but "presuming" (l. 52) and proceeds toward the conclusion that poetry is, in effect, impossible.

Imagery dominates this ode, then, in a new way. Images are not simply an end in themselves; they are the source of illumination, provide the guiding principles of the poem. They exist not to move the reader so much as to focus and clarify the emotions of the writer; they both communicate and justify the poet's emotional progression and excuse his lack of genuine intellectual progression. Yet Gray was surely right in accusing Collins of "Images with no Choice at all." Despite their high importance in this ode, individual images often seem more or less random, records of minor bits of emotional chaos. The principle that imagery should determine both the content and the structure of poetry may point toward the symbolist tradition of the twentieth century, but the embodiment of the principle in Collins, both here and elsewhere, demonstrates little of the symbolists' clarity of effect.

One reason for the incomplete success of this ode, and of so much of Collins's poetry, is that its statements and images depend upon a singularly flabby rhetoric. Josephine Miles's statistics reveal that Collins shares with many of his contemporaries the tendency to make thirty to forty per cent of his adjectives participial.[15] The relative proportion of participles and active verbs, on the other hand, differs significantly among the mid-century poets; Collins relies especially heavily on participles, using, in this ode, roughly ten more participles than active verbs. The fact suggests the emphasis which Collins's technique places on states of being rather than on process. Passive verbs occur frequently in the "Ode on the Poetical Character"; the active verbs are rarely emphatic, and two of the most striking (*o'erbrow*, l. 58, and *embrown*, l. 60), coined from nouns, describe appearance, not activity. Syntax fills no poetic function for Collins; it is rather an obstacle to poetic effects. He is capable of wild inversions:

> I view that Oak, the fancied Glades among,
> By which as *Milton* lay, His Ev'ning Ear,
> From many a Cloud that drop'd Ethereal Dew,
> Nigh spher'd in Heav'n its native Strains could hear.
>
> (ll. 63–66)

But they serve no genuine purpose: one can hardly believe that Collins wished to place special stress on *among*, say, or even *Ear*. The effect is of inadvertency. H. W. Garrod has recorded his intense irritation at the poet's repeated unconcern for syntactical logic or consistency [16] (for example, the entire strophe of "Ode on the Poetical Character" is a single long, impenetrable sentence); even so admiring a critic as Edmund Blunden is forced to apologize for Collins's "unfinished or inexact syntax." [17]

Then there is the problem of diction, the "great Variety of Words" which Gray noticed. Collins prefixed to his odes a motto from Pindar beginning, "May I be deviser of diction." Hazlitt remarked, of the "Ode on the Poetical Character," "a honeyed paste of poetic diction encrusts it, like the candied coat of the auricula." [18] If Collins's syntax is frequently an obstacle to his effects, his diction is crucial to them, although not necessarily satisfactory to a modern reader in its "poetic" and derivative nature.

The diction depends heavily on adjectives, through which the poet records his value judgments and substantiates his visions. It is sometimes difficult to tell which he is doing. So strongly visual is Collins's conception of the world — indeed, of the universe — that his moral adjectives have almost physical force. Thus, as he elaborates the image which equates the physical beauty of Spenser's "unrival'd Fair" with the spiritual beauty of the poet, he pauses to consider the non-chaste, non-fair (by extension, non-poet), for whom the "magic Girdle" bursts, to leave "unblest her loath'd dishonour'd Side" (l. 13). The three participles convey so emphatic a value judgment that they hint physical as well as moral horror, evoking perhaps, anachronistically, Coleridge's Lady Josephine with her unspeakable blemish. The personifications in the epode, intended to suggest the moral qualities connected with poetry, have great physical vividness. There is, for example,

> *Truth*, in sunny Vest array'd,
> By whose the Tarsel's Eyes were made.
>
> (ll. 45–46)

Sunny, in this context (the scene is heaven), has essentially the force of *made from sunlight*; the idea of Truth's eyes as the pattern, almost the Platonic Idea, of the hawk's is vividly evocative, suggesting (like *sunny*) both the appearance of personified Truth and the nature of the quality she represents. Some such duality of implication resides, of course, in all good personifications, but the adjective of both physical and moral weight is characteristic of Collins in other contexts as well. Indeed, it is one of his most striking poetic characteristics to make virtually no distinction between his treatment of personifications and of other sorts of figures. He gives even the inanimate universe almost human dignity. The "Eden" which Milton inhabits rests on the "rich ambitious Head" (l. 61) of a "jealous Steep" (l. 57). The adjectives, once more, are doubly effective: they remind us of the physical situation, the cliff so steep that it "jealously" keeps away all aspirants, its head "rich" in natural luxuriance, "ambitious" in reaching nearly to heaven; but they are also obviously metaphors connecting the hill with human experience. This is the hill of poetry, its riches the untold wealth of the imagination, its "jealousy" and its "ambition" reminders of the poet's limitless aspiration and of the great difficulty of achieving poet's status.

Collins uses individual adjectives with sensitivity and precision, but there are simply too many of them. Collins's notion of loading every rift with ore was to multiply image-producing modifiers, to demonstrate the riches of his visual and highly individual imagination. Contemporary ideas about the value of images, the exaltation of the ode, the poetic appeal of embodied abstractions, encouraged him in his vices. The poetic credo embodied in the "Ode on the Poetical Character" is fresh and vivid, but the absence of "judgment" as an element in composition is in practice an intolerable loss. Collins's rhetoric could not meet the demands of his idea of poetry. His realization that imagery could lead poet as well as reader toward insight is valuable; his willingness to commit himself to his images admirable. But the danger of his position was close to what Mrs. Barbauld suggested: that the poetry thus created would sometimes become "obscure, by aiming at impressions stronger than [the poet] had clear and well-defined ideas to support." Since idea, in this method of writing poetry, seems not to precede image, it is obvious that intellectual structure is likely to suffer. The weaknesses of Collins's poetry are characteristically structural and rhetorical; its strength is the vividness and power of its images.

Yet even the images seem fully justified only when the process of seeing is intimately related to that of feeling. In Collins's most successful odes, visual images both derive from and define emotion; in his weaker poetic efforts, the relation between vision and feeling becomes tenuous, and all sense of coherent structure disappears. The difference between the unsatisfying "Ode to Pity" and the far more successful "Ode to Fear," for example, can be largely defined in these terms.

"To Pity" contains one of Collins's best-known personifications in its description of Pity with "skyworn Robes of Tend'rest Blue,/ And Eyes of dewy Light! (ll. 11–12). Characteristic in their selectivity and evocativeness of Collins at his richest, the lines stand out sharply from the rest of the poem, for the emotional quality they suggest is never otherwise made real in the ode.

One striking aspect of the description is its lack of developed visual detail. Oliver Sigworth remarks, "Pity here is less vividly visualized than some of Collins' other personifications; the most vivid part of the poem is the description of the temple of Pity." [19] But Professor Woodhouse provides an appropriate qualification to the implied negative judgment of the personification, observing,

"The effect is not merely visual, but visionary. The figure of Pity, thus realized, becomes a correlative, a symbol, of the 'idea' and its attendant emotion." [20] The slight visual suggestions of the personification are so rich in meaning that they give Pity almost supernatural vividness and reality. *Sky-worn* suggests Pity's heavenly habitation and associations and defines more precisely the nature of the blue which colors these robes. *Tend'rest* emphasizes the implicit reference to the Virgin Mary, whose color is blue. The adjectives establish a triple association: Pity as an entity relates both to the benign aspects of nature (an unclouded summer sky) and to the powers of heaven. "Eyes of dewy Light" stresses further the metaphoric connection with nature; it also defines the tearfulness of Pity as a source of her radiance, implies a fundamental relation between compassion and beauty. It avoids the bathos of presenting Pity as a weeping figure while it recalls the constant imminence of tears as a response to suffering.

Pity's function in the poem as a whole, though, is essentially literary; she is to come "by Fancy's Aid" (l. 25), not as a result of experience or perception; her temple may "raise a wild Enthusiast Heat" (l. 29) in all who view it, but this "Heat" is only abstractly and arbitrarily associated with pity, which seems hardly an emotional phenomenon. Artificially conceived, this ode, like so many of its contemporaries, seems finally a mere literary exercise.

The same accusations do not apply to the companion "Ode to Fear," whose weaknesses derive from an excess rather than a deficiency of intensity. Fear's power is first a special power of seeing: to Fear "the World unknown/ With all its shadowy Shapes is shown" (ll. 1–2); she sees an "unreal" scene (l. 3), one which appals, but one perceptible only by the aid of Fancy. The ambiguous value of Fear's vision is fully recognized — at the beginning and throughout the poem. The perceptions this emotion makes possible may be dangerous; they are by definition frightening. But perception is for Collins self-justifying, worth the taking of risks. The heightening of perception involved in concentration on the idea of Fear immediately reveals to the poet, with sharp visual clarity, the monsters who compose Fear's train; his contemplation of them leads him to more vivid realization of the emotional drawbacks of commitment to Fear:

The Poetry of Vision

Who, *Fear*, this ghastly Train can see,
And look not madly wild, like Thee?

(ll. 24–25)

As in the "Ode on the Poetical Character," the progression of visual images has now defined more fully an idea implicit at the beginning of the ode: that fear's power is destructive as well as inspirational. The epode explores this insight more fully, pointing out that Aeschylus the soldier scorned fear, although Aeschylus the poet was the first to invoke its power. Yet the fact that virtue is no concomitant of fear soon seems irrelevant, as Collins's imagery reveals the creative force in a poet's acceptance of vulnerability. Sophocles, "With trembling Eyes" (l. 36; the phrase emphasizes the close association for Collins of the visual and the emotional), committed himself to Fear; he could therefore create archetypal tragic figures. And the epode ends with the poet's realization — direct product of the image of Oedipus and Jocasta which he has just evoked — that the emotional power of fear is well worth its dangers:

O *Fear*, I know Thee by my throbbing Heart,
Thy with'ring Pow'r inspir'd each mournful Line.

(ll. 42–43)

The "with'ring Pow'r" is also inspirational; the destructive and the creative aspects of Fear are finally identical.

The logical movement of the ode might seem, at this point, to be complete. The poet's images have led him to examine first the negative, then the positive aspects of fear as a literary resource, with full recognition (and the parallel recognition is conspicuously missing from "Ode to Pity") that fear must be known both as personal emotion and as imaginative possibility. The antistrophe, however, recognizes that an important question remains unanswered: what, exactly, is the nature of the commitment a poet must make in order to find fear a valuable imaginative resource? The answer emerges through another series of images, which reveal that Fear is a "mad Nymph" and describe the setting appropriate to her nature. The scene, Collins realizes, must be one of horrors: a "haunted Cell,/ Where gloomy *Rape* and *Murder* dwell" (ll. 48–49), or a cave through which echo the cries of drowning seamen. And this vivid perception that fear is a product of the truly dreadful in human experience necessarily implies that a commitment to fear is a commitment to the reality of horror, and to the reality of one's perceptions and intimations of horror.

> Dark Pow'r, with shudd'ring meek submitted Thought
> Be mine, to read the Visions old,
> Which thy awak'ning Bards have told:
> And lest thou meet my blasted View,
> Hold each strange Tale devoutly true.
>
> (ll. 53–57)

The bards of fear "awaken" to the essential reality of experience usually considered fanciful; the poet willing to submit his thought to his emotions may share their perceptions. Eighteenth-century psychology of course made a distinction between the images perceived by the eye and those conceived by the imagination. Sense perception was for Locke "the inlet of all knowledge in our minds"; [21] it recorded the eternal world, however incompletely. But the imagination can alter and combine the remembered records of reality in new ways, to create "all the varieties of picture and vision that are most agreeable to the imagination." [22] Collins, however, seems almost to obviate the distinction between literal and imaginative imagery in the antistrophe of "To Fear" — and in his characteristic poetic practice. What is imagined may be as real emotionally as what is seen; the emotions are, ultimately, the most valid test of reality. "To Fear" concludes with an implicit statement of this idea, as the power of fear becomes associated with that of Shakespeare, and Collins adjures Fear

> By all that from thy Prophet broke,
> In thy Divine Emotions spoke:
> Hither again thy Fury deal,
> Teach me but once like Him to feel: . . .
> And I, O *Fear*, will dwell with *Thee*!
>
> (ll. 66–69, 71)

Collins's imagined visions have led him to an almost religious awe of the power of imagination and emotion (the diction toward the end of this poem is suggestively similar to the religious language used to describe Fancy in the "Ode on the Poetical Character"), and to the position that visions are — or can be — more significant than vision, that feeling rather than logic must test the poet's material. And his meaning has been ordered, once more, by a pattern of imagery which appears to have been dictated more nearly by free association than by an a priori conception of logic or meaning.

The ideas about vision and feeling, emotion and reality, that are implicit here dominate to a considerable extent Collins's longest and most complex poem, the incomplete "Ode on the Popular Superstitions of the Highlands of Scotland, Considered As the Subject of Poetry." Here Collins demonstrated finally the extent to which his concern with the images of the imagination and those of the eye, and the relation of both to feeling, could provide a principle of growth and control for so undisciplined a form as the eighteenth-century ode. In Collins's odes, Wylie Sypher has pointed out, "Progress occurs by indirection." [23] The nature of that indirection is worth examining.

The pretext for the poem was Douglas Home's return to his native Scotland, with all its poetic resources, a pretext which led inevitably to contemplation of the Highland poet's special subject matter. The entire ode depends on a variation of the classical rhetorical trick of *praeteritio*: as it insists that the Scot has opportunities denied to other poets, it simultaneously makes use of the very resources it denies the Englishman. What is interesting for our purposes, though, is the extent to which Collins's sense of Scotland's special value depends on his conviction about the crucial poetic relevance of imagery. Scotland differs from England specifically in providing more images. It offers exotic sights: the vaults in which "a pigmy-folk is found" (l. 143), the bleak rocks and virtuous people of Kilda (st. x), the romantic scenery which has power over the poet:

> All hail, ye scenes that o'er my soul prevail,
> Ye [spacious] friths and lakes which, far away,
> Are by smooth ANNAN fill'd, or past'ral TAY,
> Or DON's romantic springs, at distance, hail!
>
> (ll. 204–207)

But more important is the fact that it provides images which are the product of imagination and tradition, and which are taken as seriously as those produced by sight alone. The Highlands are explicitly "Fancy's land" (l. 19), inhabited, "'tis said," by fairy people (l. 20) and by wizard seers (l. 54), alive with the memory of Runic bards (l. 41) and heroic clansmen (ll. 50–52). All these inhabitants provide visions for the inner eye. The poet is "possest" (l. 40) by the images offered him. He accepts, in effect, the validity of his own imaginings about "the swart tribes" (l. 23); he participates vicariously in the experience of the seer — an experience of seeing so intensely that the wizards themselves "With their own visions oft astonish'd droop" (l. 58): a paradox reminiscent of that in the earlier line about fear's withering power.

As the importance of Scottish scenery comes from its power to prevail over the poet's soul, so the importance of the imaginative visions is also their emotional force. Invocations of conventional social feeling frame the poem. It opens with reference to Collins's friendship for Home:

> think far off how, on the southern coast,
> I met thy friendship with an equal flame!
> (ll. 11–12)

The concluding lines of the final stanza appeal to the "Pow'rs" which guard the plains of Lothian:

> To him I lose, your kind protection lend,
> And, touch'd with love like mine, preserve my absent friend.
> (ll. 218–219)

This feeling is no less convincing for being conventional: in some real sense it explains the impulse behind the poem. Collins chooses to express his friendship by suggesting how he and Home are united in their concern for imaginative reality. Yet the contrast between the expression of feeling in the first and last stanzas and that in the body of the poem rather undermines the protestations of friendship. Only a conventional mode seems to exist for the expression of friendship; the rest of the ode demonstrates that other sorts of feeling may find new forms of expression, and places such emphasis on the demonstration that the final return to convention seems anticlimactic. The life of feeling here once more is Collins's real subject. After the opening stanza, the succeeding three stanzas (and presumably the missing stanza five as well) discuss the legendary material which Scotland offers the poet. In each individual instance, Collins explicitly describes or hints the emotional significance of this material.

> These are the themes of simple, sure effect,
> That add new conquests to her [the muse's] boundless reign,
> And fill, with double force, her heart-commanding strain.
>
> (ll. 33–35)

This assertion refers directly to the popular tales of fairies, but it supplies commentary for the entire poem. The "heart-commanding" power of Scottish superstition makes it worth the attention of the poet — makes it, indeed, crucially important to the poet concerned with emotion.

After the central stanzas about the fate of the peasant destroyed by the water-kelpie, the poem turns to the physical realities of Scotland: these too are important, clearly, for their emotional value — the vision of magic splendor provided by old tombs, that of "primal innocence" (l. 167) offered by the peasants of Kilda. Yet the real moves immediately, in the poet's imagination, toward the unreal: the image of primal innocence is not, after all, realistic, nor is the concept of "tasteful toil" (l. 169), imagined as enlivening the peasants' existence. This instantaneous imaginative transformation, the creation of myth out of geographical and historical fact, is the poet's special achievement, blurring the distinction between the actual and the fantastic — as it is blurred also, the "Ode to Fear" suggests, by strong emotion. Collins's disclaimer for dealing with "such false themes" occurs in stanza xi, immediately after the discussion of Kilda, rather than earlier in the poem, where he is more obviously concerned with the imaginary, not the actual. His evocations of the Hebrides are not accurate — but, as he points out,

> scenes like this, . . . daring to depart
> From sober truth, are still to nature true,
> And call forth fresh delight to fancy's view.
>
> (ll. 188–190)

The union of literal and metaphoric vision is the poet's highest achievement.

Collins: The Controlling Image

For this reason, the episode of the drowned peasant is truly central to the poem: the fact that it occupies the middle stanzas is no accident, for it is the ode's fullest demonstration of the welding of literal and metaphoric truth. The opening line of this section (l. 104), "Ah, luckless swain, o'er all unblest indeed!", sets the tone for the rest of the passage. The word *unblest* has a curious force in Collins (as in the line from the "'Poetical Character" ode: "It left unblest her loath'd dishonour'd Side"). As opposed to *unfortunate* or *unhappy*, two obvious possibilities in the present context, it suggests an almost theological view of the circumstances. And the state of blessedness implied by the use of the negative in this instance is simply normalcy, the ordinary, uneventful life of the typical "swain," now abruptly to be cut off.

After describing the peasant's drowning, Collins introduces the next stanza with a vignette which has familiar analogues in Thomson and Gray:

> For him, in vain, his anxious wife shall wait,
> Or wander forth to meet him on his way;
> For him, in vain, at to-fall of the day,
> His babes shall linger at th'unclosing gate!
>
> (ll. 121–124)

Comparison with the other passages is instructive. Thomson's peasant is deprived of family joys by being frozen in a snowdrift; Gray's is merely one of many in the country churchyard, the manner of his death not mentioned. But Collins's victim suffers a special fate:

> On him enrag'd, the fiend, in angry mood,
> Shall never look with pity's kind concern, . . .
> To his faint eye the grim and grisly shape,
> In all its terrors clad, shall wild appear.
> Meantime, the wat'ry surge shall round him rise,
> Pour'd sudden forth from ev'ry swelling source.
>
> (ll. 108–109, 114–117)

His death is the result of supernatural intervention, made inevitable by the malice of a fiend. And the fact is important. The most significant effects of this little narrative derive from the alternation and juxtaposition of the mundane and the supernatural. The sentimental evocation of the expectant family immediately follows the account of the fiend-dominated drowning; the drowned man's spirit pleads that his wife return to normalcy ("dear wife, thy daily toils pursue/ At dawn or dusk, industrious as before" [ll. 133–134]). Collins combines his realistic if vague sense of the nature of peasant life with his imaginative response to legend. Both produce images, of very different sorts. And the combination of the two provides a genuine function for the legendary material. Instead of being relevant simply as the stuff of imaginative stimulation, the legend becomes an emotive objectification of the horror always potential immediately outside the bounds of normalcy, the terror that lies in wait for all. The water-kelpie is an unnatural being; he becomes a way of expressing the emotional unnaturalness of any sudden death. The word *unblest* is fully justified by the narrative which follows it, a narrative about the relation between a God-dominated (because natural and orderly) pattern of life and a demonically caused death.

This fusion of opposing sorts of vision is one of Collins's great accomplishments. When he strays too far into the world of imaginative vision, without explicit reference to the human relevance of his imaginings, we may sympathize with Dr. Johnson's complaint that he reveled in "those flights of imagination which pass the bounds of nature, and to which the mind is reconciled only by a passive acquiescence in popular tradition." [24] But the process demonstrated by the "Ode on the Poetical Character," the process of discovery through images, produces Collins's largest successes. Collins lacked the theory to justify his practice fully, but his practice belongs to a grand poetic tradition. He has put many critics in mind of Coleridge; his success at combining the natural and supernatural may recall Coleridge's special function in the composition of *Lyrical Ballads*: "it was agreed that my endeavours should be directed to persons and characters supernatural, or at least romantic; yet so as to transfer from our inward nature a human interest and a semblance of truth sufficient to procure for these shadows of imagination that willing suspension of disbelief for the moment, which constitutes poetic faith." [25]

To emphasize so strongly Collins's "images" is perhaps misleading, for such emphasis may suggest that he relies far more heavily than in fact he does on the specifically visual. His "Verses to Sir Thomas Hanmer," with their stress on the relation between poetry and painting, supplied the title for Jean Hagstrum's study of one aspect of the visual in eighteenth-century poetry, and Professor Hagstrum finds in Collins abundant examples of iconic representation.[26] Yet close examination of the poet's visual presentations, particularly of the personifications which are his most characteristic rhetorical and structural device, reveals a singular lack of specificity in his typical imagery. Collins relies more on the suggestive than on the precisely visual. A. S. P. Woodhouse, in his final essay on Collins, points out that the success and the originality of *Odes on Several Descriptive and Allegoric Subjects* "depend on Collins's development — one might almost say, on his discovery — of the latent potential of personification as a poetic medium." [27] Collins's view of the imagination, Professor Woodhouse believes, is also crucial to his success. "For him its power extends beyond providing, through fiction, for vicarious emotional experience: it bears a relation to truth, and can seize on and present the idea of things — of pity, of fear, of liberty, of evening, what you will. The means which it uses to this end, in the *Odes* of 1746, is essentially that of symbol. This is Collins's great discovery, and it is the basis of his best achievement in poetry" (p. 123).

Although there is little critical agreement on precisely what constitutes a poetic "symbol," the nature of symbolism is usually considered to be more complex, richer, than that of allegory. Professor Woodhouse's suggestion that Collins's personifications are essentially symbolic is particularly valuable because it calls attention to the special richness of implication which these figures have at their best, and hints that this richness resides more in conception than in details of presentation. Collins's visions of "a world unknown" have often the haziness of a dream — but also, on occasion, the peculiar potency of dream imagery.

At the age of seventeen, Collins wrote and published a "Sonnet" strangely metaphysical in its imagery:

> When *Phoebe* form'd a wanton smile,
>   My soul! it reach'd not here!
> Strange, that thy peace, thou trembler, flies
>   Before a rising tear!

The Poetry of Vision

From midst the drops, my love is born,
  That o'er those eyelids rove:
Thus issued from a teeming wave
  The fabled queen of love.

This is not in any obvious way characteristic of Collins's later pre-occupations and techniques — unless in its oddity of syntax (*drops,* implausibly enough, is the subject of *rove* in line six). Yet its curious mixture of visual with non-visual suggestion foretells much that was to dominate Collins's later verse. The analogy between Venus rising from the waves and the speaker's love issuing from Phoebe's tears is farfetched but striking. It transforms the metaphorical, abstract meaning of *born* into its literal equivalent. "My love" thus becomes, by implication, a Cupid figure; yet it is impossible to maintain a sense of love's concrete being because the image of a Cupid rising from among "roving" teardrops is uncomfortably grotesque. The reader is left in a state of tension between the abstract and the concrete, a tension foreshadowed in the previous stanza by the strain between the abstract diction of "My soul" and the subsequent address to the soul as "thou trembler" — a formulation which, like *born* in the second stanza, allows the possibility of a concrete reference without insisting on it. It would be difficult to define fully the exact rôle of the visual in this little poem, and one encounters similar difficulties frequently in the later Collins.

By 1742, when he was twenty years old, Collins had turned to *Persian Eclogues,* expressing his appreciation of Oriental poetry for its "Elegancy and Wildness of Thought," and explaining that the style of Persian verse is "rich and figurative," in contrast to the "naturally Strong and Nervous" mode of English poetry.[28] His own version of the Oriental style bears strong affinities to the techniques he was soon to develop in his avowedly original verse.

sweet and od'rous, like an Eastern Bride,
The radiant Morn resum'd her orient Pride.
          ("Eclogue the First, Selim," ll. 13–14)

Blest were the Days, when Wisdom held her Reign,
And Shepherds sought her on the silent Plain,
With Truth she wedded in the secret Grove,
The fair-eyed Truth, and Daughters bless'd their Love.
          ("Selim," ll. 43–46)

With Thee be Chastity, of all afraid,
Distrusting all, a wise suspicious Maid;
But Man the most — not more the Mountain Doe
Holds the swift Falcon for her deadly Foe.
Cold is her Breast, like Flow'rs that drink the Dew;
A silken Veil conceals her from the view.

(ll. 57–62)

These personifications are successively more elaborate, and their elaboration takes characteristic forms. The first instance is the only one in which the subject of the personification has visual reality in itself: the morning is not, like truth and chastity, an abstraction. In inviting his readers to imagine Morn as a woman, Collins directs attention specifically to the non-visual attributes of the "Eastern Bride": she is "sweet" — an adjective which may refer to her perfume but has also far more general, expansive implications — and "od'rous." ("Eastern Bride," of course, suggests clearly the point of view of the western observer; it is not an image likely to be used by a Persian poet.) By implication the visual qualities inherent in the actual morning — its "radiance," its "orient Pride" — are also transferable to the personified figure, although both mean something very different when applied to a woman. "Orient Pride" calls attention to the splendor of the dawn, as well as to its location in the East. The fact that the personification depends on a simile (without "like an Eastern Bride," the second line could be taken as direct statement) maintains the separation between the morning as reality and the morning as imagined figure: once more Collins seems to depend on a curious tension and balance of implication.

No such tension is apparent in the second example, where the personifications delineate abstractions and the only visual adjective is *fair-eyed*: even that suggests the moral quality conveyed by Truth's eyes more than it describes appearance. The daughters of Truth and Wisdom, it turns out, are the Virtues. This is, then, a conventional genealogy of personifications, which conveys the nature of an abstraction (virtue) by explaining its origins. If these personifications succeed in evoking the "idea" of things, as Professor Woodhouse suggests Collins's embodiments are able to do, they create their ideas entirely through dwelling on relationships and contexts (the reign of Wisdom, the "silent Plain" and "secret

Grove," the atmosphere of almost religious exaltation suggested by the repetition of *Blest*); they do not really work by giving physical life to abstractions.

In the third instance, on the other hand, Collins "characterizes" his personified figure at some length. Chastity's qualities of character (she is fearful, distrustful, wise, suspicious) are clearly more significant than her appearance, but the final couplet hints a visual reality as well. The primary purport of the simile is not visual at all. Yet the comparison of the maiden with the flowers, while it interestingly qualifies the nature of her coldness, also suggests her delicacy and physical beauty. Collins's chief "point" about this being, however, is that we must not be able to see her: this is the ultimate exemplification of her modesty. The most nearly specific visual detail supplied is the "silken Veil" whose function is to conceal the maiden from view.

These three personifications may be inadequate as representations of Collins's poetic ability, but they do indicate the direction his talent was to take. The retreat from physical description enabled him to find unexpected and suggestive details that convey the very essence of phenomena. The silken veil, for example, expresses both the glamor and the mystery of Chastity. In the *Odes* of 1746, Collins's gift of selectivity operates with maximum forcefulness. Some of the visionary figures which have, even for modern readers unacquainted with personification tradition, particularly vivid physical reality, gain that reality through a single striking appearance rather than as a result of careful description. Of Vengeance, for example, in the "Ode to Fear," we see only an arm:

> *Vengeance*, in the lurid Air,
> Lifts her red Arm, expos'd and bare.
>
> (ll. 20-21)

The redness and bareness of the arm have the horror of flayed flesh; the context makes a more commonplace interpretation implausible. To evoke the dreadfulness of a supernatural being by providing a glimpse of one of its limbs is the sort of accomplishment peculiar to Collins. He defines Danger almost entirely through activities: we know of the figure's appearance that he has "Limbs of Giant Mold" (l. 10), is "hideous" (l. 12), but no more — yet he assumes spectral reality.

Collins: The Controlling Image

The kinds of visual detail Collins selects fall into some clear classifications. He uses clothes, with both positive and negative reference, to suggest essence: Simplicity, for example, disdains "Gauds, and pageant Weeds, and trailing Pall" ("Ode to Simplicity," l. 9) — dramatic and ostentatiously tragic garments — to come "In *Attic* Robe array'd" (l. 11): her attire is both appropriately simple and suggestive of an associated range of artistic and literary values. Truth, on the other hand, appears "in sunny Vest array'd" ("Ode on the Poetical Character," l. 45); she partakes by implication of the illumination associated with the primary source of light. The appearance of Evening's robes is not specified, but they are rudely rent by Winter ("Ode to Evening," l. 49), and that fact suggests that the external landscape over which Evening sheds her pale light may also be considered her garments: the intimate association between Evening and nature which the rest of the poem has suggested is thus substantiated. The "injur'd Robes" which Peace is invited to "up-bind" ("Ode to Peace," l. 13) are totally unspecific; the point of this reference seems to be merely to intensify one's sense of the outrage of War, which ravages even clothing. In "The Manners,"

> *Science*, prank'd in tissued Vest,
> By *Reason*, *Pride*, and *Fancy* drest,
> Comes like a Bride so trim array'd,
> To wed with *Doubt* in *Plato's* Shade!
>
> (ll. 15–18)

In this case, the beings responsible for Science's dress are as important as the dress itself; but the splendor and neatness of Science's attire themselves convey the point: that the very elaboration with which the university decks the knowledge it provides contributes to its compromise (or enrichment) by doubt.

Through these significant details — dress, a glimpse of eyes, or suggestions of its nature — Collins gives the essence of a personification. Visual exactitude, surprisingly often, detracts from meaning. The famous "Ode, Written in the Beginning of the Year 1746" seems a rescension of parts of the vastly inferior "Ode, to a Lady on the Death of Colonel Ross in the Action of Fontenoy." It is worth comparing the final couplet of the later ode with the equivalent stanza in the piece on Colonel Ross. In the 1746 ode we learn that

> *Freedom* shall a-while repair,
> To dwell a weeping Hermit there!

The earlier poem provides a more extended account of Freedom —
this time in female form:

> But lo where, sunk in deep Despair,
> Her garments torn, her Bosom bare,
> Impatient *Freedom* lies!
> Her matted Tresses madly spread,
> To ev'ry Sod, which wraps the Dead,
> She turns her joyless Eyes.

(ll. 37–42)

In both odes, the image of saddened Freedom simultaneously
asserts and qualifies the value of heroic death in battle. The fallen
soldiers have died for freedom, yet freedom is not automatically or
immediately achieved as a result of their deaths. In the 1746
couplet, where the appearance of personified Freedom is suggested
only by his weeping and perhaps by his rôle as hermit, the intricacies of suggestion and the subtly controlled tone convey a complex
attitude. With superb economy Collins suggests that these graves
are in some sense appropriate objects for religious devotion, that
they are intimately associated with Freedom, that the isolation and
sadness which Freedom suffers in the loss of these young men will
be only temporary ("a-while") but that it is none the less significant. The delicacy and gentleness of tone add sweetness to the
statement.

In the portrait of Freedom as demented woman, on the other
hand, each specific detail subtracts from the complexity of evocation in the far mistier single couplet. As we dwell on the reality
of her matted tresses, we became less conscious of her significance;
mention of her "joyless Eyes" — (we have previously learned that
she is "sunk in deep Despair") seems ludicrously unnecessary
understatement. The stanza is descriptively far clearer, more vivid,
than the later couplet, but its accomplishment is almost entirely
visual.

Thomson (whom Collins greatly admired) experimented in *The
Castle of Indolence* with a wide range of emotional suggestion. Collins's *Odes* (published three years before the *Castle*) display a

similar emphasis on feeling, although their kind of emotional suggestion is different from Thomson's. Collins does not retreat from the visual in order to emphasize the emotional; his lack of visual specificity, his heavy reliance on isolated details, are a form of economy; they help him to suggest large meanings. Thomson, on the other hand, seems to luxuriate in emotion for its own sake. Emotional suggestion actually defines the meaning of the first canto of *The Castle of Indolence*. For Collins, meaning, although to a great degree it depends upon such suggestion, is not so nearly contained in it. Vengeance's presentation as an extended arm rather than a fully described figure is at least partly explicable by the fact that this sort of sketchy presentation makes possible the coexistence in relatively little space of many similarly evoked figures. But Collins's practice, like Thomson's, reveals that even during the period when the visual was almost unanimously agreed to be the very essence of poetry, innovative poets were conscious of its limitations as poetic material and were straining against these limitations.

V

THOMAS GRAY:
Action and Image

THOMAS GRAY was far more famous than Collins in his own time; Adam Smith described him as joining "to the sublimity of Milton the elegance and harmony of Pope, and . . . nothing is wanting to render him, perhaps, the first poet in the English language, but to have written a little more." But his reputation has diminished, except for the churchyard elegy. Dr. F. R. Leavis dismisses his other poetic production; Donald Davie relegates him to the limbo reserved for those whose diction is impure, and A. R. Humphreys attacks him for embodying the worst poetic evils of his day. Time has not on the whole been kind to Gray, although critics are now beginning once more to give him serious attention.

One reason for modern dissatisfaction with this poet is the insistent artifice of his diction, its extremity suggested by his own famous pronouncement that "the language of the age is never the language of poetry." William Wordsworth and Coleridge were among the first to disapprove. Although they disagreed about which details were farthest removed from true poetry, both used Gray's sonnet to exemplify all those eighteenth-century poems which consist merely of "translations of prose thoughts into poetic language."[1] Gray believed that "sense is nothing in poetry, but according to the dress she wears, & the scene she appears in."[2] Most modern commentators, following Wordsworth and Coleridge, have thought his muse rather overdressed, seeing in his poetry all the vices of eighteenth-century poetic diction without perceiving that he also exemplifies the possibilities of that diction. In 1963, however, F. Doherty provided a new approach. Examining Gray's

90

language in some detail, he concluded that the poet's productions are of two kinds: those dominated by his "public," highly rhetorical "voice," and those in which his "real voice" is discernible.[3] The latter category includes most of the poems which seem relatively acceptable (in comparison with, for instance, Gray's long "Pindaric" odes) to the modern reader.

Mr. Doherty's analyses of individual passages are highly perceptive, but his examination of Gray raises further questions when one realizes how often the poems which he describes as manifesting the poet's "real voice" make use of a diction as contrived as that of the more formal pieces. Some of the poems written in 1742, usually taken as fairly direct expressions of personal emotion, demonstrate not only the artifice of technique in even Gray's most "sincere" poetic statement, but the way the poet manipulates various sorts of artifice in opposition to one another. In the "Ode on the Spring," "Ode on a Distant Prospect of Eton College," and "Sonnet on the Death of Richard West," he exploits structural patterns of alternation, passages of direct statement paired with those of highly artificial and indirect suggestion. The combination of a diction which deliberately conceals with a more personal mode of expression is largely responsible for the impact of these poems.

The "Ode on the Spring" is the most clearly "Augustan" of the 1742 group. Twenty-five years ago A. R. Humphreys summed up economically the objections that can be made to it: "It is impossible to accept, say, the *Ode on the Spring* seriously. It has a baroque charm; its warmth of colour, decorative personification, and playful solemnity give it individuality, though hardly perhaps of a different sort than if it were a scene painted on an opulent ceiling." [4] Its weaknesses, as defined by Professor Humphreys, are that it is imitative, pedantic, full of "classical pretence" and "anthropomorphic banality." It is clumsy, with "disconcerting hesitations of tone"; and it is totally lacking in personal observation.

Most of these objections are valid enough; yet the poem creates its highly individual effect through its exploitation of "classical pretence," its deliberate avoidance of personal observation, in conjunction with its ironic self-revelation. The poem's diction and its "pedantry" are alike most elaborate in the opening stanza, where conventional classical references jostle one another. We are offered

The Poetry of Vision

Venus and the "rosy-bosom'd Hours," the "Attic warbler," "Cool Zephyrs": the classical paraphernalia of a sort of "nature poetry" which has little to do with nature. The effect of the stanza is to lead the reader's eye away from the object: "long-expecting flowers" insists on the flowers' role in the pattern of nature, removing stress from their appearance; "purple spring," as Geoffrey Tillotson has pointed out, refers not at all to the actual look of an English spring; even the lovely line, "The untaught harmony of spring," about the birds' songs, generalizes rather than describes. One may possibly imagine from all this such a scene as is painted on ceilings, but the stanza is not really pictorial. It evokes an atmosphere rather than a picture, a delicate, unrealistic, faintly mythological atmosphere, quite remote from actuality. P. F. Vernon has pointed out, in a perceptive treatment of Gray's early poems, that what description the stanza contains is essentially symbolic, suggesting by its symbolic implications the meanings which the poem explicitly states only in its last two stanzas.[5]

At the beginning of the second stanza there is a shift in language: this sounds more convincingly like the poet's "real voice." The description now sketches a scene with more particularity, more solidity, than the one suggested by the poem's opening lines. It is, however, hardly less literary in its origins than the panorama which preceded it. Shakespeare now is the source instead of Virgil. Gray notes a specific allusion to *A Midsummer Night's Dream,* but the scene of poet in rural landscape, as well as the reflections the setting immediately inspires, remind us too of Jacques in *As You Like It.* The description also foretells that of the rural poet in the "Elegy Written in a Country Churchyard": [6]

> There at the foot of yonder nodding beech
> That wreathes its old fantastic roots so high,
> His listless length at noontide would he stretch,
> And pore upon the brook that babbles by.
>
> (ll. 101–104)

Both portraits derive indirectly and generally from a more ancient tradition: that of the poet as a figure in pastoral, the swain as poetic orderer of his own experience, in harmony with the world of nature he inhabits.

The language of the second stanza is more concrete and direct than that of the first, its images more specific (the "broader, browner shade" of the oak versus "long-expecting flowers"; water with a "rushy brink" as opposed to the vague and evanescent "Cool Zephyrs"), its literary references less exclusively classical. Its tone also shifts radically. Metaphorically as well as literally, the first stanza concerns "the clear blue sky." Its tone is elevated; its concentration on aesthetic pleasure implies an optimistic view of the natural universe and of man's relation to it. The environment of the second stanza, on the other hand, is a "broader browner shade." If the first stanza floats away into the heavens, the second (which, as Mr. Vernon points out, creates an image of maturity to oppose the one of youth which precedes it) remains very much tied to earth; the reflections of the poet who inhabits this landscape are accordingly melancholy:

> How vain the ardour of the Crowd,
> How low, how little are the Proud,
> How indigent the Great!
>
> (ll. 18–20)

This is an easy sort of melancholy, as automatic a response as the optimism which the introductory mythologizing might produce. The reason for its automatic quality is immediately apparent in its source: Gray seems at pains to point out that these ideas about the world are the immediate product of poetic artifice.

> Beside some water's rushy brink
> With me the Muse shall sit, and think
> (At ease reclin'd in rustic state),
> How vain . . .
>
> (ll. 15–18)

To stress the presence of the Muse in this setting is to emphasize the deliberate artificiality of the presentation as a whole; the description insists on the actual physical existence of the Muse as well as the poet in the landscape by dwelling on her posture ("At ease reclin'd") and hinting, through the oxymoron of "rustic state," the faintly humorous overtones implicit in the literal presence of this mythological figure in the concrete English setting. She reminds us that these particular lines about the futility of worldly endeavor have little to do with the *nature* of worldly endeavor. Their source is poetic convention; they represent an attitude rather than a perception.

The succeeding two stanzas continue the pattern of alternation between different modes of poetic artifice and the attitudes associated with them. In the third stanza the images, less emphatically classical (although there is a specific echo of Virgil here), remain conventionally "poetic" and once more stress physical elevation ("The insect youth are on the wing") and the emotional elevation associated with it. The fourth stanza, more closely connected with the preceding one than the second is with the first, shifts, like the second, to a melancholy perspective and an emphasis on earth rather than air ("their airy dance/ They leave, in dust to rest"). Its subject matter and point of view, however, are clearly as contrived and as arbitrary as the earlier concern with the way "The busy murmur glows!"

The importance of this insistent artifice, artifice emphasized by the alternations of mood, theme, reference, emerges fully only in the concluding stanza, where the speaker for the first time considers himself not as poet but as man. Until now, the ode has both presented and implied an image of its speaker as poetic contriver, and reminded us, by the nature of the language itself and by Gray's footnotes, how much the poem consists of contrivance. But at the end the artificial, decorative metaphor of insects which has been manipulated through two stanzas turns on itself and its creator, becoming suddenly strangely real. Artifice has controlled the poem, kept us from taking its insights very seriously; now that very artifice reveals something important about the poet as human being. The conventional "poetic" assertion that insects are like people leads to the forcible realization that people may be like insects — and judging himself as an insect, the poet discovers his limitations as a man ("Poor moralist! and what art thou?/ A solitary fly!"). He looks at the reality of his isolated life in terms of his own metaphor, which reveals reality. The method which produces the speaker's self-discovery, however, modifies and enriches its poignance. The poem achieves a wry irony which discloses the genuine pathos of Gray's sense of himself, but also tempers it. If the poet's "voice" is less conspicuously "public" here than in his grander poems, it is still far from intimate: self-revelation emerges specifically through Gray's awareness of himself as poetic contriver. The poem may, as Lord David Cecil suggests, be an utterance of a sensitive spirit in a tragic world,[7] but it is more: in a sense its subject is the relation between artifice and reality. Artifice, perceived first as a device for arbitrarily shaping one's perception of reality (toward optimism or toward pessimism), ultimately provides new insight into reality. The full logical and emotional movement of the poem is in a sense the direct opposite of that in the churchyard elegy, in which the problems of finding a personal rôle in the world are finally resolved in the figure of the poet. In the "Ode on the Spring," on the other hand, the position of poet does not help the man to solve his private dilemma: it only reveals that dilemma to him.

In the "Sonnet on the Death of Richard West" the chief tension in the expression is not between two forms of artifice but between artifice and personal statement. Its importance has been recognized by Mr. Doherty and by Geoffrey Tillotson. At the poem's opening, Professor Tillotson points out, Gray "means us to take the 'poetic diction' as dramatic — for though it is himself who is speaking, he speaks by means of quotations from others. . . . These things are stock-in-trade, and that is the point of Gray's rejection of them." [8] The sonnet's most conventional rhetoric, however, like that in the "Ode on the Spring," serves a double purpose: it exists not simply to be rejected, but also to convey a complex structure of ideas.

Five years before his death, West included in a letter to Gray a long poem entitled "*Ad Amicos.*" One section of it sheds light on Gray's later sonnet:

> I care not tho' this face be seen no more,
> The world will pass as chearful as before;
> Bright as before the Day-Star will appear
> The fields as verdant, and the skies as clear:
> Unknown and silent will depart my breath,
> Nor Nature e'er take notice of my death.
> Yet some there are (ere sunk in endless night)
> Within whose breasts my monument I'd write:
> Loved in my life, lamented in my end,
> Their praise would crown me, as their precepts mend.[9]

The conjunction between the attitude of "Nature" and that of the friend toward death is here crucial, as it was to be in Gray's sonnet, which supplies an ironic commentary on his friend's poem: for West's assurance that there is value in the lamentations of friendship, Gray substitutes the bitter conviction that his own isolation emblemizes the futility of mourning:

> I fruitless mourn to him, that cannot hear,
> And weep the more because I weep in vain.

Like the "Spring" ode, the sonnet on West proceeds by alternations of technique. Its opening quatrain is richest in conventional diction, which functions here, as so often in eighteenth-century poetry, to insist upon the essential tie between man and nature. Mornings, in the universe here invoked, are "smileing," the sun is animated as Phoebus, birds sing an "amorous Descant," fields, "chearful," "resume their green Attire." So emphatic is the insistence that even the inanimate universe partakes of the nature and values of man that it becomes almost painful — which is, of course, precisely the point.

In the second quatrain, one's attention is forced to the "lonely Anguish" of the poet. All is red, golden, green, in the opening lines; in the quatrain which follows them, all is bare and comparatively abstract. The hardly perceptible metaphors are embodied entirely in verbs: the poet's ears "repine" for other notes than those of the birds; his heart "melts"; joys "expire" in his breast. Nouns and adjectives carry the weight of the figures in the opening picture of joyous nature; in the description of solitary grief, there is no picture at all.

The third quatrain reveals fully the significance of the contrast, explaining the vital fact — not explicitly recognized in West's poem — that all parts of nature function together, in a union which includes "happier Men," and all parts have a purpose. Appropriately, Gray here returns to that "poetic diction" so well-adapted to the presentation of optimistic views of the natural world. The lines are less colorful than the opening ones, but as highly figured; they convey also a new poignance (partly the result of the contrast that has been established), exemplified in the beautiful line, "To warm their little Loves the Birds complain." [10] Here is a fine emblem of the terrible difference Gray perceives between himself and the rest of the world: the "complaint" of the birds has a function and a value, it participates in the demonstration of love; his own quite different complaint reaches no hearer and produces no positive effect. West maintains that nature and friendship both provide compensations, of different sorts, for death; his point of view is that of the man conscious of his mortality, contemplating the prospect of his own dissolution. Gray, considering death from an equivalent viewpoint in the "Elegy," was to express a similar attitude:

> For who to dumb Forgetfulness a prey,
> This pleasing anxious being e'er resign'd,
> Left the warm precincts of the chearful day,
> Nor cast one longing ling'ring look behind?
>
> On some fond breast the parting soul relies,
> Some pious drops the closing eye requires;
> Ev'n from the tomb the voice of Nature cries,
> Ev'n in our Ashes live their wonted Fires.
>
> (ll. 85–92)

The prospective victim needs to believe in the existence of "some fond breast," needs to feel that he will not be entirely prey to "dumb Forgetfulness." The "voice of Nature" cries from the tomb to the survivors who may preserve the "wonted Fires" of their departed friends perhaps by their memory alone; more specifically, Gray's footnote reference to Petrarch and the context of the entire elegy suggest, by the power of poetry to preserve life. But the ultimate faith in the human significance of the poet which dominates the elegy is not so strong in the earlier sonnet, where the artifice of poetry, as in the "Ode on the Spring," reveals its inadequacy to compensate for the ravages of feeling. Gray's viewpoint, in the West sonnet, is that of the survivor; he writes from direct knowledge rather than from observation. And, as the poet-survivor, he contradicts the more speculative conclusion of the passage from West's poem, insisting that nature, through its denial of grief, only intensifies one's solitude in sorrow (solitude more intensely poignant than that perceived by the speaker in the end of the "Ode on the Spring"), and that the monument which West imagines within the breasts of his friends must be shaky indeed, when the natural universe refuses it any real foundation.

The Poetry of Vision

Wordsworth obviously perceived the deliberate alternation of rhetorical patterns in this sonnet. The five lines that he italicizes as "the only part of this Sonnet which is of any value" include all but one of the lines where Gray evokes, in deliberately bare language, his own isolation in suffering. (The sixth presumably fails to receive Wordsworth's accolade because it includes an "alas!".) Modern readers may more readily see the extent to which Gray here — as often elsewhere — employs contrasting modes of poetry as a technique of cross-commentary. Certainly he does not reject the elaborate diction of his opening lines: he recognizes and exposes its value in conveying the beauty and unity of the natural world. But he recognizes also its limitations, as a mode of insight and of expression. It is not adequate to express the misery of solitary grief; the poet as artificer cannot merely through convention communicate the sorrow of the poet as man.

In the long "Ode on a Distant Prospect of Eton College," rhetorical variations are more complex in technique and in function. Here too Gray's shifts of rhetoric deepen and complicate his meaning; the ode's form directly illuminates its content.

That content, simply stated, seems to be the glorification of boyhood at the expense of adulthood. Wordsworth praised the child for his supernal wisdom; Gray envies him his ignorance: "where ignorance is bliss,/'Tis folly to be wise." But the ironies of this aphorism are so inclusive that they virtually transform the entire poem.

Sir Leslie Stephen complained about this ode that it "comes into conflict with one's common-sense. We know too well that an Eton boy is not always the happy and immaculate creature of Gray's fancy." [11] Certainly a more unrealistic picture of boyhood can seldom have been offered. The poem opens with a stanza so highly rhetorical that it might have been designed to provide examples of various figures and tropes. In ten lines we find repeated instances of apostrophe, metaphor, personification, alliteration, inversion, repetition, parallelism. The invocation to the towers of Eton has little reference to real experience, and the elaborate description it introduces of the joys of Eton's inhabitants is hardly more convincing. "Gray thought his language more poetical as it was more remote from common use," complained Dr. Johnson,[12] with particular reference to the phrase, "redolent of joy and youth," which Gray here uses to evoke the "gales" that blow from Eton; we may be tempted to agree. Perhaps even more "remote from common use" is the description of youthful sport:

> What idle progeny succeed
> To chase the rolling circle's speed,
> Or urge the flying ball?
>
> (ll. 28–30)

The rhetorical tone continues, although the language is more immediately evocative, in the succeeding description of boyish enterprise:

> Some bold adventurers disdain
> The limits of their little reign,
> And unknown regions dare descry:
> Still as they run they look behind,
> They hear a voice in every wind,
> And snatch a fearful joy.
>
> (ll. 35–40)

Finally, Gray presents a list of the students' attributes, including

> buxom health of rosy hue,
> Wild wit, invention ever-new,
> And lively chear of vigour born;
> The thoughtless day, the easy night . . .
>
> (ll. 45–48)

In the three-stanza treatment of the denizens of Eton, the movement has been from particularity to generalization, from the concrete to the abstract. It may be hard to feel "particularity" in such a phrase as "the rolling circle's speed," but, elevated though it is, it, like all periphrases, refers to something specific (in this case, a hoop). The final stanza of the triad, on the other hand, deals solely with abstractions: "hope," "health," "wit," "fancy," "invention," "chear," "vigour." The poet's language now is less pretentious than that which he expends on swimming, bird-catching and hoop-rolling; his nostalgic tone is more marked. But vague nostalgia and pretentious periphrasis have the same general effect: to make the reader acutely aware of the element of distance in this "distant prospect" of Eton. A light that never was on sea or land glows about the blissful young scholars; the prospect is so distant as to seem unreal. The pervasive artifice of the presentation, the unrelieved insistence of the rhetorical distancing, keep the reader conscious of the poet as manipulator of reality.

From the joys of youth the poem proceeds, after a transitional stanza, to the evils of maturity. The transition, intensely emotional, concludes, "Ah, tell them, they are men!" In its highly charged bareness, this line foretells the technique of the poem's final stanza; yet immediately after it Gray returns to his more elaborate style. He relies now almost entirely on heavy use of personification, a new form of artifice in this ode, and one which provides its own kind of "distancing" for the image of adulthood's horrors.

The personifications are expert. Like most such figures in their period, they are strongly traditional in conception, yet Gray individualizes them. Here as in so many other eighteenth-century poems the passions are "the fury Passions." They are also, however, "The vulturs of the mind": an addition which removes their dignity, makes them more concretely destructive, may recall the tortures of Prometheus, sordid and endless. Despair is "grim-visag'd" and "comfortless." These are obvious epithets, but they evoke despair's special qualities: its almost deliberate grimness, its inability either to offer comfort to its victim (like gentler forms of sorrow) or to receive comfort from any source. Infamy is "grinning," Madness, "moody"; Poverty "numbs the soul with icy hand." In each case, the relevant detail insists both upon the horror which these qualities have in common and on the special dreadfulness of each specific state.

Indeed, the descriptions of maturity — despite the fact that they are allegorical — are on the whole a good deal more concrete than those of youth. This parade of personifications comprises a metaphorical vision of adulthood to parallel the glamorized vision of youth that precedes it. Gray seems — appropriately enough — to feel far more vividly the realities of manhood than those of youth, although certainly his nostalgia for childhood is as acute as his horror of the adult's universal fate.

The allegorical presentation of phenomena, however vivid, is not "realistic"; lack of realism is as striking in the description of man's fate as in the evocation of childhood. In both cases, the high rhetorical tone reminds us that Gray's rhetoric is often associated with imaginative vision: his elaborations, decorations, heavy use of rhetorical tricks indicate his concern with something other than literal truth. In the sonnet on West, a vision of natural unity is placed in conjunction with the harsh reality of individual pain; in the "Ode on the Spring," two "literary" visions ultimately reveal the actuality of the solitary poet. In the Eton ode, too, there are two visions: of childhood and of adulthood, both deliberately removed from actuality, both containing elements of truth.

The truth of the vision of manhood is immediately and forcibly apparent; the imaginative and emotional power of the personifications attests the conviction of the author. The remoteness of personifications from actual experience, the "distancing" involved in the use of this device, emphasizes the horror of maturity in reality: it is too dreadful to be discussed more directly; the poet must find metaphors to make his perceptions tolerable. If a man's perceptions about maturity are essentially insights into its horrors, it follows that he may need to glamorize his perceptions about childhood; if beauty cannot be located in the present, it must be asserted of the past or the future. Gray's clearly artificial presentation of childhood as "paradise" emphasizes the agony of his experience of adulthood. Mr. Doherty comments that in Gray's "more plangent poems" he reveals himself as "a man whose historical sensibility demands of him that the present be always seen as part of a movement of time" (p. 229). A sense of that movement is clearly present in this ode, but it is a movement relentlessly downward. Both visions emphasize this fact.

The final stanza of the Eton ode returns to the barer style which Gray used so effectively in the sonnet on West. In it there is only one strong metaphor, no striking inversions; the diction, with the exception of one rhetorical "ah!", is such as Wordsworth might approve. But the simpler style in no way denies the validity of the affirmations which the rhetorical sections have made; here emotion derives from vision without conflicting with it. Resignation is a result of perceptions which provide a more than "realistic" insight into the nature of reality.

That resignation, faintly bitter, is summed up in the final assertion that wisdom is folly "where ignorance is bliss." Although the aphorism has the form of a general statement (and is frequently taken, out of context, to be one), its reference in the poem is particular, to the nature of youth and of manhood. Its fundamental ironies are twofold. First, the entire poem has demonstrated that the bliss of ignorance and the folly of wisdom are alike inevitable in human life. The concluding statement (like the earlier rhetorical question, "why should they know their fate?") appears to offer the possibility of choice, but in neither case does an alternative really exist. The nature of childhood and of maturity is foreordained: one may perhaps hope to be aware of it, but can do nothing to change it. It is the fate of mankind to move from blissful ignorance to foolish wisdom; it is perhaps man's nature to coin aphorisms which justify both states.

Second, the poem as a whole has defined both "ignorance" and "wisdom" with built-in ironic overtones. "Ignorance" here is specifically ignorance of the horrors that lie in store for all human beings; "wisdom" consists in awareness of those horrors. A few years after Gray wrote his Eton ode, Dr. Johnson, in "The Vanity of Human Wishes," suggested his scorn of the suppliant for long life who

> Hides from himself his state, and shuns to know,
> That life protracted is protracted woe.
>
> (ll. 257–258)

Scorn was possible for Johnson because he saw his characters in a religious context: it is shortsighted and ridiculous to pray for length of life on earth if one is convinced that a better existence may be the aftermath of human suffering. In Gray's ode, the language of religious hope evokes only departed childhood. That is the state of "bliss," the "paradise" which thought can only destroy. The wisdom of adulthood is damning.

The sudden shift to relatively undecorated language in the final stanza emphasizes the despair which awareness of the ironies can produce. The stanza's first line echoes the earlier line which most clearly prepared for the ending. "Ah, tell them, they are men!" the poet cried before, of the schoolboys; now he reminds us, "To each his suff'rings: all are men." Children and adults alike participate inevitably in the miseries of being human. The straightforward language throws into sharp relief the earlier elaboration and reveals the intimate relation of form and content in the ode. For the artifice and formality which controlled the presentation of child-hood's joy and maturity's misery reflect a further meaning of "wis-dom." To this extent alone does the wisdom derived from experience have power: it can formulate its record of experience so as to make it artistically viable. The suffering of mankind is no less intense for being embodied in personifications, but the use of such figures sug-gests a kind of order and meaning in that suffering. The joys of boy-hood are purged of imperfection by being rhetorically described; the conjunction of the two visions, of suffering and of joy, provides a perception of pattern in human life. But this function of wisdom, too, is merely folly. When rhetoric is virtually abandoned, as in the concluding stanza, and the poet speaks directly of his sense of the ultimate disorder of experience, his revelation is the more forceful for its contrast with what has gone before. Once more Gray has demonstrated his extraordinary skill at playing off highly con-trolled rhetoric against simple, direct statement.

The rhetorical oppositions manifested in these poems are by no means characteristic of Gray's later work. They dramatize a sense of tension which was to remain important in his poetry, although in different forms. These relatively early poems are perhaps experi-mental in their playing with technique; their manipulation of arti-fice seems largely responsible for the conspicuous success of the experiments. In the direct verse of the "Elegy" and the highly for-malized patterns of the 1757 odes, however, Gray does not employ any clear alternations of technique, nor does he point to his own reliance on artifice. Instead, the conflicts of values which both interest and perplex him as a poet are directly expressed as part of the subject. These later poems pose complicated problems, best dealt with through other formulations than those which describe the function of artifice in the poems of 1742.

Gray's Pindaric ode, "The Progress of Poesy," completed in 1754, concludes with an odd definition of the "way" of the poet:

> Beyond the limits of a vulgar fate,
> Beneath the Good how far — but far above the Great.

The antithesis in the last line, Joseph Warton complained, is "un-suited to the dignity of such a composition." [13] It is, moreover, in content peculiarly unrelated to the rest of the poem, which considers neither the poet's social nor his moral position. Both in form and in content, however, the line reveals Gray's characteristic preoccupations. It suggests the weaknesses of the poem which contains it; it may also provide a key metaphor for a conflict vital to Gray's most compelling effects.

The weaknesses of "The Progress of Poesy" apparent to the modern eye were obvious also to earlier critics. Two reviewers complained that the poem's abundant figures were strangely ineffective. "Though it abounds with images that strike, yet, . . . it contains none that are affecting," wrote Goldsmith in the *Monthly Review*.[14] An anonymous notice in the *Quarterly Review*,[15] raising the question of Gray's "obscurity," asserts that in this poem it is "entirely produced by the resolution to tell everything in the high figurative style" (p. 48). Dr. Johnson wrote (of "The Progress of Poesy" and its companion piece, "The Bard"): "they strike, rather than please; the images are magnified by affectation; the language is laboured into harshness. The mind of the writer seems to work with unnatural violence. . . . He has a kind of strutting dignity, and is tall by walking on tiptoe. His art and his struggle are too visible, and there is too little appearance of ease and nature." [16] Roger Martin, the twentieth-century critic who has examined Gray most thoroughly, makes essentially the same points, complaining, like Johnson, about the affectation and lack of ease in such poems: "La mythologie toujours créatrice de Pindar, qui appelait dans l'imagination des auditeurs de vivantes association, est remplacée par des secrets de philologue, des figures figées, usées et refroidies qui n'éveillent que de faibles échos, et ne sous-entendent que l'indigence des ressources." [17] And F. Doherty's close analysis of specific images in Gray's "public" poetry points likewise to the failure of the poem's figurative language.

"Extreme conciseness of expression, yet pure, perspicuous, & musical, is one of the grand beauties of lyric poetry," Gray wrote to Mason. "this I have always aim'd at, & never could attain." [18] A year later, also to Mason, he observed, "The true Lyric style with all its flights of fancy, ornaments & heightening of expression, & harmony of sound, is in its nature superior to every other style." [19] The lyric meant the ode. Norman Maclean has described the importance of the ode in the eighteenth century: "However low we may appraise the moments in which the neoclassical age felt it was lyrical, we should also realize that this 'non-lyrical' age regarded the highest form of the lyric — the Great Ode — as one of the supreme expressions of poetry and itself a supreme epoch in the history of the lyric, with its first master, Cowley, at least rivaling Pindar, with Dryden secure among all competitors, and with Gray the last and the best." [20] By the mid-eighteenth century, as Mr. Maclean and others have abundantly demonstrated, the ode was assumed to rely primarily on images rather than action. Indeed poetry could be defined, a few years after the publication of Gray's odes, as "a species of painting with words, in which the figures are happily conceived, ingeniously arranged, affectingly expressed, and recommended with all the warmth and harmony of colouring: it consists of imagery, description, metaphors, similes, and sentiments, adopted with propriety to the subject." [21]

"The Progress of Poesy" is a straightforward attempt at high lyric achievement (its form as a "Pindaric" ode is an announcement of this goal) in the fashionable pictorial mode, relying heavily on "imagery, description, metaphors, similes, and sentiments." It impresses with the remoteness of its language, but its vocabulary is not itself unduly "poetic," although the frequent classical allusions give a special flavor. Ian Jack's reminder (in connection with Gray's "Elegy") that " 'language' consists of *words as they are used* and not as separate and independent entities" [22] is highly relevant here. Yet some of the best lines in "The Progress of Poesy" are as direct in structure as in vocabulary. Gray describes Death as "sad refuge from the storms of Fate" (l. 45); the key monosyllable *sad* reverses a Christian cliché with poignant effect. The poem's one vivid personification is "coward Vice, that revels in her chains" (l. 80; Gray was to employ a similar image more effectively in his "Ode for Music": "Servitude that hugs her chain"); the unexpected *revels* sharpens the line and the paradoxical perception behind it. A more extended example of relatively direct language is the characterization of Milton, especially effective in juxtaposition with the bathetic description of Shakespeare ("The dauntless Child/ Stretch'd forth his little arms, and smiled"; ll. 87–88), but good verse in its own right:

The Poetry of Vision

> He pass'd the flaming bounds of Place and Time:
> The living Throne, the saphire-blaze,
> Where Angels tremble, while they gaze,
> He saw; but blasted with excess of light,
> Closed his eyes in endless night.
>
> (ll. 98–102)

The tone of this is elevated, its imagery characteristically compressed, its literary allusions abundant (Gray's own notes point to four), but the actual language is straightforward and even fairly concrete for an essentially metaphysical conception. The strong participle *blasted* imparts energy which is heightened by the preponderance of verbs and participial adjectives. With "extreme conciseness of expression" the lines convey the poetic and philosophic association between spiritual vision and physical blindness, and elaborate that association by suggesting vision as the cause of blindness.

But these are samples of the poem at its best. At its worst it is less forceful, more high-flown. Even in its most extravagant sections of "pseudo-poetry," however, its rhetoric is more dependent on syntax than on diction. Syntax is the key to many of the ode's effects; vocabulary is far less important than structure to its rhetorical patternings.

The chief syntactical peculiarity of this and of many of Gray's poems is the inversion.

> Her track, where'er the Goddess roves,
> Glory pursue, and generous Shame,
> Th'unconquerable Mind, and Freedom's holy flame.
>
> (ll. 63–65)

> Tho' he inherit
> Nor the pride, nor ample pinion,
> That the Theban Eagle bear
> Sailing with supreme dominion . . .
>
> (ll. 113–116)

The obscurity of reference which Gray's contemporaries found in his odes has disappeared since the poet appended his scornful notes; the obscurity of syntax remains. The reader must be always alert, conscious of whether verbs are singular or plural, willing to puzzle out the reference of participles. Syntactical strain seems almost a poetic end in itself.

One purpose of syntactical distortion may be to control the emphasis of the rhyme. *Pursue* would be the natural word to end line 64, but Gray clearly wishes here to stress the nouns rather than the verb. Conversely, and more characteristically, the inversion in line 115 accents the verb, *bear,* which governs both *pride* and *pinion* and controls the zeugma through which Gray comments on Pindar.

The inversions have also a cumulative effect. Helping to control the rhythmic patterns, they frequently provide dignity, and contribute to the tone of elevation appropriate to the Pindaric ode. In lines 63–64, quoted above, the inversions force the reader to consider glory and shame as individual phenomena ("Glory and generous Shame pursue" would call far less attention to each quality in itself); they also slow the movement of the thought and lend it rhetorical weight. On the other hand, those inversions which emphasize verbs contribute, like the emphatic syntax of apostrophe, imperative and direct address which Gray here employs, to the poem's controlled energy. The stress on *bear,* in the lines about the eagle, echoes an earlier inverted line:

> Behold, where Dryden's less presumptuous car,
> Wide o'er the fields of Glory bear
> Two Coursers of ethereal race.
>
> (ll. 102–104)

In both cases, the verb suggests the "weight" which must be borne and — even more significantly — the force necessary to sustain it. The evocation of Milton begins

> Nor second He, that rode sublime
> Upon the seraph-wings of Extasy,
> The secrets of th' Abyss to spy.
>
> (ll. 95–97)

The rhyme-stress on *spy* emphasizes the rôle of the poet as *doer,* a rôle vitally important in the poem.

Most significantly, the syntactical difficulties created by the inversions call attention to the process, the movement of the ode. In order to understand it on the simplest level, one must trace the relationship of subject, verb, object, modifiers, the structure through which ideas succeed one another. Readers unwilling to meet the demands of the syntax must comprise a large proportion of those who find Gray's Pindarics unbearable. The poet, however, made no allowances. (His motto for the two Pindaric odes was, "Vocal to the intelligent; but for the crowd they need interpreters.")

Gray's syntactical emphasis on the function of words in "The Progress of Poesy" reflects the stress on function which dominates this ode; the attention such emphasis produces to the movement of ideas is appropriate for a poem whose nominal subject is the movement of ideas. "The Progress of Poesy" is the very type of the eighteenth-century "progress poem"; it relates, in more extended fashion than Collins's "Ode to Simplicity" but with similar emphasis, the steps by which poetry is conceived to have deserted Greece for England. But perhaps more important is the fact that it also outlines a view of the nature of poetry, revealing that for Gray poetry is preeminently functional. Poetry "gives life and lustre to all it touches": so Gray's footnote interprets the opening lines. It enriches its subjects, provides beauty, controls the cares and passions (ll. 14–16). It creates grace and intensifies emotion (ll. 25–41). Poetry is a divine dispensation to compensate for human misery (ll. 42–53). It is a source of virtue, an inspirer, in particular, of love of liberty (ll. 54–65). Itself inspired by nature, poetry can offer insight into physical and psychological reality (ll. 83–94). At its best, it supplies "Thoughts, that breath, and words, that burn" (l. 110). It becomes clear that the poet must be "far above the Great," and although he must remain "Beneath the Good," he has been shown to fulfill a vital moral function.

In structure the poem's final couplet, through its precision of classification, reflects and emphasizes the schematic pattern of the whole. This ode is intellectually organized; the process by which Gray proceeds from the Aeolian lyre at the beginning to the neatly classified poet at the end is more logical than imaginative. This fact largely accounts for the ode's peculiar coldness. In "The Progress of Poesy" thought is translated into imagery because such, Gray conceives, is the method of the ode. The translation, however, is by no means entirely accurate or adequate, as Mr. Doherty has demonstrated.[23] Metaphors are sometimes mechanically conceived and incompletely integrated.

> Oh! Sovereign of the willing soul,
> Parent of sweet and solemn-breathing airs,
> Enchanting shell! the sullen Cares,
> And frantic Passions hear thy soft controul.
>
> (ll. 13–16)

The lines refer, as a footnote explains, to the "power of harmony to calm the turbulent sallies of the soul"; their movement from personification ("sovereign," "parent") to the metaphor of the lyre ("enchanting shell") is abrupt and arbitrary. Although each image is individually justifiable, the conjunction of the two suggests a rather cavalier attitude in the poet. Similarly, the shift from "They sought, Oh Albion! next thy sea-encircled coast" (l. 82) to "In thy green lap was Nature's Darling laid" (l. 84), with its radical change in point of view, hints that what Gray has to say interests him more than the specific devices through which he conveys his meaning, that form and content are not here so intimately related as one expects in poetry. Many of the personifications seem equally perfunctory:

> Man's feeble race what Ills await,
> Labour, and Penury, the racks of Pain,
> Disease, and Sorrow's weeping train.
>
> (ll. 42–44)

One realizes how perfunctory these personifications are by comparing them with the rather similar group in the "Ode on a Distant Prospect of Eton College."

> Lo, in the vale of years beneath
> A griesly troop are seen,
> The painful family of Death,
> More hideous than their Queen:
> This racks the joints, this fires the veins . . .
> Lo, Poverty, to fill the band,
> That numbs the soul with icy hand . . .
>
> (ll. 81–85, 88–89)

Here the emblematic figures, more fully visualized than their counterparts in "The Progress of Poesy," also serve a more complex purpose: Gray dwells at length on the horrors of the human situation because that is his main concern, as it is not in the ode on "poesy." Indeed, the personifications of the later poem exist mainly to be dismissed:

The Poetry of Vision

The fond complaint, my Song, disprove,
And justify the laws of Jove.

(ll. 46–47)

In the context they do not need to be vivid because they concern Gray only incidentally — as do many of the images in his poem.

"The Progress of Poesy," for all its energy and splendor, demonstrates many of Gray's characteristic poetic weaknesses. But it also enunciates a theory of poetry as justified by its effects, and implies, through its stress on syntax (and perhaps inversely through its perfunctory imagery), a view of poetry as process. Such a view does not necessarily imply weakness of actual poetic achievement, but it helps to explain why this particular poem does not show Gray at his best. For the fact is that *progress* — particularly in the eighteenth-century sense — is not the same as *process,* and no real *process* takes place in this ode, however convoluted its syntax. It is a display poem, designed to manifest the poet's powers; it causes nothing to happen, and nothing really happens in it. The progress it relates is an artificial sequence of scenes. Paradoxically, this poem asserting a functional view of poetry itself fills little genuine function. The ode does not demonstrate the weakness of Gray's poetic theory; it fails to put that theory into effect.

As I have noted, one curious aspect of the "Good-Great" antithesis set up in the last line of "The Progress of Poesy" is that its terms seem singularly irrelevant to the rest of the poem. The poet's relations to other sorts of men have not previously been an issue; the nature of poetry rather than the rôle of the poet is the ode's announced subject. Unlike the characteristic Popean antithesis, moreover, this pairing of opposites does not begin to define a balance; rather, it adumbrates a conflict implying no prospect of reconciliation. There is, to be sure, no necessary opposition between "the Good" and "the Great"; to assert the inevitability of such an opposition would ordinarily be a satirist's device. In this case, where no purpose of social criticism is apparent, the idea is peculiarly disturbing; it ends the poem with an implicit question and offers no suggestion of an answer.

"The Bard" also concludes with an antithesis. "Be thine Despair, and scept'red Care," cries the bard to King Edward I, "To triumph,

and to die, are mine." Gray wrote to Mason that his friends Nich-
olas Bonfoy and Thomas Nevile had seen the poem, and "both somehow dislike the conclusion of the Bard, & mutter something about
Antithesis & Conceit in *To triumph, to die,* wch I do not comprehend, & am sure, it is alterd for the better. It was before

> Lo! to be free, to die, are mine.

if you like it better so, so let it be."[24] The terms of the antithesis
in the form which he obviously preferred, despite the cavils of his
friends, recall the conflict hinted at the end of his other Pindaric
ode. Once more there is an opposition between the "Great" ("scept-
'red Care") and the "Good"; in this case the poet does not stand outside the conflict but participates in it. Indeed, he defines the nature of "the Good," and in voluntary death — the sign of his sacri-
ficial "goodness" — he "triumphs": achieves the grandeur of "the
Great" without the cares.

The concluding antithesis in "The Bard" is more closely related
to the body of the poem than is the one in "The Progress of Poesy,"
yet it, too, suggests some peculiarities of Gray's technique. In its
most interesting aspects, "The Bard" deals emblematically with the
problems of being a poet — more precisely, with the conflicts of
being a poet. "I felt that the Bard was I," wrote Gray to Nichols.[25]
The poet is particularly in opposition to the Great: the king murders
all the bards, they revenge themselves through their visionary power
to perceive the horrible future of the royal line. The poet is identified with the forces of nature (*e.g.*, ll. 23–28) as well as with the
supernatural. The representative of moral pattern, he both perceives and asserts the necessary restoration of order; he is thus profoundly "Good" throughout. The familiar opening lines of the ode
dramatize the conflict forcefully:

> 'Ruin seize thee, ruthless King!
> 'Confusion on thy banners wait,
> 'Tho' fann'd by Conquest's crimson wing
> 'They mock the air with idle state.'

Suggesting that nemesis attends the great, they promise a poem of
energetic clashings, seem the preamble to action rather than description.

But the poem is not the one promised. Gray's "draperies are always of brocade," writes a modern historian of the ode, "but they are nowhere so stiff and gilt as in 'The Bard.'" [26] The poem, says Jean Hagstrum, consists "so exclusively and rigorously of picture and music as to eliminate virtually all rhetorical statement." [27] Although it is less remote than "The Progress of Poesy," "The Bard" resembles the other ode in its ultimate dependence on image rather than action. "Visions of glory, spare my aching sight," cries the Bard toward the end of the poem. Despite its energetic opening, most of the ode has consisted of a panorama, a visual presentation of the exact relation between conqueror and conquered, the precise nature of nemesis. Its artificiality and stiffness derive largely from this fact: the syntax of this ode is characteristically energetic, the poem's allusions wide, its concerns both national and cosmic, yet its conception is severely limited. Commitment to the doctrine that the poet must deal primarily in images opposes the natural form of this ode, the form that would dramatize clash and struggle, that would justify the final action (the Bard's plunge "to endless night") as something more than a bit of stage business. The poet's effort to objectify the Bard's inner conflict has resulted in the virtual elimination of external struggle; one loses sight of meanings as the images proliferate. Gray's poetry of large pretensions leaves a sense of potentiality unfulfilled.

The same points can be made of Gray's "public" poems. More striking than any peculiarity of their diction is the fact that all establish the possibility of conflict, then avoid the dramatization of that conflict by escape into the convention of image rather than action as central to a poem. Even "The Triumphs of Owen," a piece whose main subject is battle and the hero's success as warrior, deals in scenes, not actions. "The Dragon-Son of Mona" poses in statuary attitudes:

> Where his glowing eye-balls turn,
> Thousand Banners round him burn,
> Where he points his purple spear,
> Hasty, hasty Rout is there.

Although the spear's purpleness indicates that it has been employed as a weapon, the poet focuses on it merely as pointer; he personifies Rout, and thus emblemizes confused action with minimal stress on activity. The "Ode for Music," most "public" poem of all, contains few hints of potential conflict, yet it begins with an exorcism of various forces opposed to academic harmony. The device is conventionally Miltonic. Yet in comparison with the opening of "L'Allegro," the beginning of Gray's ode suggests, through the vigor of its personifications, a much more intense interest in conflict. Those ordered away include

> Ignorance, with looks profound,
> And dreaming Sloth of pallid hue,
> Mad Sedition's cry profane,
> Servitude that hugs her chain, . . .
>   painted Flatt'ry [who] hide[s] her serpent-train in flowers . . .

The conjunction of personages is itself interesting, and rather fresh; the sharp and suggestive detail insists on the relevance and immediacy of these enemies to peaceful learning. One is made newly aware of the constant dangerous presence in the academy of ignorance disguised as wisdom, of political agitation that questions fundamental values, of self-seeking and cynical servility. But the scheme of the ode does not allow further development of this theme of opposition, and the poem degenerates into conventional processions and sentiments, never again approaching the vigor of its opening. Only "The Fatal Sisters," of Gray's more formal pieces, sustains the sense of conflict, and then at one remove, within the framework of the sisters' song.

That Gray relies heavily on images is well-known; in this respect he differs not at all from his contemporaries. What is remarkable in Gray is the extent to which the "public" poems, composed of images, reveal the interest in action which emerges more directly in the avowedly personal poems.

It has been argued before that Gray's poems, public and private, are all more or less disguised discussions of his own sensibility. Roger Martin, for example, asserts, "Dès le début, Gray avait fixé le centre de la poésie dans la sensibilité. La notion qui désormais se précise chez lui, c'est que la primordiale sincérité n'est jamais plus certaine que lorsque le poète s'écoute lui-même; que nulle émotion n'est plus touchante que l'émotion saisie en soi aux heures tristes et recueillies." [28] M. Martin goes on to suggest that this notion of poetry implies a reliance on images: "Si l'émotion a pour cause la perception sensible, et si la poésie réside en l'émotion, l'art de la poésie est un jeu d'images" (p. 351). But it could be argued as well that the poet who "listens to himself" in search of valid emotional experience to use as poetic raw material will concentrate on the subtleties of psychic conflict, and that the conflict itself will be more important to him than the images through which he expresses it. Certainly the poems which reveal Gray more directly than his elaborate odes deal with emotional and intellectual conflicts. For the definition of those conflicts the opposition between "the Good" and "the Great" adumbrated in "The Progress of Poesy" is relevant.

> The hues of Bliss more brightly glow,
> Chastised by sabler tints of woe;
> And blended form, with artful strife,
> The strength and harmony of Life.
>> ("Ode on the Pleasures Arising
>> from Vicissitude," ll. 41–44)

Martin Price has described as characteristic of the late eighteenth century "the self-consciousness of a mind turned at once upon the world and upon itself, constantly surprised by what it discovers in the self and as constantly eager to induce the self to reveal its mysterious feelings." [29] Gray, looking within and without, finding conflict in both realms, was only rarely and precariously able to assert the Augustan balance of opposing forces, to perceive in the alternation of bliss and woe the meaningful pattern which defines "The strength and harmony of Life." The fragmentary "Ode on the Pleasures Arising from Vicissitude" is a poem in praise of tension. Seeking to objectify internal conflict, to discover in the external world images for inner turmoil, it moves from its assertion of harmony toward the familiar description of the opposition between the virtuous peasant and the high-born wretch — or so Gray's own note hints, concluding a description of the projected poem. "Sloth envy Ambition. How much happier the rustic that feels it [the joy of spring] tho' he knows not how." [30] The fragment itself ends with the image of

> Indolence and Pride,
> Softly rolling, side by side,
> Their dull, but daily round.

114

Gray: Action and Image

The moral vision which governed the ode's opening, through which Gray perceived the succession of the seasons as analogous to the equally inevitable succession of joy and grief in human experience, is far broader than that suggested by this quotation, which derives from a more limited perspective. The contrast between the poor but feeling peasant and the proud, indolent, ambitious "great man" is sentimental and stereotyped; it implies no perception of complex order, but Gray finds it compelling.

What is particularly striking about Gray's recurrent use of the "Good-Great" opposition, is the way he makes this conflict focus personal tensions of a larger, vaguer sort. This fact is apparent in the "Elegy Written in a Country Church-yard," in which F. W. Bateson[31] and Cleanth Brooks[32] among others have seen a significant clash between village and town, the values of the poor but good and those of the great. The resultant struggle takes place mainly within the sensibility of the poet; it is primarily a psychic conflict, not an economic or philosophic one. As Mr. Brooks points out, the speaker's final choice resolves his conflict: he makes a personal commitment to rural virtue, rejecting the poetic and personal dangers of a more ambitious course. The Good, the Great, and the Poet: the three classifications focus — indeed, create — the "action" of the churchyard elegy, and the poet demonstrates his status "far above the Great," here as in "The Bard," by his final identification with "the Good." Jean Hagstrum argues that the elegy is most significantly "a succession of visually rendered scenes," that it "is not basically dramatic or narrative."[33] Yet the psychic drama which unfolds through these scenes is surely more important than the scenes themselves, and the overtones of the language gain their fullest value in relation to that drama.[34]

The city-country conflict here subsumes other issues: "What should one do in life?"; "What *can* one do?"; "How is a man to feel about what he is?" For these implicit questions the final epitaph provides no adequate answer; perhaps this is one reason why it seems not entirely a satisfactory conclusion to the poem. In the elegy's last stanzas, the poet recreates himself as an imagined, a contrived, figure. This artificial personage reconciles the conflict of city and country, avoiding the pitfalls of both. The limitations of country existence are lack of learning and restricted emotional life:

The Poetry of Vision

But Knowledge to their eyes her ample page
Rich with the spoils of time did ne'er unroll;
Chill Penury repress'd their noble rage,
And froze the genial current of the soul.

(ll. 49–52)

The "Youth" of the epitaph, on the other hand, has not been frowned on by "Fair Science"; his soul is "sincere" (l. 121); he pities misery and values friendship. The melancholy that "mark'd him for her own" seems more an asset than a liability, the emblem of his rich emotional experience.[35] If he lacks the fame and fortune of the great, he lacks also their unscrupulosity, their willingness to prostitute art.

Yet the problem is not so readily soluble, partly because it is more complex than it has been directly asserted to be. Frank Brady, in a recent discussion of the "Elegy," has defined the poem's central problem as "the relationships among potentiality, assertion, limitation, and resignation, or to combine these relationships into one question: to what extent can man fulfill himself?"[36] Mr. Brady demonstrates that the epitaph answers this question by revealing that finally "only the individual can know to what extent he has fulfilled himself" (p. 186). His argument is complex and convincing, inasmuch as the "Elegy" is concerned with the private problems of an individual trying to come to terms with the meaning of his own life. But the poem also deals, more specifically, with the problem of the poet's public rôle. One penalty of poverty, the speaker speculates, may be the creation of "mute inglorious" Miltons (l. 59); hands that might have "waked to ecstasy the living lyre" (l. 48) function only in more immediately practical fashion. Their possessors thus avoid the danger of prostituting the Muse (see ll. 71–72), but they also avoid significant accomplishment. The universal human desire to be remembered after death may be fulfilled through the preserving power of the poet; the "Elegy" is full of references to memorial verse, of which the final epitaph is, of course, an example. To order the image of the poet into an amalgam of harmonious characteristics does not finally reconcile all the difficulties implicit in the rôle of poet, any more than to assert that "artful strife" comprises "The strength and harmony of Life" helps one to deal with the situations in which strife seems anything but artful. Gray's power as a poet derives largely from his ability to convey the inevitability and inexorability of conflict, conflict by its nature unresolvable. Opposed visions of life appear in conjunction in many of his poems. His ironic "Sketch of His Own Character" suggests his sense of the ineffectuality of merely being "good." Gray can describe himself as more virtuous than his distinguished contemporaries, but he is forced to conclude,

> A place or a pension he did not desire,
> But left church and state to Charles Townshend and Squire.

Elevating himself above corruption, he thereby leaves church and state a prey to corruption — but, seeing the world in terms of irreconcilable alternatives, he can find no better choice. At his most optimistic, he may perceive some universal law which inevitably restores order, using evil to destroy itself. Thus the powerful lines "On Lord Holland's Seat" rest on the assumption that Lord Holland's greatness, unalterably opposed to goodness, is for that reason necessarily self-defeating. The nobleman seeks to create true rather than merely "mimick" desolation, but since his depravity must destroy all virtue he cannot count on loyalty or dependability in his "venal friend[s]," and his defeat is therefore inevitable. The identification between the man, Henry Fox, and the animal whose name he bears becomes the emblem of his self-destruction, rather than, as he had imagined, of the destruction of a London in which foxes would have "stunk and litter'd in S^t. Pauls."

The most personal of the poems Gray wrote in 1742, of course, provide vivid examples of the poet's interest in life's incessant and intolerable presentation of opposites as a theme. The oppositions which dominate these poems are characteristically between innocence and experience — the same sort of opposition characteristic of *The Castle of Indolence* and of much of Cowper's work. In the "Ode on the Spring" images of youthful inexperience clash with those of mature pessimism, as Mr. Vernon has demonstrated; in the sonnet on West's death the opposition underlined by the rhetorical shifts is between naive optimism and the dark view which experience enforces; in the Eton College ode, youth and age, again sharply opposed, provide the poetic subject. The tension between the "good" and the "great" so important in the later poems seems a special case of the same fundamental conflict, for the "great" are those mature and experienced in the world's realities, and the "good" must be innocent: the only alternative to innocence, in Gray's vision, is corruption.

It is notable that in the sonnet on West, the "Ode on the Spring," and the Eton College ode, the figure and function of the poet focus or resolve conflict. The poet is the subject of the "Spring" ode; the nature of poetic language is a vital issue in the sonnet; the poetic ordering of experience provides the only viable standard of order in the Eton ode. In the churchyard elegy and the two Pindaric odes of 1759, the subject of the poet's proper rôle and responsibility becomes more clearly central. It was a subject fraught with possibilities of conflict, for which Gray's most effective techniques seem appropriate.

Gray's poetic theory, clearly, was fully justified in his actual achievement long before the publication of his odes, which, in their emphasis on the pictorial, did not allow full expression of his interest in conflict as a theme. By relying primarily on imagery he could not fully implement his sense of poetry as process, as a record of creative activity. His images often seem inadequately felt, his Pindaric odes forbiddingly formal and remote. He was not the sort of man, or the sort of poet, to create and enforce new poetic conventions. But when he used conflict as the explicit subject of his poetry he produced his most successful pieces, whether or not the conflicts that concerned him were capable of poetic resolution. In these poems form and content are triumphantly interfused, the true subject is frequently the universal plight of mankind, the statement peculiarly personal.

Gray seems to stand virtually alone in his time with a concept of poetry as action. He was, of course, by no means alone in his concern with the poet as poetic subject. Thomson's examination of the temptations and dangers of indolence focused on the image of the poet; Collins's preoccupation with the nature of poetry involved him inevitably in consideration of, for example, the emotions valuable as a means to poetic achievement. For Smart and Cowper, the rôle of poet was essentially religious: this fact made it an assumed state of being, the condition of their existence, more than a poetic issue. Yet for them, too, human responsiblity necessarily involved poetic responsibility, and poetic responsibility therefore became a subject for their verse — a subject dealt with largely through experimentation with the limits of imagery.

VI 🌿

CHRISTOPHER SMART:
The Mystique of Vision (I)

"FOR IN MY nature I quested for beauty, but God, God hath sent me to sea for pearls."[1] This magnificent line from *Jubilate Agno* suggests, both in content and in technique, one of Christopher Smart's central preoccupations: his pervasive concern with the intricate and subtle relation between inner experience — what a man seeks in himself — and outer — what he may find in the world, in the sea. This is also a relation between what man, by his very nature (the line's opening phrase is wonderfully ambiguous), feels impelled to search for, and what God demands of him; and it is a relation between the abstract and general (beauty) and the concrete and particular (pearls). The hopefulness of man's nature, that nature which is also the field of his quest, contrasts with the sorrow implied by the traditional association of pearls with tears; the vastness of the sea through which the speaker must search both contrasts with the limitations of his solitary being and seems an analogue for the unplumbed depths of that being. In the middle of the line, the repeated "God" rings like a cry — a cry that echoes throughout Smart's poetry.

The rôle of poet in Smart's verse seems as natural and inevitable as that of honeybee, or cat. Unlike Gray and Thomson, he expresses no doubts or insights about the poet's special moral responsibilities; unlike Collins, he does not examine the function of poetry. He accepts the position of poet as given, concerns himself largely with problems and functions shared by all men, sees his poetry as a mode of participating in the universal activity of praise for the Creator. This universal activity itself, however, interests him less than its complexity, the way in which opposites become identities when perceived in the light of a relationship to God. Considering all his experience and knowledge in terms of this central relationship, Smart achieves a special mode of "seeing," a unique form of perception which depends heavily on the establishment of such intricate connections and contrasts as those in the line touched on above. Directed simultaneously outward and inward, it evaluates all perception and knowledge of the outside world against the poet's personal intuitions, and validates those intuitions by reference to their universality of implication. It is a way of seeing peculiarly responsible for Smart's personal and frequently overwhelming achievement.

"I have seen his Song to David & from thence conclude him as mad as ever," wrote Mason of Christopher Smart.[2] About the same time — shortly after the first publication of the *Song* — James Boswell wrote to Sir David Dalrymple, "I have sent you Smart's *Song to David,* which is a very curious composition, being a strange mixture of *dun obscure* and glowing genius at times."[3] *The Critical Review,* after an opening reservation about "the propriety of a Protestant's offering up either hymns or prayers to the dead," granted that "great rapture and devotion is discernable in this extatic song," and concluded that it was "a fine piece of ruins," which "must at once please and affect a sensible mind."[4] For the eighteenth century, although *A Song to David* might seem in many ways impressive, even moving, its "madness" disqualified it as a subject for serious literary judgment, made its critics almost unanimously patronizing. By the end of the next century, after Robert Browning's rhapsodic praise of Smart, that "madness" was the basis for high critical approbation, since it seemed to demonstrate a poetic repudiation of the accepted standards of eighteenth-century verse. "Smart was possessed by his subject . . . ; and where there is true possession — where the fires of the poet's imagination are not choked by self-consciousness or by too much fuel from the intellect — idiosyncrasy, mannerism, and even conventional formulae are for the time 'burnt and purged away.'" So wrote a reviewer in *The Athenaeum*;[5] if it is difficult to understand how he could find Smart's poem even relatively "purged" of idiosyncrasy, it is easy to see that it represents for him the very type of the anti-eighteenth-century lyric. *The Saturday Review,* in 1896, was explicit in attributing the virtues of the *Song* to its rejection of eighteenth-century standards. "To an age which made 'sense' the highest glory of poetry, its ecstatic vein, its mystic ardent chant, its bold images and colour, must have seemed wild and improper." "Alike in its incoherency and in its glowing speed of inspiration, the poem is unique in its century, unique perhaps in our literature." [6]

Recent criticism of Smart has only begun to define precisely the special sources of his poetic power. With less bias against the eighteenth century than our grandfathers had, we can now discern the extent to which the *Song to David* (as well as Smart's extensive other work) represents not just a repudiation of the poetic assumptions of its time, but also a demonstration of them. It is, to be sure, a risky matter at best to try to define the critical standards of the second half of the eighteenth century. Gordon McKenzie sums up the situation. "There were so many tentative advances, recoils, and, at times, such obliviousness to what had been written that a description of the state of development of criticism in any one year can be contradicted by a description of almost any later year." [7] Smart's demonstrated point of view toward literature was only one of several traditionally acceptable ones, but important among them.

A significant contemporary influence on Smart was Bishop Lowth, whose *Lectures on the Sacred Poetry of the Hebrews* (first published, in Latin, in 1753) dominated the poet's ideas about Hebrew verse patterns. These lectures not only analyze Hebrew poetic style, they also comment extensively on the nature of effective poetry. "The origin and first use of poetical language are undoubtedly to be traced into the vehement affections of the mind," wrote Lowth. "For what is meant by that singular frenzy of poets, which the Greeks, ascribing to divine inspiration, distinguished by the appelation of *enthusiasm,* but a style and expression directly prompted by nature itself, and exhibiting the true and express image of a mind violently agitated?" [8] If "the study of art as the evoker of emotion is perhaps even more characteristic of the aesthetic thought of [the eighteenth century] than the study of the rules," [9] another recurrent theme was emotion as the evoker of art. Bishop Lowth's view that poetical language derives from strong emotion was hardly unique, and its implications for poetic technique were far-reaching. If true poetic style and expression were "directly prompted by nature itself," the poet could hardly hope to achieve them by study of versification or attention to the details of language: he must wait for the spark from heaven to fall, test the quality of his language by the quality of his inspiration. As early as 1701 John Dennis had insisted that "Poetical Genius in a Poem is the true expression of Ordinary or Enthusiastick Passion, proceeding from Ideas, to which it naturally belongs; and Poetical Genius in a Poet, is the power of expressing such Passion worthily." This power, Dennis explains, comes automatically as a result of "enthusiasm": "never any one, while he was wrapt with Enthusiasm, wanted either Words or Harmony; and [it] is self-evident to all who consider, that the Expression conveys and shows the Spirit, and therefore must be produced by it." [10] By 1756 Robert Lloyd's magazine, *The Connoisseur,* complained that "there is this material difference between the former and present age of Poetry; that writers in the first *thought* poetically; in the last, they only *express* themselves so. Modern poets seem to me more to study the manner how they shall write than what is to be written." [11] Lord Kames, a few years later — the year before the publication of *A Song to David* — insisted that in effective poetry "the impression made by the words" must echo that made by the thought, indeed, that the very structure of the writer's sentences should reflect the structure of his thought.[12] This modern sounding idea is amplified by Hugh Blair, whose lectures, published some twenty years after Smart's great poem, were written long before, and codify theories current in Smart's time. Concerned, like so many of his contemporaries, with the nature of "the sublime," Blair believes that no description can be more sublime than the object which inspires it. Such an object "must be set before us in such a light as is most proper to give us a clear and full impression of it; it must be described with strength, with conciseness, and simplicity. This depends, principally, upon the lively impression which the poet, or orator has of the object which he exhibits; and upon his being deeply affected, and warmed, by the Sublime idea which he would convey. If his own feeling be languid, he can never inspire us with any strong emotion." [13] Again, more generally:

It is a very erroneous idea, which many have of the ornaments of Style, as if they were things detached from the subject, and that could be stuck to it, like lace upon a coat . . . And it is this false idea which has often brought attention to the beauties of writing into disrepute. Whereas, the real and proper ornaments of Style are wrought into the substance of it. They flow in the same stream with the current of thought. A writer of genius conceives his subject strongly; his imagination is filled and impressed with it; and pours itself forth in that Figurative Language which Imagination naturally speaks. He puts no emotion which his subject does not raise in him; he speaks as he feels; but his style will be beautiful, because his feelings are lively.[14]

Such a view of the relation between form and content would tend to produce in critics intense preoccupation with the nature of the poetic process, the psychology of the act of composition. In the poet who took it seriously, it might help to encourage a special mode of "seeing." We do not know or need to know that Smart was influenced by Blair's criticism; but such contemporary critics as Blair provide a plausible rationale for much that seems idiosyncratic in Smart's technique and the kind of perception it records. It is not necessary to assume that Smart was so much outside his century's poetic mode that only a more modern aesthetic theory could justify his peculiarity.

The difference between Thomson and Smart, Laurence Binyon remarks, is between observation and illumination.[15] Such a distinction, although unfair to Thomson, may suggest the potential significance of comparing these poets. Radically different as they are in every superficial respect, Thomson and Smart had similar views of the relation between the natural and the supernatural, views which they held in common with many of their contemporaries. Their ways of expressing these attitudes place them poles apart, but the difference is not simply one of quality. In Thomson, meaning derives from observation; in Smart, meaning precedes observation. Thomson begins with a general attitude which his particular descriptions support, but the process of thought and emotion which *The Seasons* records is clearly the product of repeated stimuli. The same large movement occurs over and over: first description, of "real" or imagined objects; then reflection on the description's implications or associations; finally exaltation. The exaltation is the end product, its origins clear and explicit. Although *The Seasons* ultimately achieves a complex — if precarious — unity, it seems not essentially predetermined; no a priori concept of the poem's form is apparent.

The Poetry of Vision

Several critics have noted, on the other hand, that the special quality of *A Song to David* depends upon the combination of careful structure and rhapsodic tone; [16] Smart himself claimed — perhaps ironically — that the poem's greatest fault was its extreme "regularity." In the Advertisement to the *Poems* of 1763 he remarks, "This Song is allowed by Mr. *Smart's* judicious Friends and enemies to be the best piece ever made public by him, its chief fault being the exact Regularity and Method with which it is conducted." [17] The unity of Smart's poem is not the unity of emotional process; *A Song to David* does not, like *The Seasons*, record the movement of feeling and thought through which the poet achieved his intense conviction of the participation of the entire created universe in the great exercise of praise. Its logic is rigorous. Natural details do not occur together in the poem simply because they occur together in nature, or because — like the flowers in Thomson's famous garden passage in "Spring" — they are phenomena of similar sorts which may be incorporated in an imagined panorama. The relation among them is far more complicated; it participates in the elaborate patterning of the poem.

Robert Brittain, who has suggestively elucidated the nature of much of that patterning, has also translated portions of an essay by Federico Olivero which examines some relations among the poem's images. "In this lyric," writes Signor Olivero, "each image is not independent of the others, but they respond from stanza to stanza in a harmony that echoes long and far; it is not a rapid succession of unrelated pictures, but these images, which at a superficial glance appear disconnected, are disposed — although each forms a picture in itself — with skillful artifice into an intricate garland. The poet proceeds by comparison and contrast, which finds a counterpart in the progression of the thought, with perfect symmetry." [18] Mr. Brittain elaborates this point, elucidating the ways in which Smart introduces minor themes while supporting a major one, pointing out, for example, the recurrent contrast between the natural and the cultivated which runs through *A Song to David*.[19] The relations among Smart's images are complicated; they demonstrate a union of form and content more integral, perhaps, than can be found in any other poem of the eighteenth century.

The most common pattern controlling the images is, as Signor Olivero suggests, that of comparison and contrast — with strong emphasis on contrast. Even when the opposition between, say, two members of the animal kingdom is inherent in their natures, Smart frequently makes of it something complicated.

> the beaver plods his task;
> While the sleek tigers roll and bask,
>   Nor yet the shades arouse;
> Her cave the mining coney scoops;
> Where o'er the mead the mountain stoops,
>   The kids exult and brouse.

(st. xxv)

Smart here explores the contrast between animals which "work" and those which play. When this contrast appears the second time, in the opposition between the coney which "mines" and the kids which "exult and brouse," the religious overtones of the language enrich it. The "mining coney" is not the English rabbit but the Biblical rock-badger of Proverbs 30. "There be four things which are little upon the earth, but they are exceeding wise: . . . The conies are but a feeble folk, yet make they their houses in the rocks" (verses 24, 26). The kids "exult" in the literal Latin sense: they leap up. But the metaphorical meaning of the word is also present — there are overtones of its near-homonym, *exalt,* in the context — and the activity of the kids, like the rolling and basking of the tigers, is not mere self-indulgence, but part of the universal religious exercise of praise and rejoicing. If the coney is an image of wisdom, the kids are images of joy. Work and play come to seem not opposed but analogous activities: both can be religious enterprises.

The coney appears again in the opening section of *Jubilate Agno,* used for a similar purpose: "Let Merari praise the wisdom and power of God with the Coney, who scoopeth the rock, and archeth in the sand" (Frag. A, 20). The beaver and the tiger are also here: "Let Ishmael dedicate a Tyger, and give praise for the liberty, in which the Lord has let him at large" (Frag. A, 10); "Let the Levites of the Lord take the Beavers of ye brook alive into the Ark of the Testimony" (Frag. A, 16). Neither the beaver nor the tiger is a Biblical animal,[20] but both blend into a Biblical context; *A Song to David,* too, absorbs them into the religious atmosphere of the whole. Smart's stock in trade is the unexpected. From the opening line of the stanza, with the intransitive verb *plods* used wonderfully economically in a transitive sense, through the surprising image of tigers acting like house cats in a version of the "peaceable kingdom," to the personified mountain near the end, the stanza constantly refreshes the reader's sense of the implications of ordinary phenomena. Here, as in *Jubilate Agno,* the tiger is an image of liberty, and the contrast between freedom (the tigers, the kids) and servitude (the plodding beaver, the mining coney) reinforces the contrast between play and work, while reversing the ordinary value judgments attached to the earlier terms. ("Play" ordinarily seems merely frivolous, while "liberty," which Smart associates with it, has clearly transcendent value; the reverse pattern holds for "work" and "servitude.") This maneuvering of value judgments is part of the freshening of perspective which culminates in the reiterated insistence that all forms of activity participate in the universal praise of God.

The references to "the shades" and the mountain call attention to inanimate as well as animate nature. The tigers will arouse the shades, whose state, then, is directly dependent on the animals which inhabit them. The mountain, on the other hand, seems already to participate in the active scene, stooping protectively over the mead and perhaps over the kids on it. But the syntax is perfectly ambiguous: it is equally probable that the kids are on the mountain rather than the mead. The mountain may protect the kids, or the kids play on the covering mountain: in either case the point is the same — that even the most static elements of the natural world participate in the divine activity of the whole.

The relationships of contrast in this single stanza are multitudinous and complex. In this respect, and in its thematic implications, the stanza, like many other individual sections, provides a microcosm of the entire poem. *A Song to David* concerns the complexity and meaning of the natural world; in structure and in statement, the poem constantly demonstrates the nature of that complexity.

The contrasts which emerge in the course of the demonstration are frequently unexpected.

Open, and naked of offence,
Man's made of mercy, soul, and sense;
   God armed the snail and wilk.

(st. xlii)

The explicit assertion is that man is inoffensive, and "open" suggests praiseworthy frankness. But "open" and "naked" also evoke
an image of man as unprotected: created of complicated components ("mercy, soul, and sense"), he lacks the armor of simpler
creatures, the elaborate whorled shells of the snail and whelk.
Smart moves directly from this characterization to a series of moral
injunctions, largely adaptations of the ten commandments in terms
of New Testament values. The implication is that complex man,
lacking simpler armor, must create for himself an equivalently
complex "armor" of rectitude. Once more, a physical image expands
to demonstrate the wisdom and intricacy of God's way.

Even the physical contrasts which the poem explores are frequently surprising.

With vinous syrup cedars spout;
From rocks pure honey gushing out,
   For ADORATION springs:
All scenes of painting croud the map
Of nature, to the mermaid's pap
   The scaled infant clings.

(st. liv)

Beginning with fantastic images of Golden Age fertility — wine-
spouting cedars and honey gushing from rocks — which remind
one of the Biblical closeness of God and His people ("he made him
to suck honey out of the rock"; Deuteronomy 32:13), the stanza
finally suggests that the most fanciful ideas are literally true.
Verbs enforce the central contrast; the active energy of spouting,
gushing, springing opposes the relatively passive energy of crowd-
ing, clinging. In the first half of the stanza, inanimate nature is
full of energy; in the second half, the animate becomes a static
"scene of painting," nature is a "map," a work of art. (One of the
poem's subjects is art as religious activity; David merges for Smart
with Orpheus, the type of the poet-artist.[21])

But the most important relationships in this poem do not occur within a single stanza; they are part of much larger intricacies. The mermaid and her infant, for example, occur in a sequence of parent and child images: the humming bird building a nest for her eggs (st. liii), "The spotted ounce and playsome cubs" which run through the flowering shrubs (st. lv), and "Israel" who "sits beneath his fig" while "The wean'd advent'rer sports" around him, playing with the "coral root and amber sprig" of the tree (st. lvi; this image reminds us of the "art" in nature). All participate in the "adoration" of God; their adoration of one another establishes their participation: earthly love leads to heavenly love. Smart often demonstrates a single phenomenon as relevant to birds, animals, fishes and men; here the mermaid provides a variation on this method, and the fact throws her into sharp relief. She seems not merely a decoration on the edge of an old map, but an inhabitant of the genuine map of nature, which is both art and reality. An amalgam of fish and woman, she unifies two worlds: her "adoration" is doubly significant.

Stanza lii establishes the theme of this part of the poem:

> For ADORATION seasons change,
> And order, truth, and beauty range,
> Adjust, attract, and fill.

R. D. Havens, in one of his illuminating essays on Smart, has analyzed the structure of *A Song to David*; he considers the adoration stanzas to comprise three groups of seven.[22] His groupings are convincing, but they do not exclude alternate ones. Thus, one may see the adoration stanzas as beginning with an introductory stanza, then four groups of three concerned with each of the four seasons. (Smart's own "contents" for the poem suggests this arrangement, describing verses lii-lxiv as "an exercise upon the seasons and the right use of them.") The notion that "beauty is truth" is implicit throughout this section, which makes no distinction among fanciful phenomena (the honey-spouting rocks, the mermaid, "halcyon's ark"; st. lv), personifications ("Now labour his reward receives,/For ADORATION counts his sheaves,/ To peace, her bounteous prince"; st. lix), and facts of natural history. Wine-yielding cedars, honey-gushing rocks, mermaids with their infants are all part of the fertility of spring, and the order, truth and beauty of the rich natural universe. The "order" is partly the order of plenitude, of a world teeming with varied, even fantastic, phenomena. For the Great Chain of Being Smart substitutes an image of the universe as a work of art incredibly rich, decorated, abundant. But it is a mistake in emphasis to say that in these stanzas "Smart is scarcely more than half poet and all but half painter," [23] or even that "il jette sur toute la nature un regard rapid de peintre." [24] He sees not as painter, but as poet; and the distinction is important. His images may have the vividness of paintings; his universe may even be composed like a painting; but his vision is fundamentally dependent on an organization not spatial, not visual at all, but emotional and — as a strange result — logical: he forms the intricacies of emotion into patterns intellectually analyzable, and those intricacies — not the images derived from them — are the foundation of his work.

The word *impress* has for Smart a peculiar weight. In his best-known critical utterance, with explicit reference to Horace, he writes, "Besides the Curiosa Felicitas, there is another poetical excellence: I mean the beauty, force, and vehemence of Impression . . . a talent or gift of Almighty God, by which a Genius is empowered to throw an emphasis upon a word or sentence in such wise that it cannot escape any reader of sheer good sense and critical sagacity." [25] Again, in *Jubilate Agno,* Smart attributes this particular quality of genius to himself: "For my talent is to give an impression upon words by punching, that when the reader casts his eye upon 'em, he takes up the image from the mould wch I have made" (Frag. B_2, l. 404). "For every word," he observes at another point, "has its marrow in the English tongue for order and for delight" (Frag. B2, l. 597). His desire to uncover the "marrow" of words, to make an impression by "punching," explains many of his poetic devices. The deliberate juxtaposition of opposites, the constant insistence on the likenesses within opposition, the opposition in likeness — these are modes of revelation. The revelation is uniquely poetic; it has to do not with the appearance of things but with their meaning. And it insists on full attention to the meaning and possibility of words. One of the stanzas describing David's virtues, for example, deals with cleanliness, through Smart's characteristic contorted syntax. Its juxtaposition of virtues

is itself surprising: one does not associate cleanliness particularly
with love, much less with exercise of sword and spear.

> Clean — if perpetual prayer be pure,
> And love, which could itself innure
> To fasting and to fear —
> Clean in his gestures, hands, and feet,
> To smite the lyre, the dance compleat,
> To play the sword and spear.

(st. ix)

Smart's central technique here is characteristic: he enlivens abstractions by association. The idea of cleanliness appears frequently
in the Bible, in both a literal and a metaphoric sense ("cleanse me
from sin"). The two senses coexist in Smart's treatment, which
demonstrates, like so much of this poem, his detailed knowledge
of David's career and of his Psalms. "Wherewithal shall a young
man cleanse his way?" inquires the Psalmist, and answers immediately: "by taking heed thereto according to thy word" (Ps.
119, v. 9). Later in the same psalm he promises, "I will run the way
of thy commandments, when thou shalt enlarge my heart" (v. 32);
then asks God to "stablish thy word unto thy servant, who is de-
voted to thy fear" (v. 38). "I will delight myself in thy commandments, which I have loved" (v. 47); "Consider how I love thy
precepts: quicken me, O Lord, according to thy lovingkindness"
(v. 159). Cleansing is here explicitly associated with the keeping
of God's commandments, and such rectitude involves both fear
and love. Elsewhere, in other accounts of his efforts to be upright,
the Psalmist speaks of having "humbled" or "chastened" his soul
with fasting (Ps. 35, 13; 69, 10). The association of virtues and
virtuous activities in the first half of the stanza, then, has explicit
Biblical sanction; Smart's major contribution is his extreme condensation. The second half, as usual, establishes a balance. Here
the poet concerns himself with physical rather than spiritual
exercise; but as spiritual cleanliness involves physical purification
through fasting, so physical cleanliness merges with the spiritual
purity that makes gestures "clean." Smart's concept of man as a
totality whose activities, however diverse, are part of the single
activity of devotion, parallels his concept of the universe as a single
entity in which the most bizarre components join to praise the

Smart: Mystique of Vision (I)

Lord. David, who excelled as musician, lover, king, warrior, religious man, is a fitting emblem of the many-sidedness which Smart perceives as unity. The completion of a dance is the type of greater completions; the lyre, the sword, the spear are accessories employed alike in the central work of man. And the self-conscious balancing of "*smite* the lyre" with "*play* the sword" underlines the vital theme of likeness in opposition.

The abstractions in this stanza belong to the ordinary language of religion; there is nothing especially "eighteenth-century" about them. But the relation between the abstract and the concrete was an important issue in eighteenth-century poetry. As the notion that poetry should deal primarily in images became increasingly dominant, lyricists typically sought ways to embody the abstract in the concrete. Thomson created his patterns of conjunctions between large general statements or abstract scientific or theological concepts such as "etherial nitre" or "light ineffable" and concretely imagined scenes; Collins, obsessed with abstractions (fear, peace, liberty, bravery), gave them local habitations in his gallery of personifications; Gray was fond both of personifications which embodied abstractions (Rapture waving her many-colored wings) and of those which represented generalizations ("Youth on the prow and Pleasure at the helm"). Smart's great skill was to make the abstract concrete in varied ways. But his attitude toward abstraction, as demonstrated by *A Song to David*, seems more complex than that of many of his contemporaries: he gives full value to abstractions in their own right as well as embodies them brilliantly without heavy reliance on personification. His extraordinary sensitivity to language is indicated by his ability to manipulate, to fresh purpose, conventional eighteenth-century poetic diction.

A case in point is stanza lxxviii. The first half is characteristic of Smart in its use of adjectives (as well as in its originality of material: armies and armadas are curious opening examples of the "beauteous.") The technique of the second half-stanza is as different as possible from the first; its images are as radically opposed, evoking a pastoral rather than a military scene.

> Beauteous the fleet before the gale;
> Beauteous the multitudes in mail,
>   Ranked arms and crested heads:

The Poetry of Vision

Beauteous the garden's umbrage mild,
Walk, water, meditated wild,
And all the bloomy beds.

Ranked and *crested* offer precise, calculated visual detail. The first adjective emphasizes the sheer mass of soldiers, calls attention to the beauty of repetition and order, the soldiers as a group; the second focuses attention on a single emphatic visual element in the appearance of each individual soldier, although one imagines the crests as almost infinitely duplicated.

Umbrage sets the tone for the second half-stanza: the shadowiness it refers to dominates the succeeding lines; the diction it represents is likewise in control. The language is as shadowy as the scene. *"Bloomy* beds" offers no specific picture. *"Mild* umbrage" is emotionally evocative but visually meaningless; "meditated wild" has the effect of Popean zeugma: it helps to define the scene's meaning, man's calculated creation of a "wild," but hardly its appearance.

The rhetoric of this stanza provides a particularly dramatic example of the way in which, for Smart, form follows content. Elsewhere in *A Song to David* the poet demonstrates his ability to make a garden scene come vividly to life; his reliance on vagueness here is obviously deliberate. It intensifies the contrast between the life of clearly focused, intense activity and that of less directed meditation. To assert that beauty resides in both these modes of existence implies the corollary that beauty may be the product either of sharp, specific language or of vague, "emotive" diction, a fact that Smart repeatedly demonstrates.

At his best, Smart makes little distinction between the abstract and the concrete. The key device of the group of stanzas which describe various manifestations of beauty, strength, sweetness and the like is to pair the abstract with the concrete as though they were precisely similar phenomena. Thus, the evocation of sweetness suggests appeals to various senses: the falling dew, the leafy limes, "Hermon's fragrant air," the lily's bell, the smell of the taper (st. lxxii). The second stanza of the group describes the sweetness of the "young nurse'" who, "with love intense . . . smiles o'er sleeping innocence"; then it moves to more abstract ideas:

Smart: Mystique of Vision (I)

Sweet when the lost arrive:
Sweet the musician's ardour beats,
While his vague mind's in quest of sweets,
The choicest flow'rs to hive.

The "sweetness" of the arrival of the lost is a generalizing idea, a way of evoking a whole complex of emotions; the sweetness of the musician's ardor is a yet more complicated notion. His ardor "beats" like his music; his mind is "vague" — imprecise in some respects because involved in the search for beauty, analogous to the bee through the Latinate sense of the adjective. In describing the musician's mind as a bee, Smart seems hardly to create a metaphor; instead, he simply draws out the literal meaning of the words, with his customary precise attention to the implications of his diction. The final stanza in the sequence continues the consideration of music: "Sweeter" than all that has been described before is the "language" of David's turtledove in harmony with David's own music; sweetest of all is "The glory of thy gratitude,/ Respir'd unto the Lord." The reason why these final phenomena are "sweeter" than those that have preceded them is that they have a direct spiritual orientation, represent conscious rather than unconscious praise of God — not the song of the turtledove in itself, but David's music in conjunction with it; the gratitude which for David is "respir'd," as natural as breathing, but still turned toward God. So the theoretical and abstract idea of devotion finally dominates, and in a sense the "point" of the entire exercise on sweetness is that the same adjective can describe both physical and spiritual phenomena, and its significance is the greater for this reason. The language itself, which makes possible the obviation of distinctions between the abstract and the concrete, demonstrates Smart's thesis about the unity of all experience.

Variations on this pattern govern the succeeding four triads of stanzas concerned with the exploration of key adjectives: stronger than the ostrich, the lion, or the whale is "the man of pray'r" (st. lxxvii); more beauteous than garden, moon, or church is "the shepherd king upon his knees" (st. lxxx); most precious is "that diviner part/ Of David, even the Lord's own heart" (st. lxxxiii); "the crown/ Of Him that brought salvation down" (st. lxxxvi) is more glorious than sun, comet, or even "the catholic amen" and "the martyr's gore" (st. lxxxv). The explicit assertion is usually that the spiritual is more important than the physical (sometimes that the more spiritual exceeds the less spiritual), but the groupings also insist that distinctions between physical and spiritual, concrete and abstract, are more a matter of degree than of kind, and force the reader's attention to the wonder and complexity of a language which readily expresses such subtle and involved relationships.

On a smaller scale, as well, Smart treats the abstract as though it were concrete — not finding concrete equivalents for abstractions, it seems, so much as describing directly the effect the abstraction has on him. The most closely analogous technique in eighteenth-century poetry — and it is not, after all, very close — is Collins's. In Collins's gallery of personifications, one often feels, we are offered visions rather than creations, glimpses of the uncanny way in which the poet sees his world, more richly inhabited than that of most people. Yet these personifications (partly, of course, because the rhetorical figure itself is not widely current in the poetry of our own time) seem far more artificial than Smart's creations, which often demonstrate some affinity with modern poetic technique.

> 'Twas then his thoughts self-conquest prun'd
> And heavenly melancholy tun'ed,
>   To bless and bear the rest.
>
>   (st. xi)

The puzzling mixed metaphor seems a product of exactly the sort of thought which accounts for the strength of the passages considered above. We are to imagine David's thoughts first as a tree, to be "prun'd" by self-conquest; immediately afterwards as a lyre, or some other musical instrument, which "heavenly melancholy" can tune; then as an entity capable of blessing and of bearing. The "rest" which must be borne and blessed is presumably that associated with the sabbath; it is a test for David because his forte is worship through activity rather than through passivity. The entire stanza considers David's efforts to achieve the way of contemplation; in these efforts self-conquest's "pruning" and "tuning" of thought are vitally important. Yet there remains no relation between the two metaphors except that both describe David's thoughts as objects rather than agents of action. Smart is simply capable of imagining vividly in one way, then equally vividly in another, with no apparent sense of disparity.

He also works in terms of large patterns. Tuning is one of a long series of musical allusions especially appropriate to the David-Orpheus identification; David's singing, in each of the two preceding stanzas, expresses his greatness of talent and of devotion. The idea of agricultural activity suggested by "prun'd" continues in the next stanza, where David sows "the seeds of peace" and plants "perpetual paradise"; further linkages of abstract and concrete. The world as orchestra, the world as garden: both ideas are equally viable for Smart, and he alludes with equal ease, and with no sense of incongruity, to both. In his universe, "hell, and horror, and despair" are "as the lion and the bear" (st. xiii); the muse is one moment a "bright angel," the next described by analogy with women important in David's life: "The more than Michal of his bloom,/ The Abishag of his age" (st. xvii); fish are the beings "Which nature frames of light escape" (st. xxiv); a man can "pile" his thoughts "up to heaven" (st. xxix). The gap between the material and the immaterial disappears completely: with more complexity than John Bunyan but with equal clarity Smart dramatizes his super-animated universe.

"When a picture is given us in a single word, to make out which, in our own imagination, we must go through a succession of ideas, then we are surprized in the most agreeable manner, and the beauty, of course, is consummate." [26] This ideal of imagery belongs to Smart's own time, and it seems strikingly relevant to his poetic practice, in which extreme condensation is typical. Although obscurity remained a critical bugaboo — Blair, for example, as late as 1783, asserted repeatedly that "perspicuity" was the highest poetic virtue — complexity of reference was valued in 1763 as in 1963. "It is the peculiar design of the figurative style," wrote Bishop Lowth. ". . . to exhibit objects in a clearer or more striking, in a sublimer or more forcible manner." [27] "More striking" is a significant alternative to "clearer": the ideal of perspicuity might be modified, if not suspended, for the sake of emphasis — for the sake, in other words, of Smart's "impression." Such words as *striking* and *force* appear often in the criticism of the period. Even such a critic as William Duff, well aware of the danger of too much imagery (which was likely to be obscure and tiring, and to disgust the mind with tracing resemblances,[28]) praises the resources of "well chosen images" which "give force as well as grandeur to the stile of Poetry, and are a principal source of those exquisite sensations, which it is calculated to inspire" (pp. 146–147). For Duff as for Bishop Lowth, the idea of "force" seems linked to some notion of "sublimity" ("grandeur"). And Smart, who at the climax of his poem systematically employs the traditional "sublime" images of thunder, comets, northern lights (see stanzas lxxxiv-lxxxv), relies heavily on the "force" of highly condensed imagery.

The force of that imagery, its power to impress itself on the mind by "punching," is frequently the force of the unexpected. The systematic pattern of contrasts in the poem relies heavily on the unexpected juxtapositions which it makes possible; the value of Smart's special treatment of abstractions is partly its power to surprise. A third important mode of achieving the unexpected, in *A Song to David,* is the manipulation of points of view. The poet's way of looking at things, the way he invites the reader to look at things, is constantly and dramatically shifting. A corresponding discontinuity of syntax modifies the formality of *A Song to David* and increases one's sense of the personality of the poet behind the poem. That personality emerges as extraordinarily rich and flexible. During an account of the subjects of David's songs, for example, Smart suddenly shifts his tone with startling effect.

> Trees, plants, and flow'rs — of virtuous root!
> Gem yielding blossom, yielding fruit,
>   Choice gums and precious balm:
> Bless ye the nosegay in the vale,
> And with the sweetness of the gale
>   Enrich the thankful psalm.
>
> (st. xxii)

The first half stanza, through its diction as well as its explicit reference, evokes the exotic. The use of *gem* in the root sense of "bud" connects the flowers with jewels, emphasizing the preciousness of vegetable products; the "Choice gums and precious balms" belong to some vague Oriental realm. As so often in this poem, the second half contrasts sharply with the first, in point of view, tone and diction. The "ye" here addressed should logically be David, to whom this entire song is sung. But since David and the song he sings are the subject, in the third person, of the entire group of stanzas to which this one belongs, "ye" seems rather to refer to the reader, and the lines to be direct command that he, too, participate in the universal paean. The shift in tone is as marked as that in point of view. In place of the exotic precious balm we have now the humble English nosegay picked in the familiar vale; the diction of the English hymn replaces the more dramatic language that preceded it. Adjectives in this section have almost completely disappeared; they have carried the emphasis on value earlier; now only the vital idea of thankfulness is adjectivally stressed. The pervasive change in perspective, besides directly involving the reader, indirectly reiterates the point about the diversity within the unity of praise.

If Smart is acutely conscious of human perspective, shifting his emphasis from his semi-mythic hero to his reader, he is also sharply aware of what might be called natural perspective. In one stanza he may speak of the birds "Which chear the winter, hail the spring" (st. xxiii); the point of view suggests both a personification of the seasons, which can be "cheared" or "hailed" in the guise of human beings, and the presence of an actual observer whose winter may be cheered by the sight and sound of birds. The stanza immediately following concerns fishes "Which nature frames of light escape,/ Devouring men to shun." Now the lovely image of fishes as solidified light is explained as part of a cosmic plan by which defenceless creatures can avoid their fearful enemy, man. Smart is entirely on the side of the fish; his point of view has dramatically changed, and the agility and complexity of the poet's mind involve the reader. Similarly, jewels (*gems*: Smart uses the same word for bud and precious stone, thus underlining the fact of creation's unity) are "hid in earth from man's device." Myrtles, Smart explains, "keep the garden from dismay, /And bless the sight from dearth" (st. lxi): the double point of view creates a sort of dramatic tension appropriate to the atmosphere of the stanza's opening: "The laurels with the winter strive." The conjunction of points of view, moreover, demonstrates Smart's characteristic manipulation of balance and contrast: the dearth usually associated with the world of nature now becomes a potential lack in human vision, only fulfilled by nature's beauty. Conversely, human emotion seems potential in the garden; from the "point of view" of the garden as well as that of its human inhabitants, the myrtle is vital.

A yet more complex example of Smart's shifts is the stanza on science as religious exercise.

> For ADORATION, in the skies,
> The Lord's philosopher espies
>   The Dog, the Ram, and Rose;
> The planet's ring, Orion's sword;
> Nor is his greatness less ador'd
>   In the vile worm that glows.
>
> (st. lxvi)

The scientist — who is initially, by definition, the *Lord's* philosopher — performs his act of adoration by perceiving the order in multiplicity; the act of seeing properly is the act of worship. (It is notable, incidentally, that Smart's conception of the scientist as religious man has nothing to do with his use of the telescope: the kind of vision that concerns him is by no means scientific.) The order he sees is itself the order of diversity: in the sky he spies animals, flowers, ring and sword. But then there is "the vile worm that glows," also somehow involved in the pattern of adoration. Perhaps the adoration is still that of the scientist, who recognizes the value and significance of the glowworm; but it seems also that of the worm itself, as much as the educated man a part of the great pattern. This is one of Smart's most triumphant manipulations of conventional poetic diction: the impact of the final lines depends heavily on the contrast between the automatic response requested by "vile worm" and that evoked by the final surprising "glows." In a larger sense, the effect depends on the sudden shift of perspective: we are brought from the sublimity of the heavens (and of philosophical endeavor) to the traditional degradation of the worm, and forced to realize the sense in which degradation and sublimity are ultimately the same.

Examples multiply as one contemplates the poem. More than any of his contemporaries, Smart seems in this poem to deal directly with ways of seeing. He may remind us specifically who is seeing a particular phenomenon — as when he describes the fish "For ADORATION gilt" which are "by the coasting reader spied" (st. lvii). Or he may move in a single stanza from the general idea of sugar cane and cocoanut milk detaining the western pilgrim to a sharp, impressionistic vision

> Where rain in clasping boughs inclos'd,
> And vines with oranges dispos'd,
>   Embow'r the social laugh.
>
> (st. lviii)

The rain becomes a decorative enclosing element, like those extraordinary orange-bearing vines; both combine with the "clasping boughs" to embower — the final surprise — "the social laugh": another remarkable use of eighteenth-century poetic diction in which the abstract, placed in a vividly concrete setting, becomes itself concretely embodied. Or — the most dramatic shift of perspective in the whole poem — the sudden time change in the final stanza:

> Thou [David] at stupendous truth believ'd; —
> And now the matchless deed's atchiev'd,
>   DETERMINED, DARED, and DONE.
>
> (st. lxxxvi)

The believing of the great truth mysteriously creates its reality; Christ's sacrifice, freshly perceived, takes place in the immediate present, and the entire poem backs up this perception and makes it possible.

The special quality of A Song to David has much to do with the way it succeeds in keeping the reader involved in its total action — the action of devotion — through its manipulations of language and of detail. Owen Barfield has asserted that "poetic pleasure — the stir of aesthetic imagination — is caused by a change of consciousness from one level to another." [29] This sort of pleasure Smart richly creates for his readers; his poem is a triumphant demonstration of the possibilities inherent in the poetic standards and language of the eighteenth century.

VII 🎋

CHRISTOPHER SMART:
The Mystique of Vision (II)

EVEN WHEN ONE understands that contemporary critical theory could describe and justify the techniques of *A Song to David,* it still seems a miracle in its time. No other poet before Blake captured the peculiar clarity of perception, the visionary power of interpretation, the ability to see the mystery of the commonplace, that Smart demonstrated in this extraordinary song of praise. Was it a freak of genius, the single great achievement of a hack writer constantly on the verge of madness; or do Smart's other works display similar power? Several generations of critics have investigated these alternatives, using the varying amounts of evidence available to them. Smart wrote much of his "sane" poetry, it turns out, to the prescription of established — almost outworn — poetic convention; his most individual poem, *Jubilate Agno,* first published only in the twentieth century, is so clearly the work of a madman that it has largely defied critical analysis. Yet this "maddest" of his poems is in many respects the most illuminating: some of the special attitudes toward language and toward experience which it demonstrates are crucial also in even Smart's most conventional poetry.

Smart composed most of *Jubilate Agno,* we now know, a line or two or three a day, simply as a means of recording the passage of time during his confinement in an asylum. "I believe the poem to be a chronological record of Smart's confinement from the day he entered the asylum to the day he was released," writes Arthur Sherbo.[1] On the other hand, W. H. Bond's rearrangement of the verses into their original antiphonal pattern shows conclusively that Smart at least intermittently experimented with Hebraic forms.

Smart: Mystique of Vision (II)

"Writing in what he conceived to be the Hebrew tradition, he set out to compose a pair of poems, separate and yet intimately related, agreeing page for page and line for line."[2] *Jubilate Agno*, Bond argues, is "a conscious experiment in a form new to English poetry, none the less valid because it failed and was abandoned by its author" (p. 52). Whatever the poet's intention, his achievement demands serious critical examination.

In a letter to *The New York Review of Books* (July 9, 1964), an anonymous woman, herself recurrently psychotic and an ex-inmate of mental institutions, commented on the relation between the language of madness and that of poetry. "When a psychotic speaks, he speaks with absolute precision, and having chosen a word to precisely convey his thought, that word in turn, reverberates linguistically and merges many words and thoughts within it along with a host of ideas, concepts and feelings. . . . This multifaceted use of language with its apparent contradiction between precision and confusion is what characterizes psychotic language." Later in the same letter: "the psychotic's statements are symbolic as well as specific. Sentences teem with allusions. Words are redefined in terms of their original meaning, and invested with special meaning as the need arises."

This way of employing language is to some extent, as the writer of the letter herself suggests, characteristic of all poetry, but particularly characteristic of Smart. *Jubilate Agno* explicitly reveals the poet's attitudes toward language and its energy; it also demonstrates both the difficulties and the power created by the special sort of condensation he relies on. Smart had a primitive sense of the essentially magical force of naming, the power of the word. As he perceives colors to have a mystical relation to one another (see Frag. B_2 ll. 651–672) and spiritual meaning ("NOW that colour is spiritual appears inasmuch as the blessing of God upon all things descends in colour"; B_2, 664), so he sees words as mysteriously meaningful and related. His largely incomprehensible exercise upon the word *bull* is a demonstration of this fact (B_2, 676–686). Words have power through their sounds; from this belief derives Smart's mystique of rhymes (B_2, 586–599). They may exert force through the very shape of the letters composing them: the Hebrew letter Lamed has strange significance because its form occurs widely in the natural world (B_2, 477–492). And individual letters have meanings in themselves: three times in *Jubilate Agno* Smart attempts to define such meanings. His definitions depend partly on personal association ("For E is eternity — such is the power of the English letters taken singly"; B_2, 517), but they are also clearly attempts to capture essences which he feels to be universal ("For B is a creature busy and bustling"; B_2, 514). Words, too, have their essences and their power: the names of things are essentially equivalent to the things themselves.

> For all the stars have satellites, which are
>   terms under their respective words.
> For tiger is a word and his satellites are
>   Griffin, Storgis, Cat and others.
>   (B_2, 402–403)

God, whose power is that of the Word, is the giver of names and the object of all language:

> Let Mibzar rejoice with the Cadess [mayfly],
>   as is their number, so are their names,
>   blessed be the Lord Jesus for them all.
> For the names and number of animals are as
>   the names and number of the stars.
> Let Jubal rejoice with Caecilia [a lizard;
>   also St. Cecilia, patron of music], the
>   woman and the slow-worm praise the name
>   of the Lord.
> For I pray the Lord Jesus to translate my
>   MAGNIFICAT into verse and represent it.
>   (B_1, 42–43)

The double meaning of *translate* provides a way of expressing the power of language.

> Let Libni rejoice with the Redshank, who
>   migrates not but is translated to the
>   upper regions.
> For I have translated in the charity, which
>   makes things better & I shall be trans-
>   lated myself at the last.
>   (B_1, 11)

Smart, the translator of Horace, working in the asylum on his version — a sort of translation — of the Psalms and of the parables, finds in his efforts with language the promise of his salvation. For there is no doubt in his mind that language in general, poetry in particular, exists — like all the natural creation — to praise the Lord.

> For I am the Lord's News-Writer — the scribe-evangelist.
>> (B₂, 327)

> For a NEW SONG also is best, if it be to the glory of God;
>> & taken with the food like the psalms.
>> (B₂, 390)

> For it is the business of a man gifted in the word
>> to prophecy good.
>> (C, 57)

> For all good words are from GOD, and all others are cant.
>> (B₁, 85)

All these observations suggest certain underlying principles of Smart's work. The relation between the name and the object named, the function of language as praise, the connection between the word and the natural creation: these are the immediate subjects of *Jubilate Agno*, a poem organized to reveal them. They are by no means merely the obsessions of a madman. Donald Greene has pointed out that "interest in the nature of language and a belief in the importance of using it with all possible accuracy" is one of many important links between Smart and Berkeley.[3] Although the associations made in the poem are sometimes so private as to seem perhaps psychotic, the concern with language itself is a triumph of sanity.

> For the relations of words are in pairs first.
> For the relations of words are sometimes in
>> oppositions.
> For the relations of words are according to
>> their distances from the pair.
>> (B₂, 600–602)

The intricate geometry of language which Smart so clearly perceives forms his poem, whose theme — like that of *A Song to David* — is God's glorification throughout the universe, that central mode of unifying outer and inner experience.

The Poetry of Vision

> Rejoice in God, O ye Tongues; give the glory
> to the Lord, and the Lamb.
> Nations, and languages, and every Creature, in
> which is the breath of life.
>
> (A, 1–2)

The equation of "languages" with the two concrete nouns is characteristic; the patterning of the poem steadily insists that the activity of the poet who writes is fundamentally equivalent to that of "every Creature": the "Pygarg" (a kind of bison), the lion, the chamois unite with the personages of the Old Testament to "give glory in the goodly words of Thanksgiving" (A, 14). The connection between the word and the creature is most explicit in the charming lines about men with animal names:

> For I have a providential acquaintance with
> men who bear the names of animals.
> For I bless God to Mr Lion Mr Cock Mr Cat
> Mr Talbot Mr Hart Mrs Fysh Mr Grub, and
> Miss Lamb. . . .
> For I bless God for the immortal soul of
> Mr Pigg of DOWNHAM in NORFOLK.
>
> (B$_1$, 113–114, 116)

The bulk of the poem to this point consists of repetitions of the pattern exemplified by "Let Mahlah rejoice with Pellos who is a tall bird and stately" (B$_1$, 112): the equation of some name, usually of a Biblical personage, with some animal, then a characterization of that animal, in "a virtuoso study in imaginative association."[4] The relation between person and animal may be more or less apparent; often it is obscure, and the form of the line consequently reiterates the point that all creation is related, so that arbitrary connections are as meaningful as superficially logical ones. When Smart reflects on men with animal names, he explicitly makes the connection previously implied between name and object: his knowledge of a man named Lion seems genuinely "providential" because it provides concrete evidence of the ties uniting all creation.

Smart asserts "the relations of words" and of meanings through the antiphonal pattern of the poem's most cogent portions. Often the relations seem to depend upon the psychotic's vivid sense of the complexity of language. The thought of the mythical roc, for example, immediately reminds him of its homonym. He spells the bird's name "Rock," and asserts the essential identity of words which superficially seem related only by sound:

> Let Naharai, Joab's armour-bearer rejoice with
>   Rock who is a bird of stupendous magnitude.
> For the Lord is my ROCK and I am the bearer of
>   his CROSS.

(B₁, 94)

The name of Naharai occurs twice in the Old Testament, both times in a list of the heroes who composed David's guard; this minor figure, himself an emblem of strength because of his connection with armor, is doubly associated with power by his service to the hero-king. Smart, in one of his infinite variations on the theme of total unity, stresses the connection between this minor Biblical character — not even a character, really, only a name; but the value of mere names is also a theme here — and the "stupendous" power of the enormous legendary bird. The relatively insignificant emblem of strength and the vastest rejoice together. In the antiphonal response, the "stupendous magnitude" of the bird merges with a magnitude more stupendous still: that of God. In this way, the literal meaning of *roc* merges with the metaphorical meaning of *rock*, and an essential identity emerges where only an accidental verbal similarity appeared to exist. Moreover, Smart insists on the connection between the Old and the New Testament. As in his "translations" of the Psalms one of his key techniques was to transform Old Testament references by Christian analogies, so in *Jubilate Agno* Smart exploits similar associations. The image of God as the rock of salvation occurs frequently in the Old Testament (particularly in David's Psalms), much less often in the New. (One of the few direct New Testament references to this image is in I Cor. 10:4, during a retelling and reinterpretation of the exodus of the Jews: "they drank of that spiritual Rock that followed them: and that Rock was Christ.") Smart, too, insists on the identity between God, the Rock, and Christ; he also reveals a pattern of logical counterpoint: God or Christ as Rock provides a foundation and shelter for man, yet man can metaphorically bear the burden of Christ's cross. Smart, the speaker of the poem, is thus connected (as "bearer") with the insignificant armor-bearer of the Old Testament, and both simultaneously contrast and unite with images of ultimate might.

145

The Poetry of Vision

Like most complex lines of poetry, this takes longer to explain than to understand. Its complexity is undeniable, however, and of a sort precisely representative of *Jubilate Agno* as a whole. If it belongs to the private vision of a psychotic, is typical of the psychotic's dealings with language, it is none the less decipherable in "public" terms: the intertwining of reference depends on a web of literary and theological allusions, not merely on the arbitrary connections of a madman. And the bulk of the poem is interpretable in this way; only isolated sections seem finally incomprehensible. The poetic effect of *Jubilate Agno* depends heavily on the combination of simplicity and complexity. In its reiterative form, in the simple relation between lines beginning with "Let" and those beginning with "For," in the frequent apparent naivete of its utterances, the poem seems the product of a simple, even a primitive, mind. The antiphonal pattern, as Smart understands it, is based on formal repetition; the cumulative effect of long sequences of paired "Let" and "For" verses resembles that of Psalm 136, in which various listed evidence of the mercy and power of God precedes the refrain, "for his mercy endureth forever." Smart never employs a refrain in the strict sense, but the close identity of form between one line and the next establishes a sense of refrain, makes possible extraordinary focusing of emphasis when the pattern suddenly varies, as in the sequence concerned with Smart's renunciation of his birthright (B_1, 45–53). The "Let" verses here preserve the pattern of man-animal association, with emphasis, as W. H. Bond has pointed out (p. 48), on animals associated with cuckoldry. The "For" verses begin "For I am a little fellow, which is intitled to the great mess by the benevolence of God my father." Each of the next three verses opens, "For I this day made over my inheritance to my mother in consideration of her ——"; only the last word varies from line to line (*infirmities, age, poverty*). Then three verses begin "For I bless the thirteenth of August, in which I . . ." After this account, a single line connects Smart's giving of property to his mother with giving to Christ. Occurring at the end of this sequence, the final pair of lines is particularly noteworthy:

> Let Barkos rejoice with the Black Eagle, which
> is the least of his species and the best-
> natured.

Smart: Mystique of Vision (II)

For nature is more various than observation
tho' observers be innumerable.

(B₁, 53)

Barkos appears in the Bible only in the register of those who escaped from the Babylonian captivity, including "the children of Barkos." The line about the Black Eagle seems to continue Smart's references to himself and his rôle; perceiving himself simultaneously as father and son, he emphasizes his good nature and his smallness of stature as he has stressed these characteristics earlier in the passage. But the antiphonal response in this instance has a startling effect, moving suddenly outward from the obsessively, self-pityingly personal to the universal. It implies the poet's own recognition of the narrowing of perception involved in his earlier employment of his knowledge of animals as a means of self-justification; simultaneously it implies the realization that even the most self-centered attitude toward nature produces one of the infinite possible modes of "observation." By placing his own concerns against a broad backdrop, moving suddenly out of the pattern of statement and reference that he himself has established, Smart dramatizes the diversity of possibilities in poetry and in experience.

The direct personal references in the poem contribute to the paradoxical effect of mingled simplicity and complexity, innocence and sophistication. They may seem narrowly self-pitying, as in the lines about the inheritance; or purely naive, as in the passage about people with the names of animals; or occasionally incomprehensible in their allusiveness. Yet almost invariably the poem succeeds in establishing some larger context which radically alters the limited effect of lines taken in isolation. It can hardly be claimed that *Jubilate Agno* achieves — or even appears to attempt — any detailed unity. Yet it holds together, partly by the consistency with which Smart exploits the ambivalences of vocabulary and syntax. The structure of his lines of verse is almost invariably simple in the extreme, and its repetitiveness emphasizes the effect of direct, simple statement — which is, of course, often contradicted by the actual content of the line. Such a verse as this — quoted previously — is in many respects typical:

> For I have translated in the charity, which
> makes things better & I shall be trans-
> lated myself at the last.

The Poetry of Vision

Translated and *charity*, belonging to a fairly elementary religious vocabulary, are the most sophisticated words here: the simplicity of diction is striking. Structurally, too, the line seems completely lucid: it seems, indeed, a good deal more lucid than it actually is. The introductory *for* promises a statement of causality, and a further simple causal relation is implied by the co-ordinate clauses: "For I have translated . . . & I shall be translated." "Which makes things better" has a childlike directness, as an explication of the complicated notion of charity; "at the last" similarly reduces a Christian mystery to perfect simplicity. Yet the line remains complex, the source of its complexity Smart's idiosyncratic mode of dealing with language. The pun on *translated* is vital; so is the curious phrase, "in the charity." Both together convey an almost unparaphrasable idea: that literary translation (since "all good words come from God") is a religious activity, a mode of justification by works; that translation, like charity itself, "makes things better"; that the relation between words points to a relation of facts; that charity is single and universal (*"the* charity"). Repeatedly — indeed constantly — Smart reveals the simple as complex. And, employing his customary principle of balance, he also treats the obscure and complicated as simple. His range of reference in *Jubilate Agno* is extraordinary; the poem requires annotation probably as much as any other English poem. But Smart treats obscure animals, private reference, scientific facts, minor Biblical personages as though all belonged to a single, simple world, the world of a child. Indeed, paradoxically, *Jubilate Agno* can be read and enjoyed without footnotes: one does not really need to know what *Lepas* means, or who Patrobus is, to appreciate the line, "Let Patrobus rejoice with Lepas, all shells are precious" (B$_1$, 256). Its rhythm, its pattern, its relation to the lines which precede and follow it — these produce poetic pleasure. But it is in the other mode, that of deceptive simplicity, that Smart is most effective; the memorable passages of *Jubilate Agno* are consistently of this kind. Such are the well-known lines beginning, "For I will consider my cat Jeoffry" (B$_2$, 697–770). Far earlier in the poem, Smart prepares for this meditation on his cat by remarking, "For I am possessed of a cat, surpassing in beauty, from whom I take occasion to bless Almighty God" (B$_1$, 68). Moreover, the subject of cats has been related, like so many of Smart's preoccupations, to that of language, in a passage where Smart elaborates, with several Greek puns, his idea that "the power and spirit of a CAT is in the Greek" (B$_2$, 628), using such evidence as "For the pleasantry of a cat at pranks is in the language ten thousand times over" (B$_2$, 630). The long exercise on Jeoffry describes the cat's activities in lavish detail:

> For first he looks upon his fore-paws to see if
>   they are clean.
> For secondly he kicks up behind to clear
>   away there.
> For thirdly he works it upon stretch with
>   the fore paws extended.
> For fourthly he sharpens his paws by wood.
>   (B$_2$, 705–708)

This is Smart at his most individual. No one else in his century could have written these lines, with their simple yet personal ("he works it upon stretch") structure, their absolutely matter-of-fact vocabulary, their apparent lack of concern with any import beyond immediate characterization. Yet the larger import is always present. Immediately after reading of Jeoffry's ten routine activities we learn, "For having consider'd God and himself he will consider his neighbour" (l. 715). "He counteracts the Devil, who is death, by brisking about the life" (l. 725). He is especially beloved by God (l. 735), and his presence is significant for the activity of a poet: "For he is good to think on, if a man would express himself neatly" (l. 757).

This "larger import," however, seems after all hardly more significant than the descriptive details, which receive considerably more emphasis, occupying the bulk of the passage. The fact that Jeoffry is exactly what he is is crucial. "What he is" includes his spiritual and his physical aspects. Earlier in the poem Smart has observed, "For nothing is so real as that which is spiritual" (B$_1$, 258); the truth that Jeoffry is beloved by God informs all other truths about him. But the physical truths are not simply a means of getting to the spiritual ones; they are self-justifying simply because they are true. Smart's interest in "order, truth and beauty," clearly demonstrated in *A Song to David,* is frequently paramount also in the far more chaotic seeming *Jubilate Agno.* The order, truth and beauty of his cat's life emerges vividly and complexly as the result of a treatment which in vocabulary and arrangement seems unsophisticated, but which adds up to one more complex demonstration of the unity of all creation.

The freshness of perception, the clarity and complexity of purpose apparent in Smart's late work emerge at least spasmodically in his early productions as well; so do his curious methods of dealing with language. His diction is not outside his century's mode, but he handles it with a difference. Like Gray and Thomson, for example, Smart is fond of using words in their Latinate senses and often prefers a Latinate to an Anglo-Saxon root. But the effect of his experiments in this vein is far from Thomsonian. "A Noon-Piece, or, The Mowers at Dinner" (first published in *The Student*, 1750) begins

> The Sun is now too radiant to behold,
> And vehement he sheds his liquid rays of gold:
> No cloud appears thro' all the wide expanse;
> And short, but yet distinct, and clear,
> To the wanton whistling air
> The mimic shadows dance.

Vehement, the single unexpected word here, is vital to the passage. It establishes the sense of energy which informs these lines, and it provides a radically new perspective on the sun, thus freshly personified, given "character" as well as appearance, "shedding" his rays with maximum energy in order, it seems, to get rid of them. The root meaning of *vehement* (mindless) may be relevant too though by no means dominant; the animated universe here sketched is attractive, but purely physical: dancing shadows merely mimic, the whistling air is wanton. The effect of the word, however, has nothing to do with its reference to any specific literary tradition. Unlike Thomson or Gray, Smart does not remind his readers of Virgil or invoke the power of classical literary associations. The Latinate word is self-justifying; its emphasis depends on its sound, sharp and forceful, and on its literal meaning alone. Its employment is the product of flawless poetic tact, but the tact of a poet whose best effects are strongly personal. He can write a line as conventional and as flat as the third quoted above — but he places it in conjunction with the distinctively vivid three lines that follow it.

The entire exercise of writing a "noon-piece" is itself conventional, and this poem of Smart's sounds now like Milton ("On a bank of fragrant thyme,/ Beneath yon stately, shadowy pine,/ We'll with the well-disguised hook/ Cheat the tenants of the brook"; ll. 30–33); now strangely like Marvell ("Where Flora's flock, by nature wild,/ To discipline are reconcil'd,/ And laws and order cultivate,/ Quite civiliz'd into a state"; ll. 44–47); it uses the language of Pope ("Where Taste and Elegance command/ Art to lend her daedal hand"; ll. 42–43); and of crude romantic poetasters ("Ah! HARRIOT! sovereign mistress of my heart,/ Could I thee to these meads decoy"; ll. 26–27) — in a curious potpourri. Naturally, the poem is effective only to the degree that it unifies its disparate elements — but that degree is considerable. This is obviously not a religious poem. But as Smart was to demonstrate later the poetic power of a religious vision which absorbed divergent phenomena to make them wondrously demonstrate a single great truth, so in these earlier pieces he occasionally showed a similar unifying power in his very selection of details:

> Their scythes upon the adverse bank
>   Glitter 'mongst th'entangled trees,
> Where the hazles form a rank,
>   And court'sy to the courting breeze.
>
>   (ll. 22–25)

Glittering scythes laid casually upon a bank unite pictorially with the trees which surround them; the result is an image of formal and informal order in conjunction. Scythes flung on a bank in "natural" confusion create a pattern which provides a sort of visual counterpoint for the extreme artificiality of the whole; it is merely one among many details of the day; yet it provides a microcosm of the complex relation between man and nature which is a vital source of interest in the poem.

Even in humorous verse, Smart demonstrated his flair for the unexpected but perfectly functional word, the word which brings to life a whole complex of ideas. In his charming piece, "The Author Apologizes to a Lady for his Being a Little Man" (published in *The Student*, 1751) this couplet occurs:

> Still pouring forth executive desire,
> As bright, as brisk, as lasting as the vestal fire.
>
>   (ll. 17–18)

Executive, a striking word in this context, conveys the rich ironies of the couplet. "The soul" is the agent of action, pouring forth desire. Is it, then, some sort of "platonic," non-physical desire? Far from it: it is *executive* desire, literally concerned to "follow out" its purposes. Its relation to "the vestal fire" is complex: it is as enduring, as vivid, as "brisk" (another Smartian word) as that emblem of physical and spiritual purity; it is also simultaneously its opposite. The argument thus ironically asserts that desire is as admirable as chastity (and a little man as admirable as a big one), while keeping in reserve the point that both desire and the little man are more admirable than their opposites, because their very differences represent their most significant merits.

The entire poem depends on minute shadings and startling conjunctions of tone, achieved by control of the connotative values of diction.

> Say, is it carnage makes the man?
> Is to be monstrous really to be great? . . .
> Ask your mamma and nurse, if it be so;
> Nurse and mamma I ween shall jointly answer, no.
> (ll. 7–8, 11–12)

The modulation is expert, dependent on the divergent implications of *monstrous* and of *carnage* (great achievement in battle, the horror of that achievement), and on the poet's complete awareness of the values of his tone, so that the mock-heroic weight of the rhetorical questions is echoed in the "I ween" which interrupts the bathetic descent from concern with the warrior to reliance on mamma and nurse.

One must grant that much of Smart's early production is pedestrian in the extreme; yet his distinctive note sounds often, in the secular as well as the religious verse. *Jubilate Agno* is a more private poem than these early pieces; *A Song to David* is more complicated than its predecessors. But both demonstrate a further development of attitudes toward language, practices in using it, that were already apparent in Smart's young manhood. And these practices, these attitudes, although they often recall those of seventeenth-century poets or foretell those of Blake and Keats, are in many respects the culmination of ideas that had been important throughout the eighteenth century. In *Jubilate Agno*, Smart blesses God for the memory of Pope, Swift and Gay (B_1, 84). In his short lyric, "On A Bed of Guernsey Lilies" (written September, 1763), he concludes,

> 'Tis by succession of delight
> That love supports his reign.
>
> (ll. 19–20)

The thought is far from Popean, but the expression, in its calm restraint, its unemphatic complexity, its apparent effortlessness, its control, owes a good deal to Pope. *The Hop-Garden*, a Georgic published in 1752, provides cogent examples of Smart's ability to control and to transform his century's diction and emphases. The poem depends heavily — like *A Song to David* — on the emphatic, vivid verb:

> And silvers to maturity the Hop.
>
> (I, 2)

> Soon as bright Chanticleer explodes the night
>
> (II, 149)

(The second line, adapted from Lucretius, is more vigorous than its model.) It repeatedly produces instants of fresh perception:

> Egregious shepherds of unnumber'd flocks,
> Whose fleeces, poison'd into purple, deck
> All Europe's kings . . .
>
> (I, 36–38)

> Every unshaven arboret . . .
>
> (I, 31)

Eighteenth-century poets before Smart had repeatedly used purple fleeces as emblems of luxury and ease, taking the image from Virgil. Smart contributes a new point of view; perceiving dye as poison, not decoration, he supplies freshness to an old image. Similarly, although the technique of describing inanimate nature in human terms is commonplace enough, he freshens it with *unshaven*: the single precise adjective brings the tiny arbors to the reader's imagination.

Like every part of *The Seasons*, *The Hop-Garden* includes a description of the preamble to a storm, a description particularly revealing of Smart's relation to the poets of his own time. In many respects this is representative of its genre. The inversion in the second line, for example, seems dictated not by any special purpose other than stress of the alliteration; it belongs to the century's typical Miltonics. The details of the early lines are equally conventional.

> as the storm rides on the rising clouds,
> Fly the fleet wild-geese far away, or else
> The heifer towards the zenith rears her head,
> And with expanded nostrils snuffs the air:
> The swallows too their airy circuits weave,
> And screaming skim the brook; and fen bred frogs
> Forth from their hoarse throats their old grutch recite
> Or from her earthly coverlets the ant
> Heaves her huge eggs along the narrow way:
> Or bends Thaumantia's variegated bow
> Athwart the cope of heav'n: or sable crows
> Obstreperous of wing, in crouds combine.
>
> (II, 106–117)

The passage invites direct comparison with Thomson, who selects some of the same images:

> Snatched in short eddies, plays the withered leaf;
> And on the flood the dancing feather floats.
> With broadened nostrils to the sky upturned,
> The conscious heifer snuffs the stormy gale.
> Even, as the matron, at her nightly task,
> With pensive labour draws the flaxen thread,
> The wasted taper and the crackling flame
> Foretell the blast. But chief the plumy race,
> The tenants of the sky, its changes speak.
> Retiring from the downs, where all day long
> They picked their scanty fare, a blackening train
> Of clamorous rooks thick-urge their weary flight,
> And seek the closing shelter of the grove.
>
> ("Winter," ll. 130–142)

Smart may have been directly indebted to Thomson for the detail about the heifer. The two descriptions rely in similar ways on alliteration; although Thomson's blank verse is rather more expert than Smart's, both poets clearly attempt the same tone. In general Thomson is more expansive than Smart; he dwells in a leisurely fashion on the activities of "the plumy race," defining, by periphrasis and by details, their precise place in the order of things. And he introduces a human observer, from whose point of view all the other details become relevant. Although he deals with animate and inanimate nature, with human being, animal and fowl, he considers the relations among the various parts of creation only to the extent that they help to define the order of the universe. Thus, "the plumy race" is a periphrasis of the familiar sort which defines birds by differentiating them from other "races" — the scaly race, the fleecy race, the human race; "The tenants of the sky" suggests the patterns of tenantry which permeate the creation; the passage as a whole demonstrates systematically the different levels and forms of consciousness through which various members of the natural universe become aware of the encroaching storm.

Smart, on the other hand, after a conventional opening, begins to demonstrate his characteristic and enduring concern with patterns of analogy and contrast. The "airy circuits" of the swallows contrast with the earth-bound solidity of "fen bred frogs," as their screams provide counterpoint for the hoarse recital of the frogs' "old grutch." The activity of earthy ants joins the passive beauty of the heavenly rainbow; and the colors of that bow set off the blackness of the "sable crows" which combine in a dark, noisy mass beneath it. Man is not present in the examined creation, although as orderer, mythologizer, interpreter, observer, he is implicitly on hand. Smart makes each animal interesting by the nature of his attention. The frogs are a brilliant example: the reference to "their old grutch" calls up a host of associations (the fable about King Log, the myth of the shepherds changed into frogs for mocking Latona, the old story about the boy throwing stones at the frogs); the line's calculated roughness helps to withhold sympathy from them, and to make their recital of grudges comic rather than pathetic: it is an extended piece of onomatopoeia. Unlike Thomson, who takes a fairly general view of all the phenomena he describes, Smart moves from the most minute attention to the ant and her eggs to the wide view of the rainbow. If the compound *thick-urge,* with its compressed insistence on both the numbers and the energy of the birds, yet its faint awkwardness of formulation, exemplifies Thomson's special vocabulary, Smart's is represented by *obstreperous,* an adjective traditionally used of crows and rooks, but by him freshly and complexly employed of their wings. His usage insists on the root meaning of the word (from Latin *obstrepere*, to make a noise against); it thus suggests the multiplicity of birds, but it also hints the later meaning, unruly, and characterizes the ceaseless activity of crows even on the ground.

One of Smart's poetic ideals was economy, the "perspicuity" so much admired by eighteenth-century critics. In a poem published in 1752 he mourns, "Oh! had I Virgil's comprehensive strain,/ Or sung like Pope, without a word in vain" ("Epithalamium," ll. 54–55). His comprehensiveness and his economy were different from that of Virgil and Pope, but even in his most conventional pieces he demonstrates repeatedly that these were indeed his special gifts, that his curious vocabulary, his extraordinary range of reference, both contribute constantly to these ideals, in his secular and his religious verse alike.

One of Smart's principal contributions to the body of English religious verse was his group of hymns, a product, like his translations of the Psalms, of his interest in reforming Anglican church procedure. Arthur Sherbo has argued convincingly, on the basis of striking parallels in language, that the *Song to David*, the translations of the Psalms and the hymns themselves were all composed between March 1759 and August 26, 1760, early in Smart's stay in the asylum, while he was also writing *Jubilate Agno*.[5] Even critics who have been unwilling to see signs of genius in Smart's earlier work frequently grant that all of this late religious verse is recognizably the product of a single mind. Thus McKenzie concedes, "à l'égard des poèmes qui entourent le Song, et surtout à l'égard des psaumes et des hymnes, nous sommes obligés de modifier un peu l'idée que l'on se faisait de Smart comme de l'auteur d'un poème unique."[6] And Ainsworth and Noyes describe the *Song* as "of a piece with his other religious verse — finer, stronger, sweeter, but of the same substance."[7]

The writing of hymns for the Church of England was in the eighteenth century an unorthodox activity. Metrical psalms were far more common than original hymns; hymns were associated with the evangelical movement.[8] Karina Williamson has examined Smart's hymns extensively, and defined some of their important differences from the evangelical pieces being produced at the same time. She insists that "all the evidence suggests that Smart looked upon the writing of hymns as a deliberate exercise of creative skill, and it is in this way that he differs most fundamentally from the evangelical hymn writers of the eighteenth century."[9] Unlike the products of his Evangelical contemporaries, Smart's hymns were not characterized by simplicity and plainness of diction, she argues (pp. 421–422); Biblical phraseology is modified and absorbed into "the native texture of his verse" (p. 419); the hymns are extensively based on or related to the Anglican prayer book (pp. 416 ff.). More important than any of these peculiarities, in the light of Smart's other work, is the fact that he was able often, in a limited and conventional form, with set subject matter, to speak most distinctively in his own voice.

The cycle of the Christian year provides a loose organizational principle for the thirty-five hymns, entitled *Hymns and Spiritual Songs for the Fasts and Festivals of the Church of England.* Yet more significant are the organizational links suggested by the relations between succeeding hymns. Hymn II, "Circumcision," for example, concludes " 'This is my HEIR of GRACE,/ In whose perfections I rejoice.' " The next hymn, "Epiphany," opens, "Grace, thou source of each perfection . . ." Links of this sort are common; links of *some* sort are almost invariable, although the connection sometimes depends rather on general ideas than on specific words. Moreover, the entire cycle receives genuine cyclical form both through its emotional patterning and through its beginning and ending with characteristic Smartian emphasis on "the Word." The first hymn, "New Year," begins,

> WORD of endless adoration,
> Christ, I to thy call appear;
> On my knees in meek prostration
> To begin a better year.

Hymn XXXV, "The Holy Innocents," ends,

> Though the heav'n and earth shall fail,
> Yet his spirit shall prevail,
> Till all nations have concurr'd
> In the worship of WORD.

Both stanzas look to the future, thus dramatizing the continuous necessity of Christian worship; both insist on the Word as the fundamental power. The hymns contain repeated references to the problem of language and communication, the responsibility of Englishmen in general and of the poet in particular; they evidence in this respect the continuity of Smart's thematic concerns.

His interest in the intricacies of creation and the ways in which all creation combines to praise the Lord is as explicit here as in *A Song to David,* and often even more appealing.

> Praise him thou sea, to whom he gave
> The shoal of active mutes;
> (Fit tenants of thy roaring wave)
> Who comes to still the fiends, that rave
> In oracles and school disputes.
> (Hymn VI, "The Presentation of Christ in the Temple")

This hymn presents with exceptional complexity the vision of a universe united in praise; its perspective is broad enough to permit Smart's characteristic constant shifts of viewpoint. The pattern of contrast perceived in the relation between noisy sea and quiet fish serves more than formal purposes; it becomes an emblem of the relation between quiet Christ and roaring fiends. As tenor and vehicle reflect on one another, the raving of those who engage in "school disputes" seems as meaningless as the noise of the waves (also, paradoxically, "fiendish"; this relation suggests, to use Hannah Arendt's phrase, "the banality of evil"); and the relation between fish and the sea they inhabit seems one in which the fish, types of the meek victim (like, in one aspect, Christ Himself) mysteriously dominate the vast ocean.

The hymns are particularly compelling in their exploration of this sort of symbolism. Although symbolic implications are frequently suggested by *A Song to David* and *Jubilate Agno,* they are rarely exploited as they are in the hymns, the best of which are surely among Smart's most impressive work. Hymn VI, a stanza of which is quoted above, concludes, after an investigation of various parts of creation (birds, fish, beasts, human workers, snakes, flowers, bees, gems),

> Praise him ye cherubs of his breast,
> The mercies of his love,

Smart: Mystique of Vision (II)

> Ere yet from guile and hate profest,
> The phenix makes his fragrant nest
> In his own paradise above.

After stanzas like the one about Christ and the fishes, we may expect such equivalents as these: abstract "mercies" and concrete cherubs are in apposition; Christ as phoenix, a metaphor not previously suggested in the poem, is the logical culmination of various images of the natural world as partaking of the nature of Christ.

Such a hymn as this is in every respect a rich and accomplished poem. Smart makes no compromises for the sake of his form; it is hard to imagine most of these hymns actually sung. But the subject of the church festivals and fasts peculiarly harmonized with the poet's gifts. Around such topics, for Smart, intricate meanings naturally coalesce; the result is a group of "songs" surely expressed in a more individual idiom than any other hymns in the language.

These pieces frequently explore the relation between abstract and concrete which often preoccupied Smart. Here are three stanzas from Hymn XI, "Easter Day":

> Herodians came to seal the stone
>   With Pilate's gracious leave,
> Lest dead and friendless, and alone,
>   Should all their skill deceive.
>
> O dead arise! O friendless stand
>   By seraphim ador'd —
> O solitude! again command
>   Thy host from heav'n restor'd.
>
> Watchmen sleep on, and take your rest,
>   And wake when conscience stings;
> For Christ shall make the grave his nest
>   Till God return his wings.

The modulations of tone from blatant irony ("Pilate's gracious leave") to the quiet assurance of the final two lines are superbly controlled; but the special effect of these stanzas depends largely on their use of abstractions. Reading "dead and friendless, and alone," one waits for the noun these adjectives are to modify. The discovery that, by metonymy, these negative qualities (lack of life, friends, company) can substitute poetically for the person of the Christ has shock value; Smart exploits it by turning the negatives immediately into their positives: the very qualities which should make activity impossible are the source of activity. The nature of the Christian paradox lends itself to this sort of treatment; Smart makes the most of its possibilities. His special note occurs most distinctively in the image of Christ as bird which concludes the passage, where the grave becomes the emblem of perfect security and comfort in the final and most involved paradox, simply and directly expressed.

The interrelations of abstract and concrete are perhaps most complex in the best-known of Smart's hymns, number XXXII, "The Nativity of Our Lord and Saviour Jesus Christ." Its vocabulary combines the simple and sophisticated:

> O the magnitude of meekness!
>   Worth from worth immortal sprung;
> O the strength of infant weakness,
>   If eternal is so young!
>
> Nature's decorations glisten
>   Far above their usual trim;
> Birds on box and laurels listen,
>   As so near the cherubs hymn.
>
> Spinks and ouzles sing sublimely,
>   'We too have a Saviour born,'
> Whiter blossoms burst untimely
>   On the blest Mosaic thorn,
>
> God all-bounteous, all creative,
>   Whom no ills from good dissuade,
> Is incarnate, and a native
>   Of the very world he made.
>   (stanzas 3, 6, 8, 9)

The structure of the stanzas, and of lines within them, is disarmingly simple, and the physical details of the poem project a child-like vision of beauty, in which nature provides "decorations" and the cherubs come near the earth to sing to the birds, while birds in turn produce "sublime" songs of praise. On the other hand, the first stanza quoted and the last exemplify the poem's concern with abstractions: the conclusions to be drawn from the phenomena described have to do with "the magnitude of meekness," the bounteousness, creativeness, incarnation of God. John Middleton Murry comments, "There is a simple miracle in that last line and a half: and one need not be a professing Christian to feel that it is the miracle of the Nativity itself." [10] "Simple miracles" are crucially important to Smart; the paradox of the phrase is central to his verse, which presents the miraculous frequently in such simple terms that one hardly realizes how convoluted are the ideas implied.

It is curious that Miss Williamson should claim that Smart's hymns lack simplicity and plainness of diction. Their diction is not that of the evangelical hymns; Smart's vocabulary is extraordinarily large and the hymns sometimes make use of its great range. Yet one of the most vivid distinctions of these hymns is their capacity to reveal the significance of simplicity and directness.

> Gentle nature seems to love us
>   In each fair and finish'd scene,
> All is beauteous blue above us,
>   All beneath is cheerful green.
> (Hymn XIX, "The Nativity of St. John the Baptist")

> To the Lord your wealth resign,
> Distribution is divine,
>   Misers have no hope.
> (Hymn XVIII, "St. Barnabas")

> Study sits beneath her arbour,
>   By the bason's glossy side;
> While the boat from out its harbour
>   Exercise and pleasure guide.

> Pray'r and praise be mine employment,
>   Without grudging or regret,
> Lasting life, and long enjoyment,
>   Are not here, and are not yet.

> Hark! aloud, the black-bird whistles,
>   With surrounding fragrance blest,
> And the goldfinch in the thistles
>   Makes provision for her nest.

The Poetry of Vision

Ev'n the hornet hives his honey,
Bluecap builds his stately dome,
And the rocks supply the coney
With a fortress and an home.
(Hymn XIII, "St. Philip and St. James")

These are isolated examples of a technique which permeates many of the hymns. The first is most representative of the poet's language as purely naive. In this stanza Smart sums up the import of several previous verses concerned with the beauty of the natural world; he returns to the image of nature as artist so frequently implied in *A Song to David*: each scene is not only "fair" but "finish'd." Without resorting to language more sophisticated than that of a child, Smart manages to communicate through this simple vision a rather complicated effect: that the beauty of nature is not accident but art, and that its beauty is evidence of God's — or nature's — happiness and love.

In "St. Barnabas," on the other hand, and in a good many of the other hymns, Smart combines moral injunctions couched in adult terms with another sort of seeming naivete, this time of thought. The lines quoted conclude the poem's final stanza, offering the "lesson" of the hymn as a whole. "Distribution is divine," characteristically economical, represents the positive argument for giving up one's wealth; "Misers have no hope" is the negative. But the negative, in its simple clarity, is the more powerful, reminding one sharply that hope is God's great gift to man, its absence a horror.

The most complicated employment of the "naive" technique is instanced by the passage from "St. Philip and St. James," where Smart plays variations on his theme. The personifications of the first stanza are so unemphatic that one is hardly aware of them as abstractions; the stanza is reminiscent of the section of the *Song* beginning "Where Israel sits beneath his fig." The moral language of the succeeding stanza is also that of a child; the Christian argument that one must pray without ceasing to prepare for the life to come, couched in such terms, seems as self-evident as the beauties of nature related in the next two stanzas.

Most of this passage deals directly with some form of activity, and the forms here touched upon are numerous. The prospect of "Lasting life, and long enjoyment" justifies the activity of prayer and praise in the second stanza, but the other employments evoked are not similarly justified. Yet the familiar pattern of contrast helps to reveal their significance. Study in her arbor, exercise and pleasure in their boat; black bird and gold bird; bird blessed with fragrance and bird capable of making security from thistles; the fragile hive of the hornet or nest of the bluecap (titmouse) and the fortress of the coney: these evidence the order in variety of the natural universe. The stanza introductory to the entire sequence about nature asserts that

> All the scenes of nature quicken,
> By the genial spirit fann'd;
> And the painted beauties thicken
> Colour'd by the master's hand.

The theme of nature as art is operative here, too; part of the "art" consists in the ordering of contrasts. The art of nature and of the God behind nature is not, however, merely visual. "Pray'r and praise" as employment or the hollowing of rock to make a home may be, in the Master's plan, analogous activities. More immediately important in the context, the facts that birds are created capable of nest-building ingenuity, that the coney has the power to hollow the rocks, that man is able to pray are evidences of God's goodness. The stanza following the ones quoted reads

> But the servants of their Saviour,
> Which with gospel peace are shod,
> Have no bed but what the paviour
> Makes them in the porch of God.

The explicit point seems to be that God is less benevolent to the Christian than to the hornet, but the relationship between man and hornet is more subtle than this: God's gifts to man are less obvious but more important than His benevolence to the animal creation. The Christian, "shod" with "gospel peace," need not concern himself with beds; he has the capacity for greater concerns. Thus the hymn ultimately, with disarming simplicity of diction and structure, reveals that God's gifts of capacity to do, to endure, to understand are even more important than His gifts of natural beauty; at the same time, they are analogous to the visually apparent gifts, accomplishments, too, of the Artist of the universe.

The Poetry of Vision

Smart is not always so successful in use of the technique of naive, almost primitivistic simplicity as he is in the examples quoted; the hymns, like the secular poems — indeed, like *Jubilate Agno* — are uneven. The child-like voice or vision of the poet can produce such ludicrous couplets as this, referring to Queen Anne: "Queen of the wave, to cherish with her wing/ A Russel, Shovel, Rook, a Benbow, and a Byng" (Hymn XVII, "The King's Restoration"). Here we can discern the same sort of interest in words, in the value of names, so often apparent in *Jubilate Agno,* but the interest is not fully controlled. Lack of control mars other of the hymns as well. Yet their accomplishment as a group is great, and interestingly similar to that of the charming *Hymns for the Amusement of Children,* in which Smart writes avowedly from and to the point of view of a child, and demonstrates how harmonious such a technique is to him.

VIII 🦎

WILLIAM COWPER:
The Heightened Perception

AS A WRITER OF hymns, William Cowper is more renowned than Smart; his contributions to the *Olney Hymns* have been admired and sung for almost two centuries. If Smart's hymns gain much of their power from a vision turned freshly outward, Cowper's (to which Smart was a subscriber) depend as heavily on the quality of perception directed within. Several commentators have observed that a personal record of psychological distress and recovery is perceptible in his sequence of hymns. The hymns, says Lodwick Hartley, "represent various stages and aspects of the poet's struggle for faith: an ebb and a flow, but withal a progression, in this one respect not unlike the struggle for faith found in a more elaborate but not more poignant manner in *In Memoriam*."[1] Kenneth MacLean suggests that the unique quality of Cowper's hymns depends on the fact that they "are poems in religious, in primitive fear," an emotion "little considered by poets of Cowper's time."[2] And Maurice Quinlan observes that, in Cowper's poetic production as a whole, "even a brief consideration of [his] imagery reveals that he was one of the most subjective of English poets."[3]

What is particularly striking about Cowper's hymns as compared with his other work is their essentially slight dependence on imagery: their strength derives almost entirely from the quality of their psychological insight, and their attempts to translate that insight into images are rarely and incompletely successful. Key images identified by critics[4] include the worm, the thorn, the tempest, the fig tree, and fetters. To this we may add imagery of light, of battle, and of streams or fountains. All are commonplaces of Evangelical discourse; most are common to religious language in general. And, upon examination, few seem truly essential to Cowper's record of religious agony occasionally modified by the faint hope of salvation.

One of the most moving of the *Olney Hymns* is number IX, "The Contrite Heart."

> The Lord will happiness divine
>   On contrite hearts bestow:
> Then tell me, gracious God, is mine
>   A contrite heart, or no?
>
> I hear, but seem to hear in vain,
>   Insensible as steel;
> If ought is felt, 'tis only pain,
>   To find I cannot feel.
>
> I sometimes think myself inclin'd
>   To love thee, if I could;
> But often feel another mind,
>   Averse to all that's good.
>
> My best desires are faint and few,
>   I fain would strive for more;
> But when I cry, "My strength renew,"
>   Seem weaker than before.
>
> Thy saints are comforted I know,
>   And love thy house of pray'r;
> I therefore go where others go,
>   But find no comfort there.
>
> Oh make this heart rejoice, or ache;
>   Decide this doubt for me;
> And if it be not broken, break,
>   And heal it, if it be.

This is almost bare of figurative language; the only clear metaphor is "Insensible as steel" — the broken heart of the final stanza seems not metaphorical but literal. The hymn's power derives largely from its very bareness, and from the conviction with which the poet describes and analyzes his own emotional tension. Conflict is the essence of the poem. Initially, there seems to be a clash between the conventional — the automatic, easy assurance of the first two lines — and the personal: the bewilderment expressed in the succeeding two lines, underlined by the fact that they address a conventionally "gracious" God. Then Cowper redefines the opposition between conventional and personal as one between the expected (the speaker should "hear" the word of God) and the actual (he hears in vain). He is literally "of two minds": one weakly "inclin'd" toward God; the other, more forceful, "Averse to all that's good." Willing to go through the prescribed motions, the sufferer is constantly brought up short by awareness of his own feelings: he *thinks* himself inclined to love God, but *feels* averse to good; he cries, conventionally, "My strength renew," only to *feel* his own weakness; he *knows* that "saints" love church, does what they do, but *feels* the lack of resultant comfort.

The Donnean appeal of the final stanza is fully justified by the exposition that precedes it. It is an appeal that emotion resolve conflict — not knowledge or even faith: God can "decide" the speaker's doubt only by making him *feel* intensely and unambiguously. The extreme economy of the final two lines helps to make them climactically moving. The poet's heart is unavoidably passive: it either is or is not broken; the stress on passive verb forms (increased by the use of *be* as the final rhyme word) emphasizes the human helplessness which is so often Cowper's theme. In contrast, only God is capable of meaningful action: He can "break" (the strong physical connotations of the word increase its power, suggesting the possibility that the will of God could shatter the whole personality) or "heal" all breaks, all human maladies; and breaking as well as healing may be a mode of salvation — through the restoration of feeling.

This evocation of God as all-powerful, but apparently strangely unwilling to use His power, and of man as forced by his own divided state into a condition of helpless passivity, is central to Cowper's thought. The same ideas emerge frequently in his other hymns, but rarely with as much energy and conviction as in "The Contrite Heart." Here is another presentation of the same problem:

> My God, how perfect are thy ways!
>   But mine polluted are;
> Sin twines itself about my praise,
>   And slides into my pray'r.

The Poetry of Vision

When I would speak what thou hast done
   To save me from my sin,
I cannot make thy mercies known
   But self-applause creeps in.

Divine desire, that holy flame
   Thy grace creates in me;
Alas! impatience is its name,
   When it returns to thee.

This heart, a fountain of vile thoughts,
   How does it overflow?
While self upon the surface floats
   Still bubbling from below.

Let others in the gaudy dress
   Of fancied merit shine;
The Lord shall be my righteousness;
   The Lord for ever mine.
                    (No. XI, "Jehovah Our Righteousness")

Once more, the hymn's theme is the nature and destructiveness of the divided human spirit. This time Cowper concentrates on how good impulses can turn into their opposites: prayer into sin, praise into "self-applause," "Divine desire" into impatience; the heart, traditionally the repository of gentle feelings, is actually "a fountain of vile thoughts." Yet the final stanza somewhat smugly asserts the poet's superiority to others because he recognizes his own inability to achieve virtue and therefore relies solely on the goodness of God.

This conclusion is logical enough: the rational content of the poem consists of an elaboration of the opening two lines, and the concluding stanza defines an attitude toward the facts the poem has described. But that attitude, although logically plausible, contradicts the emotional emphasis of the stanzas that precede its statement. One may object to the imagery of serpent and fountain, but its emotional purport is clear: it insists upon self-disgust as the necessary consequence of man's awareness of his sinful nature. To deny that self-disgust in the conclusion exemplifies the very weakness pointed to in the second stanza: "I cannot make thy mercies known/ But self-applause creeps in." Although self-awareness is the subject of the hymn, there is none in the resolution. The disdain for less knowledgeable "others" implied by *gaudy*, the easy assurance of the pronouncement, "The Lord for ever mine" — these are far from the sense of doubt and questioning earlier conveyed.

The most moving stanzas are the second and third, most specifically concerned with the nature of inward contradiction, most direct in their statement of the problem. Their paucity of imagery also distinguishes them: "that holy flame" is the only clear metaphor. ("Creeps in," in the preceding stanza, has undeveloped metaphoric implications.) This rather commonplace image exists in dramatic conjunction with expression of a very different sort: the holy flame of divine desire reveals itself to be simply impatience, and one perceives the relative pretentiousness of the metaphor when the quality it refers to receives a different "name." The problem of using language properly is implicit in all but the final stanzas of this hymn: the sinner's self-examination is largely examination of the difficulty of expressing in words any inner integrity he may have. Sin contaminates the words of prayer; the effort to "speak" God's praises turns to self-applause; the name of divine desire becomes the name *impatience*.

Partly because the poem's concerns are mental (or spiritual) and verbal problems, the concreteness of sin conceived as serpent is disturbing: twining and sliding are motions too physical for the context. On the other hand, when Cowper treats sin simply as spiritual fact, in the second stanza, its force is considerably greater. The heart as "fountain of vile thoughts" is momentarily impressive, but as the image is elaborated its details become so concrete and specific as to remove stress from the main point. We may even find ourselves lost in contemplation of how and why the "self" manages to float on the surface of its own heart. The image is vivid, but its meaning becomes shadowy; the relation between the self and the heart is both obscure and grotesque.

The danger of grotesquerie is often imminent for Cowper because of his singular lack of tact in converting his ideas to images. Norman Nicholson may argue that "Praise for the Fountain Opened" ("There is a fountain fill'd with blood") makes us "aware of rituals even older than the Old Testament: of the dying god of the fertility cults and of primitive symbols that probe deeply into the subconscious mind," [5] but the argument seems singularly irrelevant to the immediate effect of the hymn, which, on non-evangelical readers, is likely to be shocking but not illuminating.

> There is a fountain fill'd with blood
>   Drawn from Emmanuel's veins;
> And sinners, plung'd beneath that flood,
>   Lose all their guilty stains. . . .
>
> E'er since, by faith, I saw the stream
>   Thy flowing wounds supply;
> Redeeming love has been my theme,
>   And shall be till I die.

The effort at fruitful paradox is unsuccessful because the sheer physical specificity of the image, with its insistence on the source of the blood in *veins* (and later *wounds*) is so intense as to overpower its meaning in Christian tradition. Cowper's frequent references to the blood of Christ make it clear that he conceives it not as an image but as a symbol: what it stands for is of course immeasurably more important than what it *is*. Yet since the poet insists on reminding us in some detail of what precisely it *is*, readers less tradition-steeped than he are likely to have difficulty making the transition from image to meaning. "Comfortable thoughts arise/ From the bleeding sacrifice," observes another hymn (number VIII, "O Lord, I Will Praise Thee"); it is difficult to imagine anyone but Cowper composing such a couplet. The adjective *bleeding* presumably reminds him of the symbolic import of Christ's sacrifice; for the reader, it turns a relatively abstract noun into a sharp and perhaps unpleasant image. The attempt to evoke a Christian paradox by speaking of *comfortable* thoughts fails; the paradox is too easy to be convincing.

The most vivid single example of Cowper's lack of control of his images is the final hymn of his Olney series, which systematically turns the natural world into a series of emblems for Christ. This can hardly be what Hugh Fausset meant when he maintained that "of all the hymns which Cowper wrote, . . . those come nearest to pure poetry in which God is invoked through Nature." [6] The final stanzas are typical:

> What! has autumn left to say
> Nothing of a Saviour's grace?

Cowper: Heightened Perception

Yes, the beams of milder day
Tell me of his smiling face.

Light appears with early dawn,
While the sun makes haste to rise,
See his bleeding beauties, drawn
On the blushes of the skies.

Ev'ning, with a silent pace,
Slowly moving in the west,
Show an emblem of his grace,
Points to an eternal rest.
(no. LXVII, "I Will Praise the Lord at All Times")

The grotesque conjunction of "the blushes of the skies" and "his bleeding beauties" is the most startling element in these stanzas, but the flatness of the first one quoted, the padding of its opening lines, the anticlimax of its conclusion, are also characteristic of Cowper the hymn-writer at his worst. Although the implied personification of this stanza is thematically appropriate, in the second stanza the personification emphasizes the awkwardness of the emblematic treatment, and in the final stanza it is simply irrelevant: how does evening conceived as a person "point to an eternal rest" in any way importantly different from that of evening as a physical phenomenon? This is poetry *voulue* with a vengeance, justifiable only by reference to its purpose, not to its effects. One recalls Dr. Johnson's strictures on metaphysical imagery: "the force of metaphors is lost when the mind by the mention of particulars is turned more upon the original than the secondary sense, more upon that from which the illustration is drawn than that to which it is applied." [7] Cowper's images, in his hymns, frequently seem to have a sort of fatality, to call one's attention inexorably to the "original" rather than the "secondary sense." And his imagery is often "metaphysical" in two ways: its references, although they may purport to deal with the realm of concrete actuality, really concern only the realm beyond the physical; and the images often embody "the most heterogeneous ideas . . . yoked by violence together." [8] Unfortunately Cowper at his most "metaphysical" resembles John Cleveland ("my pen's the spout/ Where the rain-water of mine eyes runs out") more than John Donne; his extravagances, traditional though they often are,

are imperfectly controlled, and likely to alienate rather than to attract the reader.

Yet the imagery of these hymns, when it is less extreme, is strangely revealing. Most deeply-felt of Cowper's images of the sinner's state seem to be those of storm and of battle. God may be a pilot in the storm (Hymn XXXVIII), or He may actually calm the storm (Hymn XLI); He may control the course of battle and supply the weapons (IV, V), or guard the city against besiegers (XIV), or brighten the Christian's armor in answer to prayer (XXIX); when the satanic "foe" takes the guise of bird of prey, God becomes a sheltering bird, protecting His children beneath His wings (XXIV). Only in the last of these functions, though, does God seem vividly present to the poet's imagination. Cowper's reiterated imagery of light (his favorite emblem of God) and of streams and fountains is more convincing. His most typical positive adjectives and nouns (*calm, pleasant, cheerful, peace, comfort*) suggest the state of restored innocence for which he, as a Christian, yearns, a state emblemized by the calm cheer of light, the steady flow of the fountain.

The conjunction of these facts is suggestive; two stanzas from Hymn LVIII, "The New Convert," hint their significance:

> No fears he feels, he sees no foes,
> No conflict yet his faith employs,
> Nor has he learnt to whom he owes
> The strength and peace his soul enjoys.

> But sin soon darts its cruel sting,
> And, comforts sinking day by day,
> What seem'd his own, a self-fed spring,
> Proves but a brook that glides away.

The polarities of Cowper's universe are here suggested and partly described. On the one side is the realm of "conflict." The new convert may postpone awareness of it, but he cannot avoid its actuality; he will ultimately be forced to "see" the foes which have existed all along; his comforts will "sink" as inevitably as the brook glides away. Conflict implies depletion of human resources; it involves a falling away from the state of "strength and peace," of enjoyment, calm, cheer, which is Cowper's most potent vision. He dreams, too, of a never-exhausted fountain of grace, as he dreams of, and believes in, a divine source of spiritual light. But faith and perception seem, in this hymn at least, fundamentally opposed: faith temporarily protects a man from "seeing" what is to be seen; as the power of sin counteracts that of faith, he comes to realize that the inexhaustible spring is only a transient brook. In some of the most convincing hymns Cowper's perceptions of nature support him in his non-rational conviction of the essential hostility of the universe he inhabits. Yet his fundamental effort in all his poetry was to justify, and thus to retain, his dream of idyllic peace, in which he might return to the child-like state of the new convert.

In the hymns, by their very nature, Cowper's religious conviction dominates his poetic gifts. It is not necessary to agree with Hugh Fausset that the poet's life and work demonstrate the unalterable and fundamental opposition between his poetic impulses and his religious bias ("Throughout his life Cowper's allegiance was disastrously divided between poetry and religion."[9]); one may still see that the hymn form emphasizes a dichotomy which may elsewhere disappear. In his most successful poetry, Cowper's concern with art and his preoccupation with morality unite — despite the fact that his own utterances on his poetry occasionally suggest a drastic separation between them, insisting even that all artistic devices must be a means for moral instruction. "My principal purpose," he wrote to the Rev. John Newton, of *The Task*, "is to allure the reader, by character, by scenery, by imagery, and such poetical embellishments, to the reading of what may profit him."[10] Newton was far more interested in Cowper's spiritual development than in his artistic achievement; the poet's statement of his intent may have been colored by his sense of what his mentor expected of him. But his sense of a responsibility to make his poetry "useful" emerges elsewhere as well. "I can write nothing without aiming at least at usefulness," he explained to the Reverend William Unwin: "it were beneath my years to do it, and still more dishonourable to my religion."[11]

One reason for Cowper's insistence on the didactic function of poetry seems to have been his conviction that his contemporaries subordinated matter to manner. An important subject of "Table Talk" is the deterioration of value implicit in the fact that modern standards of poetic excellence stress technique rather than content: "Manner is all in all, whate'er is writ,/ The substitute for genius, sense, and wit" (ll. 542–543). Cowper insists that poets must be judged by their subject matter:

> To dally much with subjects mean and low
> Proves that the mind is weak, or makes it so. . . .
> The man that means success should soar above
> A soldier's feather, or a lady's glove;
> Else, summoning the muse to such a theme,
> The fruit of all her labour is whipt-cream.
>
> (ll. 544–545, 548–551)

Yet Cowper's notion of the poet's proper subject matter was by no means limited to the promulgation of religious doctrine; he had also an idea of imaginative truth. His scorn for "mere matters of fact" is worthy of a nineteenth-century "Romantic": "I do not know," he writes to Newton, "that a poet is obliged to write with a philosopher at his elbow, prepared always to bind down his imagination to mere matters of fact." [12] And his concern for the substance of poetry did not prevent him from being deeply aware of the demands and resources of technique, considered in isolation from content. The struggle for technical dexterity offered a sort of salvation for him. In a touching letter to Newton, Cowper dilates upon his religious despair, describing himself as engaged in "continual listening to the language of a heart hopeless and deserted" and therefore as unfit for conversation about theological matters. He admits, however, that he is able to write verse about subjects he cannot discuss in talk or in written prose. The reason is that "The search after poetical expression, the rhyme, and the numbers, are all affairs of some difficulty; they amuse, indeed, but are not to be attained without study, and engross, perhaps, a larger share of the attention than the subject itself. Persons fond of music will sometimes find pleasure in the tune, when the words afford them none." [13] Cowper was much concerned with the "tune" of his poetry in its very specific aspects. "To make verse speak the language of prose, without being prosaic — to marshal the words of it in such an order as they might naturally take in falling from the lips of an exemplary speaker, yet without meanness, harmoniously, elegantly, and without seeming to displace a syllable for the sake of rhyme, is one of the most arduous tasks a poet can undertake." [14] This is, at least in its opening phrases, such an ideal as Wordsworth was to enunciate, and Cowper appears to have pursued it assiduously.

Yet Donald Davie is surely right in maintaining that Cowper's "work is far more the consummation of one tradition than the prelude to another." [15] Mr. Davie points out that the Augustans in general, like Wordsworth, insisted "that the poet had a duty to the spoken language. . . . But for them this requirement, this duty laid upon the poet, was one among many, others being the observance of decorum, the need for compactness, and metrical felicity" (p. 188). Cowper's adverbs in the passage quoted above (*harmoniously, elegantly*) indicate his concern with decorum and "felicity." The extent to which his poetic principles corresponded to those of his contemporaries and predecessors emerges even more vividly in his ideal of "perspicuity." "Blank verse, by the unusual arrangement of the words, and by the frequent infusion of one line into another, not less than by the style, which requires a kind of tragical magnificence, cannot be chargeable with much obscurity, — must rather be singularly perspicuous, — to be so easily comprehended. It is my labour, and my principal one, to be as clear as possible." [16] Again, six years later: "Only remember, that in writing, perspicuity is always more than half the battle: the want of it is the ruin of more than half the poetry that is published. A meaning that does not stare you in the face is as bad as no meaning, because nobody will take the pains to poke for it." [17] Years before, Fénelon had written, "We shou'd use a simple, exact, easy Stile, that lays every thing open to the Reader, and even prevents his Attention. When an Author writes for the Publick, he shou'd take all the Pains imaginable to prevent his Reader's having any." [18] The goal, and the sense of audience which determines it, remain precisely the same at the century's end as at its beginning. The most authoritative critics of Cowper's own time were unwavering in their advocacy of perspicuity as a prime — perhaps *the* prime — poetic virtue. Lord Kames exposes the logic of their view: "communication of thought being the chief end of language, it is a rule, That perspicuity ought not to be sacrificed to any other beauty whatever." [19] Blair echoes him with greater elaboration and even more emphasis: "Perspicuity, it will be readily admitted, is the fundamental quality of Style; a quality so essential in every kind of writing, that, for the want of it, nothing can atone. . . . This, therefore, must be our first object, to make our meaning clearly and fully understood, and understood without the least difficulty." [20]

For twentieth-century readers, trained to value complexity as an index to poetic merit, such an ideal may seem to promise a dull and obvious sort of poetry. These adjectives, however, do not describe Cowper's best poetic achievement (any more than they describe much of the other poetry written in the service of the same ideal). One may theorize that Cowper was wiser as a poet than as a commentator on poetry, that he did not actually attempt to achieve the goals to which he pays lip service. But the goal of perspicuity itself implies a more complicated critical perception than one may at first realize, for perspicuity can only be achieved through simultaneous awareness of the demands of form and of content: indeed, it specifically implies a union of these concerns. Style, Hugh Blair pointed out, "is a picture of the ideas which rise in [an author's] mind, and of the manner in which they rise there; and, hence, when we are examining an author's composition, it is, in many cases, extremely difficult to separate the Style from the sentiment. . . . Style is nothing else, than that sort of expression which our thoughts most readily assume." [21]

The style most readily assumed by Cowper's thoughts, in *The Task* for example, is fluent and deceptively simple. "I always write as smoothly as I can," he explained to Joseph Johnson; "but . . . I never did, never will, sacrifice the spirit or sense of a passage to the sound of it." [22] On the other hand, he scorned a poet "Too proud for art, and trusting in mere force" ("Table Talk," l. 683) and articulated a poetic ideal involving both form and content:

> Fervency, freedom, fluency of thought,
> Harmony, strength, words exquisitely sought;
> Fancy, that from the bow that spans the sky
> Brings colours, dipt in heav'n, that never die;
> A soul exalted above earth, a mind
> Skill'd in the characters that form mankind . . .
> ("Table Talk," ll. 700–705)

This passage on the poetic character develops an elaborate simile of the poet as resembling the sun:

Cowper: Heightened Perception

Like his to shed illuminating rays
On ev'ry scene and subject it surveys.

(ll. 712–713)

It was not a new comparison: Daniel Webb, for example, had pointed out that "poetry is to the soul, what the sun is to nature; it calls forth, it cherishes, it adorns her beauties." [23] Yet as an instance of Cowper's poetic technique and as a statement of conviction, this description of the poet's gifts is important. Its insistence on metaphors from nature (the rainbow, the sun) is more than accidental: the best examples of Cowper's successful and quite individual fusion of the claims of form and content characteristically develop from his concern with natural imagery. The intellectual progressions recorded in *The Task* depend heavily on the implications of images often presented quite unemphatically.

Cowper's letters sometimes expressed his worry that *The Task* might not immediately reveal its coherence. In a letter to Unwin he supplied his most detailed account of what he considers himself to have achieved in the poem. His defense of his own achievement rests on his expressed belief that his work demonstrates independence of spirit (in its use of his own experience as the sole basis for descriptions both of human and terrestrial nature, and in its "numbers"), authenticity of feeling and, he strongly implies, a rather more "regular" plan than may be immediately apparent. The explanation is worth quoting in full:

My descriptions are all from nature: not one of them second-handed. My delineations of the heart are from my own experience: not one of them borrowed from books, or in the least degree conjectural. In my numbers, which I have varied as much as I could (for blank verse without variety of numbers is no better than bladder and string), I have imitated nobody, though sometimes perhaps there may be an apparent resemblance; because at the same time that I would not imitate, I have not affectedly differed.

If the work cannot boast a regular plan (in which respect however I do not think it altogether indefensible), it may yet boast, that the reflections are naturally suggested always by the preceding passage, and that except the fifth book, which is rather of a political aspect, the whole has one tendency: to discountenance the modern enthusiasm after a London life, and to recommend rural ease and leisure, as friendly to the cause of piety and virtue. [24]

Cowper here suggests that the unity of *The Task* derives from its consistent recommendation of country over city life, its insistence that "God made the country, and man made the town"; but he explicitly excepts the "political" fifth book from the general unity of the whole. Yet the fifth book, too, fits into a more subtly articulated pattern of unity than Cowper ever explicitly claimed, a unity derived largely from the reiteration and elaboration of certain sorts of imagery and reference. Examination of the first book — which contains Cowper's announcement of his intentions in the poem along with certain well-known passages of natural description — and the fifth — largely concerned with political and theological issues — may suggest the nature of that unity.

Book I, entitled "The Sofa," begins with a mock-heroic account of the evolution of the sofa. With a rather heavy-handed piece of levity Cowper announces that, having previously sung "Truth, Hope, and Charity," he now proposes to "seek repose upon an humbler theme" (l. 5). The justification for such a concern is merely that "the Fair commands the song" (l. 7); in an accompanying note the author explains the origin of the poem in the arbitrary and fanciful suggestion of Lady Austen. In the succeeding history of the sofa's development, occasional references suggest the possibility of some allegorical connection between the creation of sofas and the creation of poems. Both may be "employed t'accommodate the fair" (l. 73); both may be based on plans simple or elaborate; both may use shepherds or flowers as decoration (see ll. 35–38). And both attain excellence only as a result of slow, hard labor (ll. 83–85). Such connections are merely hinted; their significance emerges gradually.

The transition from consideration of the sofa to presentation of the poet's experience of the natural world involves a rejection of the indoor life associated with diseases resulting from "libertine excess" (l. 106). The speaker, who prefers the outdoors, recounts his memories of the sights and sounds of the country (ll. 109–364); these lead him to reflections on their significance which occupy most of the rest of the first book. The visual perceptions he offers are organized in "scenes." [25] The value of these, the real point of their inclusion, seems to be their effect on the observer rather than any inherent meaning.

> scenes that sooth'd
> Or charm'd me young, no longer young, I find
> Still soothing, and of pow'r to charm me still.
>
> (ll. 141–143)

> Scenes must be beautiful, which, daily view'd,
> Please daily.
>
> (ll. 177–178)

> Now roves the eye;
> And, posted on this speculative height,
> Exults in its command.
>
> (ll. 288–290)

The observer is more important than the phenomena he perceives. In a revealing sequence, Cowper discusses a small cottage which he has named "the peasant's nest" and romantically yearned to inhabit. Considering the possibilities more carefully, he realizes that life in such rural isolation would offer far too many hardships, and concludes

> thou seeming sweet,
> Be still a pleasing object in my view;
> My visit still, but never mine abode.
>
> (ll. 249–251)

To make external reality into a series of pleasing objects in his view seems to be part of Cowper's goal; a partial justification for this procedure is that it does no harm: "the guiltless eye/ Commits no wrong, nor wastes what it enjoys" (ll. 333–334).

The reduction of nature to an object of aesthetic perception implies the possibility of a close relation between nature and art; this relation is a significant part of Cowper's subject, although his concern with it sometimes emerges only through his choice of metaphors. His description of rural scenes frequently insists, explicitly or implicitly, on the fact that nature provides "works of art" for contemplation. Like many eighteenth-century poets, Cowper often perceives landscapes as spatially organized like paintings, but he seems more aware than most of what he is doing. A typical passage is full of indications of spatial relationships: *there, here, there, far beyond.* But it also expresses the perceiver's conscious — or almost conscious — pleasure in having discovered a point of view from which nature and people in the natural world can be considered as purely aesthetic phenomena.

> Thence with what pleasure have we just discern'd
> The distant plough slow moving, and beside
> His lab'ring team, that swerv'd not from the track,
> The sturdy swain diminish'd to a boy!
> Here Ouse, slow-winding through a level plain
> Of spacious meads with cattle sprinkled o'er
> Conducts the eye along its sinuous course
> Delighted. There, fast rooted in their bank,
> Stand, never overlook'd, our fav'rite elms,
> That screen the herdsman's solitary hut;
> While far beyond, and overthwart the stream
> That, as with molten glass, inlays the vale,
> The sloping land recedes into the clouds.
>
> (ll. 158–171)

The sturdy swain, visually diminished to a boy, therefore need not be considered as a suffering, striving human being. The pleasures of perspective make it unnecessary to contemplate hard realities. (Cowper elsewhere in *The Task* demonstrates some capacity to participate imaginatively in the difficulties of peasant life. He does so clearly from a sense of duty; the pleasure of contemplating peasants depends on thinking of them as children, or as figures in a landscape). Similarly, the cattle, "sprinkled o'er" the spacious meads, are elements of composition, not real animals; even the "lab'ring team" is described with primary emphasis on its participation in a visual pattern ("swerved not from the track"). The Ouse is significant because, like a river in a painting, it can conduct the eye along its sinuous course and thereby "delight" the perceiver. The final metaphor of the stream "inlaying" the vale "as with molten glass" sums up many implications of the passage. The visual joys of nature are thoroughly analogous to those of art; to see the river as resembling a stream of molten glass is to assert its place in an ordered aesthetic whole. This is nature tamed and methodized in a particularly significant way, nature made comprehensible through analogy, subordinated to the aesthetic needs of the observer.

The scenes Cowper describes frequently have this sort of neatness, orderliness — frequently, but by no means always. The first book, however, describes the natural universe almost entirely from the point of view of the connoisseur of art, whose eye orders even the relative confusion of the forest.

> Nor less attractive is the woodland scene,
> Diversified with trees of ev'ry growth,
> Alike, yet various. Here the gray smooth trunks
> Of ash, or lime, or beech, distinctly shine,
> Within the twilight of their distant shades;
> There, lost behind a rising ground . . .
>
> (ll. 300–305)

Once more we have the *here-there* organization; Cowper asserts confidently, "No tree in all the grove but has its charms" (l. 307), and then specifies with sharp visual detail the individual attractions of each, providing a brilliant objectification of that Augustan ideal of "order in variety" hinted by the opening lines of the passage. He can perceive the panorama of hill and valley between wood and water as "a spacious map" (l. 321) with no implied deprecation of its beauty: the fact that it is describable in terms of human achievement suggests its praiseworthy orderliness. The effect of this reference to nature as a map is at the opposite pole from that of Smart's "All scenes of painting crowd the map/ Of nature," which dramatizes the poet's impression of an overflowingly rich universe, in which the distinction between the works of God and those of man becomes finally irrelevant. Cowper's metaphor describes a world in which the human need for perceptual order is dominant.

"The love of Nature, and the scene she draws,/ Is Nature's dictate," Cowper observes (ll. 412–413) in one of his most explicit uses of the analogy between nature and art. The purpose of the analogy is to insist on the superiority of nature to art:

> Strange! there should be found, . . .
> Who, satisfied with only pencil'd scenes,
> Prefer to the performance of a God
> Th' inferior wonders of an artist's hand!
> Lovely indeed the mimic works of art;
> But Nature's works far lovelier.
>
> (ll. 413–421)

Cowper offers a standard argument for the greater loveliness of nature: painting pleases only the eye, "sweet Nature ev'ry sense" (l. 427). But this is only a superficial justification for a preference which is in fact the key to the structure and meaning of the first book and in a sense of the poem as a whole.

The more profound significance of the poet's belief in the aesthetic superiority of nature to art emerges only gradually, although it is implicit even in the early natural descriptions. Immediately after his direct statement that nature's works are lovelier than man's — in the same verse paragraph — Cowper begins exploring the aesthetic principle of contrast which had interested Thomson and Akenside. The prisoner, the invalid, the sailor deprived of sight of land: these appreciate the "feast" spread by nature (l. 433) more than can men to whom that feast is constantly available. (In the case of the sailor, longing for the beauty of nature brings about his destruction: looking into the ocean he sees "visions prompted by intense desire" [l. 451], visions of the fields he has left behind; seeking those fields, he plunges to his death. The destructive agent is not nature but his own imagination. The dangers of fancy are an important subordinate theme of *The Task*.) Earlier, Cowper had pointed out the principle of contrast operating in other areas: nature herself subsists by constant change (ll. 367–384); man gains the greatest goods through alternation of activity and rest. "Measure life/ By its true worth, the comforts it affords," the poet commands (ll. 396–397); then one perceives that only through contrast can genuine pleasure be achieved.

The greatest pleasure for Cowper is unquestionably aesthetic contemplation, contemplation as an observer. Actual participation in life is dangerous and debilitating; life can become "A peddler's pack, that bows the bearer down" (l. 465); men cling to it although it is essentially meaningless, long for society through mere dread of solitude. Cowper's images of all but peasant life are characteristically images of deprivation and desperation. To the horrors of the urban life which, through its very gaiety, "fills the bones with pain,/ The mouth with blasphemy, the heart with woe" (ll. 504–505), the poet opposes, once more, his vision of nature as essentially designed for human contemplation:

> The earth was made so various, that the mind
> Of desultory man, studious of change,
> And pleas'd with novelty, might be indulg'd.
>
> (ll. 506–508)

Cowper: Heightened Perception

The principle of change and contrast in nature seems now to exist to fulfill man's aesthetic needs: man may become bored with individual "prospects," but other prospects always exist; he may contemplate landscapes interrupted by hedges which provide visual variety; the shapeless gorse offers "ornaments of gold" (l. 529) made more pleasing because opposed to the "deform'd" (l. 527) bush itself.

In the last third of the first book, nature as aesthetic object is not so important. The organization of episodes now begins to seem relatively random; yet subterraneously the same theme remains dominant: the theme of nature's importance as an object of contemplation and a source of the comforts life affords, its superiority in these respects to human art and artifice. We learn about crazy Kate, whose insanity results from an over-active fancy (ll. 534–556); then about the gypsies, lazy and immoral, who none the less enjoy "health and gaiety of heart" (l. 587), direct results of their contact with nature. Then comes, rather surprisingly, an extended passage of praise for civilization (ll. 592–677), in the course of which Cowper considers the limitations of the "noble savage." Finally the book moves into its lengthy denunciation of cities (a denunciation which, however, painstakingly accords credit to urban achievement) and its ultimate praise of the superiority of country life (ll. 678–774).

The need to record the glories of civilization seems to come, in the context, from recognition of the fact that man is, after all, by necessity, a being who must act as well as contemplate. In the first two-thirds of this book, Cowper has insisted upon the value of nature to man, who is the passive recipient of what it has to offer. Partly through reiterated analogies between nature and art, he has stressed the inferiority of art to nature as an object of contemplation, the aesthetic value of nature, the moral innocence of "nature appreciation," the importance of the physical and mental health which nature offers man as recipient. As long as man *sees* rather than *does*, he is secure; he may even be happy, gaining the "comforts" by which the value of life is to be judged. On the other hand, there have also been hints of darker possibility. The sailor is killed, Kate crazed as a result of the operations of fancy. The gypsies steal; as *doers* they are unattractive, though blessed as recipients of nature's power. And we have had a somber sketch of those who give their lives to the pursuit of pleasure in a social environment: a pursuit which makes life empty, valueless. On the other hand, Cowper has asserted the value of "strenuous toil" — but only because it provides, by contrast, "sweetest ease" (l. 388).

In the context of the values implied, Cowper faces a dilemma when he begins to consider the possibility of man's acting positively rather than negatively. In what context can man act properly; and what, precisely, is the relation between action and contemplation? Does action necessarily result in that "sinking" of comfort which the poet so deeply dreads? Only civilization, Cowper concludes, makes possible true and consistent virtue in action. "Here virtue thrives as in her proper soil" (l. 600): repeated uses of natural analogy insist that the patterns of nature are the models to man. Thus civilized virtue is "By culture tam'd, by liberty refresh'd,/ And all her fruits by radiant truth matur'd" (ll. 606–607). It tends to exist only in temperate climates; the inhabitant of the frozen north feels "severe constraint" (l. 612), and — more interestingly — residents of tropic isles

> Can boast but little virtue; and inert
> Through plenty, lose in morals what they gain
> In manners — victims of luxurious ease.
> These therefore I can pity, plac'd remote
> From all that science traces, art invents,
> Or inspiration teaches.
>
> (ll. 623–628)

The distaste for the inertness of ease and of over-constraint, the admiration for the accomplishments of science and art — these are standard eighteenth-century attitudes, associated with belief in the doctrine of progress. They are not, however, really compatible with Cowper's more fundamental convictions, and his uneasiness with them soon emerges through his expressed consciousness of the gap between the ideal of progress and the actuality. Ideally, civilized virtue is "gentle, kind" (l. 605). Actually, it is Omai, the South Sea Islander, who is gentle — and he is a "gentle savage" (l. 633). The real result of civilization is

> With what superior skill we can abuse
> The gifts of Providence, and squander life.
>
> (ll. 637–638)

"Doing good,/ Disinterested good, is not our trade," Cowper explains (ll. 673–674); the conflict between commercial and moral values is fundamental and unalterable. Lacking such conflicts, the South Sea Islander, despite his lack also of civilized graces, seems in all his passivity the moral superior of the energetic Englishman. Like Wordsworth, who advocated a "wise passiveness" toward nature, unlike Thomson, who felt obliged to condemn such passivity as "indolence," Cowper seems to feel the passive relation to nature as an ideal state of being. Indeed, in one of his letters he suggests that man can achieve even active virtue only in a state of nature. "I accede most readily to the justice of your remark on the subject of the truly Roman heroism of the Sandwich islanders," he wrote John Newton. "Proofs of such prowess, I believe, are seldom exhibited by a people who have attained to a high degree of civilization. Refinement and profligacy of principle are too nearly allied, to admit of any thing so noble." [26]

Cowper insists on a distinction between the "civilization" of cities — characterized by "refinement" — and that of the country. Virtue thrives "in the mild/ And genial soil of cultivated life" (ll. 678–679) — "Yet not in cities oft" (l. 681), to which flow, as to a sewer, "The dregs and feculence of ev'ry land" (l. 683). In one respect alone are cities truly praiseworthy: they are "nurs'ries of the arts" (l. 693). The poet praises Joshua Reynolds — who can turn "a dull blank" into "A lucid mirror, in which Nature sees/ All her reflected features" (ll. 700–702) — the sculptor John Bacon, and the powers of sculpture in general. He also appears to admire the achievements of "philosophy" and of commerce — although his comparison of London as the thriving mart of commerce with ancient Babylon, the city of captivity, qualifies the positive implications of his presentation. His damnation of London is far more emphatic than his praise; it centers on the evils of urban activity, the injustice and hypocrisies of a life where "civilized" forms have quite replaced moral content.

The argument of the first book is now complete: Cowper has both asserted and demonstrated the value of aesthetic contemplation of the natural world; he has opposed to his insistence on nature's aesthetic value an equally clear awareness of the dangers of participation in worldly activity. He has suggested repeatedly that art is necessarily inferior to nature, although art provides useful analogies for the understanding of nature — and nature for the proper appreciation of art. And he has hinted that commitment to the life of imagination may be dangerous: the perception through which man sees, the memory with which he recalls satisfying sights, the judgment with which he guards against moral danger — all these human faculties are more unambiguously valuable than the fancy. The final lines of the book, beginning, "God made the country, and man made the town," sum up these implications.

> What wonder then that health and virtue, gifts
> That can alone make sweet the bitter draught
> That life holds out to all, should most abound
> And least be threaten'd in the fields and groves?
>
> (ll. 750–753)

Nature's lack of threat to passive man is as significant a value as her more positive virtues. But the ultimate value is once more aesthetic. Cowper abandons city-dwellers to their own element: they "taste no scenes/ But such as art contrives" (ll. 756–757). Then he returns to the "scenes" which interest him more, the groves and birds and moonlight of the country, whose aesthetic appeal is now systematically contrasted with that achieved by human art and artifice. The conclusion strikes a strong moral note:

> Folly such as your's,
> Grac'd with a sword, and worthier of a fan,
> Has made, what enemies could ne'er have done,
> Our arch of empire, stedfast but for you,
> A multilated structure, soon to fall.
>
> (ll. 770–774)

This final condemnation of those who live in cities is justified by reference to no sin more serious than their preference of opera singers to birds, lamplight to moonlight. In Cowper's ethical system, however, such lapses of judgment, such willing acceptance of inferior sorts of perception, amount to genuine moral failing. He has not yet fully revealed the basis for his consistent association of strong perceptual response to nature with moral uprightness; it emerges completely in the fifth book, paradoxically one of the sections of the poem least obviously concerned with nature.

Cowper: Heightened Perception

Book V, despite its title ("The Winter Morning Walk"), is a record primarily of man reflecting rather than man perceiving. It begins with a hundred and seventy-five lines of description and meditation on nature and man in nature, but the succeeding seven hundred and thirty lines virtually abandon nature as subject. Yet the problem of perception is once more central to the argument of the book, although liberty and permanence are the subjects which most clearly unify the poet's concerns.

The opening lines present a direct record of perception, visual awareness modulating imperceptibly into moral. The sun, at first an image of great power, loses force as it rises. First "with ruddy orb/ Ascending, [it] fires th'horizon" (ll. 1–2); the regal associations of *orb* support the sense of potency in the image of the sun "firing" the whole horizon. By line 4, the sun is no longer an orb, but merely a disk. Two lines later, "his slanting ray/ Slides ineffectual down the snowy vale" (ll. 6–7); with an increasing sense of the sun's ineffectuality we learn that now its power consists merely in "tinging all with his own rosy hue" (l. 8) — a considerable falling-off, both visually and conceptually, from the energy which fired the horizon. Finally, the sun creates shadows; the observer in the scene is thus united with "ev'ry herb and ev'ry spiry blade" (l. 9), which, like him, cast their shadows. When the human participant in the natural scene reflects on the import of his shadow he announces, with surprising levity, one of the major themes of this book. The relative impermanence of man and his achievements will come to seem more and more important as the book proceeds; here, on the other hand, the poet's verbal attempt to assert his own transience is immediately counteracted by the enduring reality of nature, which seems infinitely more significant. The transience of man is almost a joke; recognition of it coincides with awareness of the visual grotesqueness of the shadow's transformation of well-proportioned limb to lean shank.

> Mine, spindling into longitude immense,
> In spite of gravity, and sage remark
> That I myself am but a fleeting shade,
> Provokes me to a smile. With eye askance
> I view the muscular proportion'd limb
> Transform'd to a lean shank.
>
> (ll. 11–16)

The Poetry of Vision

The observer, perceiving the natural world sharply, feels himself essentially a part of that world; his abstract awareness that he is "but a fleeting shade" is far less compelling than the comic visual reality of distorting shadow, and the pleasure derived from perception of that reality.

The revelatory power of nature is important throughout this description.

> the bents,
> And coarser grass, upspearing o'er the rest,
> Of late unsightly and unseen, now shine
> Conspicuous, and, in bright apparel clad
> And fledg'd with icy feathers, nod superb.
>
> (ll. 22–26)

Frost makes the unseen seeable, the unsightly beautiful. This natural power is meaningful not, as in Thomson, primarily for the kind of energy it manifests, but for the transformed world it displays. The display implies the great kinships of nature — weeds metaphorically unite with men by being "clad" in "apparel," with birds by being "fledged with . . . feathers" — but its chief impact is visual. Similarly, as the vignette continues, it directs our attention chiefly to the visual effect of mourning cattle, working man, scampering dog, and only secondarily to the implications of order and permanence in the description of the haystack, for example, or even of the woodman moving "right toward the mark" (l. 53).

Reflection about what happens to various kinds of animals and insects in winter leads Cowper to the two central images of Book V: the frozen surroundings of the waterfall and the ice palace of Empress Anna of Russia. The waterfall itself is too forceful to be "bound" by frost, but the mist it throws off freezes into fantastic and compelling forms. "See," the poet commands, with Thomsonian emphasis,

> where it [the frost] has hung th' embroider'd banks
> With forms so various, that no pow'rs of art,
> The pencil or the pen, may trace the same!
>
> (ll. 107–109)

Once more the specific "scene" raises the issue of nature's relation to art; once more Cowper insists that neither the painter nor the poet can capture the beauty of natural reality. Art is clearly inadequate as the "mirror" of nature; if it aspires to mirror, it must fail. (Elsewhere in the poem, Cowper explains that the mind of the artist is a mirror, and that the responsibility of the poet is

> T'arrest the fleeting images that fill
> The mirror of the mind, and hold them fast,
> And force them sit till he has pencil'd off
> A faithful likeness of the forms he views.
>
> [II, 290–293]

Art — specifically poetry — may provide a mirror for nature, but in a moral, not an aesthetic sense; Cowper describes his "stream" of poetry as "reflecting clear,/ If not the virtues, yet the worth, of brutes" [VI, 723–724].) Continuing to describe the wonders of the frozen landscape, Cowper concentrates on suggestion more than precise visual detail: "Here grotto within grotto safe defies/ The sunbeam" (ll. 117–118). The reader is invited to consider the significance, the mystery of the frost's achievement as well as to "see" its manifestations. And the poet concludes his treatment of this magical creation with yet another extended and emphatic statement of nature's superiority to art:

> Thus nature works as if to mock at art,
> And in defiance of her rival pow'rs;
> By these fortuitous and random strokes
> Performing such inimitable feats
> As she with all her rules can never reach.
>
> (ll. 122–126)

Gone is Pope's sense of the essential, inevitable harmony between art and nature; now the two are "rival powers," with nature clearly the victor. Nature's aesthetic superiority to art is clearly explained:

> The growing wonder takes a thousand shapes
> Capricious, in which fancy seeks in vain
> The likeness of some object seen before.
>
> (ll. 119–121)

The fancy, the human creative power which produces art, is limited, Locke had explained, to forming new combinations or interpretations of objects (or parts of objects) previously perceived.

It cannot create anything entirely new, completely unrelated to earlier perception. Nature as artist, on the other hand, suffers from no such limitation: its creations bear no likeness to any object seen before. Only nature can provide new material for fancy to work upon. The perceptual grounds for its aesthetic superiority to art are perfectly apparent.

The man-made ice palace contrasted with the nature-created grottoes also offers aesthetic appeals — despite the fact that it is "less worthy of applause, though more admir'd" (l. 126). Its attractiveness, however, derives largely from the illusion it creates of permanence and accordingly of man's dominance over nature.

> though smooth
> And slipp'ry the materials, yet frost-bound
> Firm as a rock. Nor wanted aught within,
> That royal residence might well befit,
> For grandeur or for use.
>
> (ll. 154–158)

But it is, after all, a "brittle prodigy" (l. 154); the moral satisfaction of considering its "evanescent glory, once a stream,/ And soon to slide into a stream again" (ll. 167–168) counteracts the aesthetic satisfaction of contemplating its apparent permanence and order. "In such a palace Poetry might place/ The armory of Winter" (ll. 138–139), Cowper observes; this idea causes him to consider the power of winter, which produces "snow, that often blinds the trav'ler's course, And wraps him in an unexpected tomb" (ll. 142–143). No human structure adequately contains the menace of winter; if the lamps within the palace seem "Another moon new risen, or meteor fall'n/ From heav'n to earth, of lambent flame serene" (ll. 152–153), it is only by an illusion of human perception. The apparently successful manipulation of nature by man is temporary, soon to vanish, offering but the pretence of permanence.

The complex combination of immediately perceived solidity with intellectually recognized evanescence makes the ice palace the type of all human achievement; for this reason it provides an underlying metaphor throughout the rest of Book V. Its metaphoric value is underlined at the end of the description:

> Alas; 'twas but a mortifying stroke
> Of undesign'd serenity, that glanc'd
> (Made by a monarch) on her own estate,
> On human grandeur and the courts of kings.
> 'Twas transient in its nature, as in show
> 'Twas durable.
>
> (ll. 169–174)

The "mortifying stroke" is the palace's sliding back into a stream. The palace is the emblem of princely endeavor, which may struggle for dominance "by pyramids and mausolean pomp" (l. 182), by building; or by destroying, provoking wars in which kings make "the sorrows of mankind their sport" (l. 186). The desire of kings to assert their power in tangible form causes war, but war originated, Cowper explains, in man's attempt to extend his dominance over nature, when he "had begun to call/ These meadows and that range of hills his own" (ll. 222–223). Continuing his discussion of warfare and of the presumption of kings, the poet defines the king's pride: it consists in thinking "the world was made in vain, if not for him" (l. 271). Man persists in believing that he is in some real sense master of the natural world; it is an odd corollary that he should believe that some are fit to be masters of others, even though a king is a man

> Compounded and made up like other men
> Of elements tumultuous, in whom lust
> And folly in as ample measure meet
> As in the bosoms of the slaves he rules.
>
> (ll. 307–310)

So it is that man loses his freedom in his political institutions: through a misinterpretation of his own humble position in the universe which remotely parallels the misinterpretation involved in believing an ice palace to be permanent or its lights to be equivalent to the moon.

We are not directly reminded of the ice palace, however, until the very end of the discussion of political liberty, when Cowper returns to the metaphor of building:

> We turn to dust, and all our mightiest works
> Die too: . . .
> We build with what we deem eternal rock:
> A distant age asks where the fabric stood.
>
> (ll. 531–532, 534–535)

The state itself can be described as an "old castle" (l. 525); the entire issue of political liberty is evanescent as the ice palace in comparison with the far more fundamental problem of spiritual liberty which Cowper next considers.

The essence of spiritual liberty is its permanence, in comparison with which nature itself seems transient. In His visible works, God,

> finding an interminable space
> Unoccupied, has fill'd the void so well,
> And made so sparkling what was dark before.
> But these are not his glory.
>
> (ll. 556–559)

On aesthetic grounds, man supposes that "so fair a scene" (l. 560) must be eternal — as he supposes the permanence of the ice palace on the basis of visual evidence (the adjective *sparkling*, like *glitter* in the lines quoted below, may remind one of the connection between the two phenomena). Yet nature, considered in terms of the divine plan, is merely another sort of artifice, the product of an "artificer divine" (l. 561) who has Himself "pronounc'd it transient, glorious as it is" (l. 563) because He values spiritual, not physical, permanence. Cowper's values are similar; he elaborates for almost two hundred lines on the value, the essentiality, of spiritual liberty. Yet the resolution of the discussion of spiritual freedom accepts once more the profound aesthetic value of nature, and makes the ability to perceive this value a touchstone of one's spiritual state.

> He is the freeman whom the truth makes free,
> And all are slaves beside. . . .
> He looks abroad into the varied field
> Of nature, and, though poor perhaps compar'd
> With those whose mansions glitter in his sight,
> Calls the delightful scen'ry all his own. . . .
> Are they not his by a peculiar right,
> And by an emphasis of int'rest his,
> Whose eye they fill with tears of holy joy,
> Whose heart with praise, and whose exalted mind
> With worthy thoughts of that unwearied love
> That plann'd, and built, and still upholds, a world
> So cloth'd with beauty for rebellious man?
>
> (ll. 733–734, 738–741, 748–754)

Cowper: Heightened Perception

The beauty of the world is God's special gift to man; visual "possession" of "delightful scenery" is more valuable than wealth. Moreover, true aesthetic response to nature depends on a proper relation with God:

> Acquaint thyself with God, if thou would'st taste
> His works. Admitted once to his embrace,
> Thou shalt perceive that thou wast blind before:
> Thine eye shall be instructed; and thine heart,
> Made pure, shall relish, with divine delight
> Till then unfelt, what hands divine have wrought.
>
> (ll. 779–784)

Understanding of God's dominance over nature (in contrast to the false belief in man's control of nature) produces the perception which distinguishes men from brutes (see ll. 785–790), gives the soul "new faculties" (l. 806) which enable it to discern "in all things, what, with stupid gaze/ Of ignorance, till then she overlook'd" (ll. 808–809). When man holds converse with the stars, the special significance of the "shining hosts" (l. 822) is that they "view/ Distinctly scenes invisible to man" (ll. 825–826); heightened perception is a metaphysical goal. The "lamp of truth" enables man to "read" nature (l. 845); and liberty itself "like day,/ Breaks on the soul, and by a flash from heav'n/ Fires all the faculties with glorious joy" (ll. 883–885).

> In that blest moment Nature, throwing wide
> Her veil opaque, discloses with a smile
> The author of her beauties, who, retir'd
> Behind his own creation, works unseen
> By the impure.
>
> (ll. 891–895)

If God is the source of proper perception, He is also the *end* of perception: this is the final word of Book V. The fired faculties which liberty creates lead man ultimately to God, healing the potential and sometimes actual split felt between God and nature as objects of contemplation. The poignant story which Cowper tells in his *Memoir* is well-known: how, exalted and soothed by contemplation of a marine sunset, he was subsequently overwhelmed with guilt at the realization that he had sinfully attributed to the power of nature the psychological healing that could only be due to the power of God. In the logic of Book V of *The Task* such distinctions virtually disappear — not because nature and God are identical ("Nature is but a name for an effect,/ Whose cause is God" [VI, 223–224]), but because the ability to perceive nature is the result of a proper relation with God, and the heightening of faculties which makes possible an enlightened aesthetic response to nature also produces an awareness of how God expresses Himself through nature. The ability to appreciate the "scenes" which nature provides becomes thus virtually a test of one's spiritual condition; the belief in the aesthetic superiority of nature to art is not a matter merely of personal response, but a product of the realization that nature has intrinsic significance which no work of art can achieve. Elsewhere in *The Task*, some of the most compelling passages of natural description attempt to define and delineate this significance. The substructure which justifies such attempts is probably most apparent in Book V, itself comparatively bare of description.

For Cowper, then, the act of visual perception, which had provided subject matter and metaphors for poets throughout the eighteenth-century development of the poetry of image rather than action, finally takes on metaphysical importance. Thomson had attempted to "see" significance as well as appearance, Collins had "seen" into a realm of fantasy as well as of reality, Gray had used contrasting "visions" to create a poetry of tension, Smart had seen the natural world and then gone beyond his own seeing to establish connections with a realm of transcendental truth. For Cowper the seeing itself implied the transcendental truth; the physical power of vision became a spiritual reality.

Donald Davie has remarked of Cowper that he is, "after Ben Jonson, . . . the most neglected of our poets." [27] The neglect is of analysis rather than simply of attention: Cowper has been written about voluminously — as a psychological case, as a representative of piety, as a phenomenon of his century. Few critics, however, have made any serious attempt to examine the source or nature of his poetic effects; those who have tried to describe his poetry often take so large a view that all possibility of accuracy vanishes. Thus we are told, for example, that " 'The Task' resembles the conversation of one dowered with no special gifts of intellect; of an interesting quiet man, of humour and austerity with an intensely human hand-grip." [28] Alternately, its form, "remarquable par sa simplicité audacieuse," is that of fragments of a journal.[29] "To Cowper," another critic observes, "nature is simply a background, . . . essentially a *locus in quo* — a space in which the work and mirth of life pass and are performed." [30] Or we are informed that "his intuition was comparatively superficial, if disinterested, because he never strove to discipline ideas to facts or to interpret facts ideally, but only to invest them with sentiment or reflect upon them." [31] All such statements seem plausible when one considers *The Task* casually as a whole; all lose their plausibility if closely examined in relation to specific passages, which reveal at least a potential unity far more rigorous than that of a conversation or a journal, demonstrate the fundamental importance of nature not as a *locus in quo* but as an object of contemplation, and suggest that Cowper at his best characteristically "interpret[s] facts ideally." It is extremely difficult to generalize accurately about *The Task* because although, as I have attempted to show, an underlying structure of ideas does in fact unify many of its apparently disparate concerns, it remains a poem of details, details which depend upon varied techniques and apparent preoccupations. The poem's variety is particularly confusing with regard to its language. The diction of *The Task* ranges from "poetic" to colloquial, from abstract to concrete, apparently depending on many different principles of control. The magnitude of the poet's concerns emerges vividly through examination of his language.

The prevailing critical attitude toward the diction of *The Task* has been that it is remarkable for its "plainness." In Cowper's own time plainness was thought to be one of his chief poetic merits; thus a reviewer of his first volume observes: "Anxious only to give each image its due prominence and relief, he has wasted no unnecessary attention on grace and embellishment; his language, therefore, though neither strikingly harmonious nor elegant, is plain, forcible, and expressive." [32] Specifically with regard to *The Task,* another of Cowper's contemporaries, remarking "the familiarity of the diction," observes, "The language may sometimes appear below the poetical standard; but he was such a foe to affectation in any shape, that he seems to have avoided nothing so much as the stiff pomposity so common to blank verse writers." [33] More modern critics have echoed this view: "the language is of the purest and finest, but it is not strikingly ornamented. It is without anything unusual in poetic diction." [34] And Thomas Quayle singles out "the moral and didactic portions" as characterized by language "as a rule, uniformly simple and direct." [35]

Yet these judgments, too, seem perplexing when one examines specific passages of *The Task* to find Cowper writing, "The verdure of the plain lies buried deep/ Beneath the dazzling deluge" (V, 21–22), or — for a more extended example —

> Now from the roost, or from the neighb'ring pale,
> Where, diligent to catch the first faint gleam
> Of smiling day, they gossip'd side by side,
> Come trooping at the housewife's well-known call
> The feather'd tribes domestic. Half on wing,
> And half on foot, they brush the fleecy flood,
> Conscious, and fearful of too deep a plunge.
> The sparrows peep, and quit the shelt'ring eaves
> To seize the fair occasion. Well they eye
> The scatter'd grain; and, thievishly resolv'd
> T'escape th' impending famine, often scar'd,
> As oft return — a pert voracious kind.
>
> (V, 58–69)

This is part of the opening description of man, animals and vegetation in a winter landscape. It is not, in its diction, fully characteristic of Cowper's technique, but it demonstrates the dexterity with which the poet turns varied conventions to personal use.

In language and in sentence structure, these lines seem to come from the mid, not the late, eighteenth century. The pseudo-Miltonic inversions, such Thomsonian formulations as "the feather'd tribes domestic," the unrealized personification of "smiling day," the automatic phrase, "the fair occasion," the periphrases of "fleecy flood," "feather'd tribes," "pert voracious kind": all these belong to well-established poetic patterns — patterns which we might expect Cowper to avoid. They seem to be used for familiar reasons: to establish metaphoric links between man and lower forms of nature which will reinforce the reader's sense of some vast natural harmony. One may note Cowper's accuracy of perception in such phrases as "Half on wing/ And half on foot," or the vividness of "brush" (in "they brush the fleecy flood"), the figurative appropriateness of "gossip'd"; still, the impression remains that the passage as a whole is almost pure convention, in language and in concept.

To understand its function in *The Task* one must turn to its context, which significantly modifies the effect of the lines considered in isolation. A few lines taken from either side of the description of the birds may suggest the nature of that context. The first of these passages focuses on an individual animal, sharply perceived in his separateness; the second, although it too is rich in specific detail, is more general. The first makes emphatic use of inversion, and offers the Thomsonian "wide-scamp'ring"; the second has no striking structural peculiarities and its diction provides no special associations. Yet these two descriptions resemble one another far more than they resemble the description of domestic fowl. The voice that speaks in them, although it is not emphatically distinctive, is none the less individual in comparison to that which speaks of a "fleecy flood." One sees here the effect of an eye trained steadfastly upon the object, a mind concerned to discriminate and to define not on the basis of relationships or of categories ("kinds") but in terms of specific individual perceptions.

> Shaggy, and lean, and shrewd, with pointed ears
> And tail cropp'd short, half lurcher and half cur —
> His dog attends him. Close behind his heel
> Now creeps he slow; and now, with many a frisk
> Wide-scamp'ring, snatches up the drifted snow
> With iv'ry teeth, or ploughs it with his snout;
> Then shakes his powder'd coat, and barks for joy.
>
> (V, 45–51)

> The very rooks and daws forsake the fields,
> Where neither grub, nor root, nor earth-nut, now
> Repays their labour more; and, perch'd aloft
> By the wayside, or stalking in the path,
> Lean pensioners upon the trav'ler's track,
> Pick up their nauseous dole, though sweet to them,
> Of voided pulse or half-digested grain.

The Poetry of Vision

The streams are lost amid the splendid blank,
O'erwhelming all distinction.

(V, 89–97)

The lines beginning with allusion to the rooks and daws deal with transformations effected by winter, and with the resulting paradoxes: birds forsake their "natural" habitat for traveled roads; the "nauseous dole" voided by the travelers is "sweet to them"; winter creates a "splendid blank,/ O'erwhelming all distinction," while the poet insists precisely on the distinctions of the chill landscape. The passage on the dog, with its emphasis on energetic verbs (*snatches, ploughs, shakes, barks*; the noun *frisk* and the participle *wide-scamp'ring* also suggest the energy of action), dramatizes the way in which the power of winter may inform the animal kingdom: if it immobilizes water, it intensely animates dogs.

Each of the three passages, then, represents a different way, almost a different principle, of "seeing." The eye focuses on an individual phenomenon in the lines about the dog, discriminates the details of the animal's appearance ("Shaggy, and lean, and shrewd, with pointed ears/ And tail cropp'd short"), then moves on to contemplate the exact nature of his activity. The language of the description is "plain," generally direct, heavily Anglo-Saxon. Interpretation is kept to a minimum, suggested only by the adjective *shrewd* and the phrase "barks for joy"; the scene is self-sufficient, containing its meaning in its details. One sentence is simple, one compound; the coordinate conjunction *and,* occurring six times in the seven lines, is vital in establishing relationships.

In the passage about rooks and daws, a single, elaborate complex sentence occupies seven of the nine lines; the increased complexity of structure is paralleled by heightened dignity of tone. Although direct, simple description remains important, with the plain diction appropriate to it, Latinate words now assume a more significant rôle. They convey the interpretive judgment of the author in such key terms as *labour, pensioners, nauseous, splendid, distinction.* Meaning as well as appearance is important here; this fact accounts for the heightened dignity of language and structure. The central paradox that privation and beauty are by winter mysteriously connected, a paradox embodied in the phrase "splendid blank," is elaborated both through the specificity with which Cowper details the nature of privation and its compensations and through the generality of his final descriptive allusion to the snow which covers everything.

The heavy stress on established poetic diction in the section on domestic fowl does not obscure the clarity of the poet's observation any more than does the complexity of structure or the relative elevation of language in the lines on rooks and daws. Here, though, the principle of "seeing" is to place observed details in the context of a tradition, to remind the reader of eternal rather than immediate patterns, to insist on the fundamental kinships of the universe. The descriptive emphasis is on characterization, the special personality of these birds. But unlike the dog's "personality," which is conceived as his specifically animal nature, the character of the birds is at least analogically human: they "gossip," "troop," compose "domestic" tribes, are "conscious, and fearful," sensitive to the "fair occasion," capable of being "thievish." Winter, which increases the dependency of the animal kingdom on man, increases as a consequence human awareness of the links that bind all creation, so that analogies between the look of sheep and of snow, the nature of chickens and of the housewife who feeds them, or between sparrows and children (this barely suggested: but children too might under some circumstances be defined as a "pert voracious kind," although this was not the typical eighteenth-century view of them), take on true significance.

These three modes of "seeing" the panoramas which winter presents, with the dictions appropriate to each mode, suggest how functional Cowper's varieties of perspective and technique can prove. In the early descriptive section of Book V, the poet demonstrates the nature of that true perception which by the end of the book he will assert to be a product of man's right relationship with God. True perception does not depend on anything so simple as constant assertion of the connections between God and His creation, but it does involve completeness, wholeness of vision. Such wholeness is the sum of many parts, many incomplete visions; in this long descriptive portion of his poem, Cowper isolates and emphasizes various ways of seeing in a fashion that may prepare us to believe in the significance of their combination. His variations of technique reflect quite precisely the shifts in emphasis of his subject matter.

One cannot always believe that Cowper's diction conforms exactly to the meanings it is intended to convey. His verse seems dependably good when its content is descriptive, its subject that perception which Cowper found both emotionally and philosophically so important. Large portions of *The Task,* however, are moralistic rather than descriptive; nor does the moralizing always resolve itself, as in Book V, in terms of the poet's commitment to the value of perception. Book II, "The Time-Piece," for example, contains no extended treatment of the external world; it is entirely reflective. Although it includes sections of great vigor and poetic skill, it also displays Cowper at his worst — and his "worst" is characteristically his most rhetorical.

Considering two particularly weak passages, we may find it hard to understand why either of them should be poetry rather than prose. By Coleridge's well-known standard ("whatever lines can be translated into other words of the same language, without diminution of their significance, either in sense, or association, or in any worthy feeling, are so far vicious in their diction"),[36] most of these lines are excellent examples of "vicious diction," in spite of the fact that, with some exceptions, the diction does not call special attention to itself. In the first passage, Cowper considers the institution of preaching; the second deals with an individual exemplar of the institution. Both treatments may be the product of deep conviction, but it is not embodied in any way likely to move a reader. "Men love to be moved, much better than to be instructed," Joseph Warton pointed out; [37] Cowper's calculated rhetoric is only "instructive." Here are the passages:

> The pulpit, therefore (and I name it fill'd
> With solemn awe, that bids me well beware
> With what intent I touch that holy thing) —
> The pulpit (when the sat'rist has at last,
> Strutting and vap'ring in an empty school,
> Spent all his force and made no proselyte) —
> I say the pulpit (in the sober use
> Of its legitimate, peculiar pow'rs)
> Must stand acknowledged, while the world
>   shall stand,

Cowper: Heightened Perception

The most important and effectual guard,
Support, and ornament, of virtue's cause.

(ll. 326–336)

The second selection describes the bad pastor,

Perverting often, by the stress of lewd
And loose example, whom he should instruct;
[he] Exposes, and holds up to broad disgrace
The noblest function, and discredits much
The brightest truths that man has ever seen.
For ghostly counsel; if it either fall
Below the exigence, or be not back'd
With show of love, at least with hopeful proof
Of some sincerity on th' giver's part;
Or be dishonour'd, in th' exterior form
And mode of its conveyance, by such tricks
As move derision, or by foppish airs
And histrionic mumm'ry, that let down
The pulpit to the level of the stage;
Drops from the lips a disregarded thing.

(ll. 551–565)

The repeated, self-conscious parentheses of the first passage, the artifice of the reiterated phrase "the pulpit," which produces an inadvertent comic effect, the factitious-seeming indignation in the denunciation of the satirist, the padding in such phrases as "solemn awe" and "well beware," even the relatively skillful play on *stand* — all these contribute to one's sense that the poet as contriver has here superseded the poet as expresser of felt, perceived or imagined reality. The passage has almost the effect of parody. One believes in the existence of the felt reality, but not that Cowper is committed to it; his obvious concern with the proper mode of expression seems strangely isolated from what he has to say, seems not a concern for the best way to convey emotion or meaning so much as for the moral posture appropriate to a man of his convictions. In the second passage, the moral posture itself seems suspect: is "*show of love,*" with its conceivable implication of hypocrisy, really adequate for the "good" pastor? or is merely "hopeful proof/ Of some sincerity"? The poet concerns himself almost entirely with appearances, with what he himself calls "th' exterior form/ And mode of . . . conveyance" of divine truths; yet he appears to make a distinction between exterior forms and what he evidently considers inner reality — reality demonstrated by "show of love" of "proof/ Of some sincerity." In the actual concerns of the passage, then, form and content blur, and exterior forms assume disproportionate importance — just such importance as they seem to assume in the poetic rendering of the ideas, which itself has some aspect of "histrionic mumm'ry." The language of the passage, with the possible exception of the word *exigence,* is quite ordinary and straightforward; its structure, with its deliberate slowness and suspension, moving with measured pace toward the calculated anticlimax of "disregarded thing," seems anything but straightforward, and its contrived complexity reflects no corresponding complexity of thought.

One striking fact about the relatively weak moralistic sections of *The Task* is that they are so radically different in technique from the worst of Cowper's hymns. If the special talent manifested in the hymns is the ability to turn the perceptive faculty inward, to define and render directly certain sorts of psychic activity and psychic stasis without significant recourse to visual metaphor, the talent which created *The Task* seems adept at rending inner states by suggestion, through reference to and reliance on imagery of the external world. Conversely, the hymns at their worst depend most heavily on metaphor; *The Task,* whose central subject is concrete reality in its spiritual context, is at its worst often almost bare of imagery, lapsing into concern only with abstractions. There is a kind of metaphor (although a weak and sketchy one) in "ghostly counsel" dropping, a "disregarded thing"; aside from that, and the vague metaphoric possibilities of *touch* in line 328, *empty school* in line 330, the only metaphor in the two passages is "The brightest truth that man has ever seen," a reference characteristic of Cowper's conventional interest in light as an emblem of spiritual reality, but hardly more than a reference

But if these passages manifest little distinct visual awareness, they also demonstrate little psychic awareness. What "perception" they display seems theoretical ("philosophical," Cowper might say) rather than direct, the product of what the poet has been told, not what he has himself "seen." Cut off from his deepest sources of feeling, he produces impoverished language; the more barren sections of *The Task*, which by implication deny the validity of that very perception that the poem at its best strongly affirms, are boring. "Where the Idea is accurate, the terms will be so too; and wherever you find the words hobble, you may conclude the notion was lame; otherwise they wou'd both have had an equal and graceful pace." So wrote John Constable,[38] and his terms suggest an appropriate vocabulary to indict Cowper at his worst.

But Cowper also had at his disposal strikingly individual language. Trying to describe the writer characterized by "simplicity" (a term which in his usage as in Collins's has rather complex implications), Hugh Blair observes, "There are no marks of art in his expression; it seems the very language of nature; you see in the Style, not the writer and his labour, but the man, in his own natural character." [39] The distinction he makes is difficult to enforce, but it seems appropriate to one of Cowper's characteristic modes, a mode which defines his most personal ways of perceiving. "All we behold is miracle," Cowper points out, "but, seen/ So duly, all is miracle in vain" (VI, 132–133). The statement might serve as text for *The Task*, which at its best uncovers the miracle of the commonplace, sometimes employing a distinctive rhetoric to emphasize its revelations. Divine power operates "all in sight of inattentive man" (VI, 120); the poet's responsibility is to make man more attentive, so that his "sight" will be more significant. Man sees the dearth of winter; he should be conscious simultaneously of the richness it foretells.

> But let the months go by, a few short months,
> And all shall be restor'd. These naked shoots,
> Barren as lances, among which the wind
> Makes wintry music, sighing as it goes,
> Shall put their graceful foliage on again,
> And, more aspiring, and with ampler spread,
> Shall boast new charms, and more than they have lost.
>
> (VI, 140–146)

Both the lines about miracle and the first line of this description employ rhetorical repetition. Unlike the reiteration of "the pulpit" in the moralizing passage, this duplication is a device of progression rather than of suspension. It intensifies an atmosphere of calm assurance (defined particularly by the grand inclusiveness of "all shall be restor'd") instead of creating, like the other repetitive pattern, merely a sense of dogged determination. Now Cowper relies heavily on metaphoric suggestion, both the conventional associations of *aspiring* and *boast*, and a more complex and personal effect in the description of "naked shoots,/ Barren as lances." The defencelessness implied by *naked* is immediately denied when the nakedness becomes that of an aggressive weapon. But the implications of *lances* are in turn opposed by the further transformation of lances into musical instruments; and the fact that the music derives from the "sighing" of the wind adds a final degree of perceptual and emotional complexity. The beauty of winter is as real as that of spring, although it is beauty of an entirely different order. Nature embodies the Christian sequence of death and resurrection. The poem directs one's attention to the beauties of winter as well as those of spring, to the beauty of apparent death and that of rebirth, reinforcing the aesthetic contrast by the opposition between the conventional language of personalization applied to spring and the more direct, personal language through which winter is evoked.

This passage continues with one of the catalogues so characteristic of Cowper, introduced by a generalization couched entirely in "poetic diction," in a form which reminds one of the associations of that diction with the language of science.

> Then, each in its peculiar honours clad,
> Shall publish, even to the distant eye,
> Its family and tribe. Laburnum, rich
> In streaming gold; syringa, iv'ry pure;
> The scentless and the scented rose; this red
> And of an humbler growth, the other tall,
> And throwing up into the darkest gloom
> Of neighb'ring cypress, or more sable yew,
> Her silver globes, light as the foamy surf
> That the wind severs from the broken wave;
> The lilac, various in array, now white,
> Now sanguine, and her beauteous head now set
> With purple spikes pyramidal, as if,
> Studious of ornament, yet unresolv'd
> Which hue she most approv'd, she chose
>   them all . . .
>
> (VI, 147–161)

This is slightly less than half the full catalogue, but it suggests the technique and quality of the whole. The imagined conjunction of flowers is complexly perceived, with reference to form (*streaming, globes, pyramidal*), color, balance and contrast ("The scentless and the scented rose," tall and short, dark and light, white and purple), and metaphor. Metaphors of richness (*gold, iv'ry, silver, ornament*) dominate the scene, and two key images insist on relationships among the parts of the created universe: the emphatic association of the "silver globes" of the rose with the bits of surf "severed" from the wave, and the description of the lilac as a human belle.

The powerful effect of this catalogue depends heavily on the relationship between the directness of the diction (only *sable, sanguine*, possibly *beauteous* and *gloom*, have predominantly poetic associations; the adjectives and nouns which carry the weight of the description are on the whole precise and limited in their individual meanings) and the elaboration of the picture and meaning created by the simple language. As Cowper saw in the naked branches of winter a rapidly shifting range of meanings, he perceives in a static panorama of spring and summer flowers so many sorts of meaning and relationship — visual and "philosophic" — that his presentation of the scene pulses with energy. The source of that energy, and its significance, become explicit at the end:

> From dearth to plenty, and from death to life,
> Is Nature's progress when she lectures man
> In heav'nly truth; evincing, as she makes
> The grand transition, that there lives and works
> A soul in all things, and that soul is God.
> The beauties of the wilderness are his,
> That makes so gay the solitary place
> Where no eye sees them.
>
> (VI, 181–188)

The "lecture" nature offers is the revelation that there is no separation, finally, between the visual glory (or, for that matter, the visual barrenness) of the natural world and its theological meaning. The vibrant "soul in all things" need only be recognized; perception of its energy is part of Cowper's direct relation-seeking poetic perception of the imagined scene itself. The force of that perception, expressed through unpretentious but intricately organized language, leads the poet finally to the realization that meaning and beauty are inherent in the natural world independently of the perceiver — "Where no eye sees them." The perceiver, even at the beginning of this passage, is only a "distant eye"; the splendor of the scene does not depend on human perception. In this pageant of inanimate nature, the vegetative world finally embodies full richness, dignity, even hints of eroticism ("her beauteous head"). God's plenty is here; religious, aesthetic, emotional meaning fuse. The greatest achievement of *The Task* (not only here; in other passages as well) is this fusion. In the hymns, Cowper conveyed his fear that man must move inevitably from an infantile state of pure dependence and complete comfort to an anguished awareness of conflict and the loss of peace, comfort. Elsewhere in *The Task*, he reminds us that the eye is "guiltless": no blame can attach to aesthetic contemplation; passivity is associated with lack of vice. In the flower passage, contemplation is not merely guiltless; it becomes essentially an act of worship, of such total worship that it involves the poet's entire sensibility — his desire for peace, for beauty, for piety; his emotional and religious yearnings, his intellectual convictions. The act of visual perception has finally become fully inclusive as it leads Cowper back to his ideal state of faith and ease.

IX 🌺

THE ACHIEVED IMAGE

For *Wit* and *Judgment* often are at strife,
Tho' meant each other's Aid, like *Man* and *Wife*.
(Pope, *An Essay on Criticism,* ll. 82–83)

The meanings of *wit* in the young Pope's critical scheme have been the subject of a good deal of intelligent and ingenious investigation. It is safe to say that those meanings are multiform and vital to the import of *An Essay on Criticism*; and that at least one of them — the one most relevant to the couplet quoted above — is close to what might also have been called *fancy*,[1] close even to some modern senses of *imagination*.

Wit was not to Pope merely a quality opposed to judgment. The couplet immediately before the one quoted has long been a critical crux:

Some, to whom Heav'n in Wit has been profuse,
Want as much more, to turn it to its use.

Dennis, assuming that Pope here expressed a characteristic sort of confusion, observed scornfully that of course the poet meant to say that some have wit without the judgment to manage it. But this is clearly not what Pope meant at all; through his revision of the *Essay* he carefully preserved the equivocal quality of his couplet. As Aubrey Williams points out, "Wit thus becomes not only a faculty which provides quickness of insight and liveliness of expression, but also a controlling and ordering faculty. Wit and Judgment seem to be, on this crucial occasion in the poem, differing aspects of the same faculty."[2]

That Pope was capable of understanding wit in this way may be taken as one index to the magnitude of his poetic accomplishment. Certainly in his best poetry one feels no division between invention and control: the discipline of his couplets participates in their imaginative power; the functional brilliance of his images is as striking as their sheer inventiveness. But his capacity to perceive wit and judgment as aspects of a single faculty and to employ them as such was a rare one. *Fancy* became a more fashionable term than *wit* after Pope's time, but the relation between fancy and judgment, too, seemed more often one of strife than of harmony or symbiosis. The conflict between fancy and judgment is, for example, a recurrent theme, explicitly or implicitly, in Collins's series of poems on poetry.

In the ode "To Pity," the vocabulary reflects the poet's dilemma about the relation of "Thought," "Art," "Fancy," and "Passion" or feeling. The second stanza of the poem, which ends with the famous personification of Pity in her "sky-worn Robes," opens,

> By *Pella's* Bard, a magic Name,
> By all the Griefs his Thought could frame,
> Receive my humble Rite.

Euripides is to be honored, almost worshipped, because he could frame by *thought* — intellectual power — the griefs which might interest the viewer of his tragedies. On the other hand, stanza four praises Otway because his singing of the female heart was "unspoil'd by Art." Pity is urged, in the next stanza, to come "by Fancy's Aid"; her temple, through its "Truth compleat," will "raise a wild Enthusiast Heat" in all who see it. Finally, the poet himself begs to retire to that temple, where he can "In Dreams of Passion melt away" (l. 38).

On the one hand, then, pity is a dramatist's asset, to be achieved through the exercise of thought, fancy, art. But it also represents a genuine power, as the personification makes clear; it is an emotion to be felt, not spoiled by art (*art* meaning, of course, something more like *artfulness*), a source even of passion and "enthusiasm." The poet finally anticipates that mere *dreams* of feeling will produce his song: he would remain in Pity's temple until she again delights "To hear a *British* Shell," presumably his own. The relation between the opposed conceptions is hardly coherent; the unexamined contradictions of outlook weaken the poem.

The Achieved Image

The "Ode to Fear," on the other hand, which relies heavily on similar contradictions, emphasizes the oppositions, insists on dual truths, and in the conclusion resolves paradox, at least implicitly. It demonstrates the poet's awareness of the conflict between the conception of fear as a genuine and powerful emotion and as a poetic and dramatic resource. The dangers of fear as emotion are as fully realized as its values for the poet; the structure of the poem largely depends upon the alternation and development of the opposed concepts of fear. Gradually fear is more and more strongly associated with imagination, for which it can provide a metaphor because its attributes are in many respects identical to those of imagination: both forces are irrational, actively opposed to reason (in Collins's conception); both provide revelation; both are similarly dangerous to their possessors, in encouraging separation from objective reality. Yet the truth of fear's revelations must be accepted; the willing suspension of disbelief is more vital for the poet than for the reader. At the beginning of the poem Fear gazes "appal'd" at an "unreal Scene"; by its end, such unreality has been perceived as incorporating a higher reality, and Fear is precisely equivalent to poetic "enthusiasm," that mysterious power which can possess the poet like a god.

> O Thou whose Spirit most possest
> The sacred Seat of *Shakespear's* Breast!
> By all that from thy Prophet broke,
> In thy Divine Emotions spoke:
> Hither again thy Fury deal,
> Teach me but once like Him to feel . . .
>
> (ll. 64–69)

The need for restraint, for the mature judgment which may control the divine madness of the poet, seems by now to have vanished from the speaker's consciousness — not by simple abandonment, but by transcendence as well. Judgment — a quality never named in this ode but an implicit focus of discussion — keeps the poet in firm contact with reality. The need for it largely disappears with the recognition that the revelations of fear, associated strongly with imagination, may put one in touch with a realm of higher reality, a region offering perceptions more profoundly and fundamentally "true" than those from the world of objective fact. As Pope arrogated to wit the qualities of judgment, so Collins here suggests that strong emotion as well as intellect may provide insight. Yet since insight seems finally the only real good of the poem, he also rejects by implication many of the other values associated with the intellectual. His fusion is by no means so complete as Pope's: the principle of control is, finally, simply not admitted as a fundamental value.

In "To Simplicity," the next in the collection of odes, the problem of control reappears. This ode raises fairly directly the question of how far imagination is to be trusted, how vital is the principle of control; it makes an unsuccessful effort to suggest the superior importance of discipline. Its tone of uncertainty is indicated by the genealogy attributed to Fancy in the first stanza: she is the child either of Simplicity or Pleasure, and the poet never decides which. His doubtfulness about the sources of poetic invention is here Collins's central problem, although he does not appear to recognize it as such. Stanza 8 expresses the confusion at greater length:

> Tho' Taste, tho' Genius bless,
> To some divine Excess,
> Faints the cold Work till Thou inspire the whole . . .

It is difficult to imagine a work blessed by genius to the point of "divine Excess," yet still "cold," and to be *warmed* by the control of simplicity, which seems to imply a sort of artful "naturalness." Indeed, in the next, concluding stanza, Collins tacitly grants that Simplicity is, after all, a sort of second-class power:

> Of These [Taste and Genius] let others ask,
> To aid some mighty Task,
> I only seek to find thy temp'rate Vale . . .

Others may do the great work of poetry; Collins will settle for pastoral piping, but not without recognizing that more significant achievement is possible.

If this poem represents a partial retreat from the position reached in the conclusion of "To Fear," "Ode on the Poetical Character" returns, of course, to a somewhat despairing faith in "enthusiasm." The paradox there asserted might have developed from the implications of "To Fear": poetry is a high achievement, founded in imagination, essentially divine in origin — it must therefore be impossible. Once, to be sure, it existed: perhaps Spenser was a true poet; certainly Milton was the very type of the inspired singer. And the idea of poetry exists: all the more reason to despair. Contemplating the image of Milton, in the antistrophe, Collins concludes unequivocally that there can be no more poets. Such a conclusion, of course, is not to be taken with undue seriousness; the act of writing an ode is itself an assertion of poetic aspiration. But it suggests the intensity with which Collins felt his dilemma: recognizing the value of imagination and its dangers he could not fully commit himself to it; respecting the idea of discipline, he could rarely reconcile it with imagination; temporarily his faith in poetry becomes the cry, *Certum est quia impossibile est.*

Poetry is impossible only if one believes the alternate views of its sources to be mutually exclusive. In some of Collins's best poetry he succeeds in incorporating dual viewpoints, with full recognition of the value of each. Merle E. Brown has demonstrated the coexistence of principles of chaos and control, simplicity and artifice, in the "Ode to Evening"; [3] the famous short ode "Written in the Beginning of the Year 1746" asserts on the one hand that truth, the truth of the soldiers' honorable death, is sweeter than fancy could possibly be, while simultaneously it creates a highly fanciful parade of mourners to glorify these soldiers. The triumph of Collins's sense of duality is the incomplete and imperfect "Ode on the Popular Superstitions of the Highlands of Scotland," which in basic conception and in execution depends heavily on awareness of paradox and contradiction, and of the interest and value of such oppositions. The central paradox of the ode is that while it insists on the special privileges of the Highland poet, it simultaneously demonstrates that these are really the privileges of all poets, that imagination provides its own romantic environment. At the end of the poem, as at the end of the "Ode on Fear," Collins suggests that scenes which depart from "sober truth, are still to nature true," that imaginative insight is for poetic purposes superior to more prosaic clear-sightedness. This is the message of "To Fear," but it is not the complete message of the "Popular Superstitions" ode; the total setting qualifies it.

It is significant that this ode should be so much the most suc-

cessful of Collins's longer poems (compare, for example, the confusion of "The Passions"), and among the most satisfactory pieces
he wrote, for it represents a genuine solution to his dilemma. On
the one hand, in it he can assert, more emphatically than ever
before, total commitment to the values of the imagination. He
postulates a realm where imaginative values are of paramount
importance, where fairies are believed in, where the heroic past
is kept alive and the supernatural associations of death make death
as vivid as life. Or he imagines an environment where poetic justice
really reigns and bliss is the immediate reward of virtue; he
recreates imaginatively and closer to the heart's desire an island
life he has only read of. Having established such images, he can
even insist that imagination is more important than truth, that it
provides a higher truth. On the other hand, he contains this
imaginative creation within a highly conventional framework of
praise and admonition. The first and last stanzas of the ode are
conventional in language and structure. Despite their slight awkwardness, they protect Collins from the dangers of too total in-
volvement in the potential chaos of his conception of the imagination; they provide the context of discipline he so badly needed.

Obviously it would be virtually impossible — certainly virtually
impossible in the eighteenth century, before the principle of free
association had taken on full psychological authority — for anyone to write poetry entirely the product of uncontrolled imagination: the act of writing implies the principle of control. The poems
in which Collins manifests his clearest sense of the need for imagination to be somehow disciplined to the claims of reality ("Popular Superstitions," "To Fear" — where, to be sure, the notion
of reality itself changes; but reality remains very much an issue
of the poem), or in which he demonstrates in practice the vital
coexistence of fancy and judgment as principles ("To Evening,"
"How Sleep the Brave") seem today his most successful accomplishments. *Fancy* and *judgment* are slippery critical terms, and they
designate kinds of creative cause, not kinds of effect: it would be a
futile exercise for the modern critic to attempt to determine what
part of Thomson's work, say, is the product of fancy, what of judgment. Yet the dichotomy between the two may help, finally, to make
some useful distinctions between the achievements of these poets

which seem strongest to twentieth-century sensibility and those which seem relatively weak.

One is likely to feel, in the weakest eighteenth-century poetry, some crucial division, a separation of principles that should be united, The nature of this separation varies: of Collins at his worst it may be said that he lacks discipline, coherence; of Gray at his worst that he has entirely too much discipline, lacks vitality. It is often urged, of "bad" eighteenth-century poetry, that it is written merely to the prescription of convention. *Merely* is the operative word: convention also controls much of the best poetry of the period, but one feels in such poetry the presence of an original impulse as well. Sometimes, though, the original impulse seems conspicuously lacking. Thomson, for example, praises great men, operating in an established mode:

> he, the last of old Lycurgus' sons,
> The generous victim to that vain attempt
> To save a rotten state — Agis, who saw
> Even Sparta's self to servile avarice sunk.
> The two Achaian heroes close the train —
> Aratus, who a while relumed the soul
> Of fondly lingering liberty in Greece;
> And he, her darling, as her latest hope,
> The gallant Philopoemen, who to arms
> Turned the luxurious pomp he could not cure,
> Or toiling in his farm, a simple swain,
> Or bold and skilful thundering in the field.
> ("Winter," ll. 486–497)

However intense Thomson's actual admiration for Agis and Philopoemen may have been, it is easy to dismiss these lines, and the long passage from which they come, as a set-piece of the most automatic sort. This is not to deny them all poetic virtue: they are fairly economical; they manifest a rudimentary sense of paradox (in the figure of the hero who alternates the roles of simple swain and bold warrior). Yet they remain unconvincing, dead, and it seems strange that a man who can make plausible poetry out of the theory that frost operates by hooked salts should fail to make his awe of great men at least equally compelling.

One reason it is not more compelling is that it relies heavily on moral counter-language to evoke an automatic response. On the one hand we contemplate a "rotten state," "servile avarice," "luxurious pomp"; on the other, men who are "generous," "gallant," "bold and skilful," "toiling," even, with all sorts of positive connotations, "simple." The moral judgments are asserted, not argued. There is no need to argue them: they are perfectly obvious. The poet provides no fresh perception of the meaning or relevance of his heroes' virtues, and the absence of fresh perception is crucial. This, after all, is what we demand of poetry: that it make us see, understand, anew. Thomson is, as we have seen, capable of providing genuine poetic revelation, but in passages of a very different sort from this one.

If one considers fancy and judgment opposed powers, this passage may be taken to be largely a product of judgment. Meaning is more important than "ornament" to its effect. Such images as "rotten state" and "relumed the soul" are virtually dead metaphor; they have no power to ramify meanings. Nor do they have the subterranean emotional force so characteristic of Thomson at his strongest. When Thomson describes a snowstorm or the state of farm animals in midsummer, when he reflects on the nature of frost or the source of rivers, even, on occasion, when he attempts an imaginative recreation of life in the tropics, one feels how deeply his vision of fruitful, ordered nature and of man's relation to it possesses him. The "something new" he offers is not freshness of descriptive detail or strongly individual imagery; it is the totality of a vision, an emotionally grasped sense of universal meaning. At his highest moments, when the imagery produced by fancy is the perfectly appropriate vehicle for the meanings which judgment creates, his verse seems to result from a fusion of intellect and emotion — in short, from a "unified sensibility."

Yvor Winters long ago pointed out that "The reasoning of the Age of Reason was very largely directed toward the destruction of the authority of Reason." He comments that "the nineteenth century judgment, which still prevails, of eighteenth century poetry, [was] that it is bad because too intellectual, whereas in reality eighteenth century poetry is commonly good and is often great but displays defects which are primarily due to intellectual deficiency." [4] Donald Greene, in his important examination of the "logical structure" of eighteenth-century poetry, shares the view that this poetry is rather too little than too much dominated by intellect.[5] Unlike Mr. Greene, who does not explicitly consider this aspect of the problem, Mr. Winters also seems to question the validity of the expressed emotion in such poets as those treated in this study. He uses *The Seasons* as an example of the kind of poetry in which "there is no attempt . . . to communicate any feeling save the author's interest in visible beauties" (p. 49). Collins's "Ode to Evening," he argues, displays "a melancholy which at moments, as in the description of the bat, verges on disorder, and which at all times is far too profound to arise from an evening landscape alone. . . . A symbol is used to embody a feeling neither relevant to the symbol nor relevant to anything else of which the poet is conscious: the poet expresses his feeling as best he is able without understanding it" (p. 50). Although Mr. Winters calls Collins "one of the best" romantic poets, he believes him to provide many examples of "pseudo-reference," a major poetic fault.

Such views support Mr. Eliot's conviction that the "unified sensibility" had vanished from English poetry by the eighteenth century. His famous formulation of the theory of unified sensibility attributes this virtue almost exclusively to the poets of the early seventeenth century. His description of Donne is well-known: "A thought to Donne was an experience; it modified his sensibility. When a poet's mind is perfectly equipped for its work, it is constantly amalgamating disparate experience; the ordinary man's experience is chaotic, irregular, fragmentary." [6] The second sentence is particularly illuminating, for it implies that the unification of sensibility is characteristic of all good poets. But Mr. Eliot goes on, "The sentimental age began early in the eighteenth century, and continued. The poets revolted against the ratiocinative, the descriptive; they thought and felt by fits, unbalanced; they reflected" (p. 288). This has long been a widely accepted view of eighteenth-century poetry: that poets like Thomson and Cowper alternately feel and think, poets like Smart and Collins feel to the exclusion of thinking, poets like Gray think rather too much — although not too well — but sometimes employ the Thomsonian technique of alternation.

Mr. Greene is unquestionably right in his contention that the structure of eighteenth-century poetry is not controlled by logic.

The Poetry of Vision

He provides — although not precisely for the purpose I am turning it to — a description by W. H. Auden of nineteenth-century romantic poetry which defines with surprising accuracy the achievement of such poets as Thomson and Collins and Cowper. "A poem that attempts to follow the motions of consciousness," writes Mr. Auden, "will have to organize itself into a whole in ways which consciousness itself suggests, not as logic dictates." [7] What Mr. Greene calls "the frank impressionism of *The Seasons* and *The Task*" (p. 334) provides exactly such a mode of organization; the characteristic development of Collins's odes, in all their chaos — even, often, of Gray's more highly disciplined presentations — is profoundly responsive to the "motions of consciousness"; and of course *Jubilate Agno* is primarily a record of psychic patterns. (*A Song to David,* on the other hand, as Mr. Greene points out, is more logically organized than most of Pope's verse.)

But to say that these poets on the whole do not depend on logic is not to say that they lack ideas. All five of the figures considered in this study turned away from the secular, urban orientation of the great satirists to concentrate more heavily on the values of nature and of contemplation, and of the personal as opposed to the social functions of poetry. Pope, in some of his greatest poems, displayed an essentially religious passion of belief in the moral responsibility and dignity of the poet; his central ideas about poetry fused with his most intense feelings about social decay and possibility, producing verse of enormous energy and conviction. The "ideas" which dominated Thomson, Smart, Collins, Cowper were perhaps vaguer, but they remain ideas: about the relation of nature to God, say, or about the importance of the imagination. Thomson and Cowper were not merely impressionistic; I have tried to demonstrate how much the unity of *The Seasons* and *The Task,* like that of the more tightly organized *Song to David,* depends upon a few central ideas which control the selectivity of the poems.

The way in which these poets think is not on the whole impressive: they often lack full coherence; they do not respond completely to the pressure of ideas. One can hardly claim that any of them could stand beside John Donne. The matters they think about, although frequently important, do not have for us the weight and immediacy of Donne's concerns, and they do not seem capable, like Donne, of following out the implications of an idea. Yet one way to define the magnitude of their greatest achievement is to describe it as the product of unified sensibility. Certainly the distinction between Thomson at his flattest and at his richest in *The Seasons* has to do with the divergent effects of poetry which seems almost dutiful in its plodding presentation of ideas, and poetry in which idea and emotion participate in one another. In Cowper, too, the most impressive descriptions — the only really impressive ones — are those which express in their very selectivity the poet's dominant ideas about the significance of nature in the life of man or the relation between nature and art. The power of Smart's great religious poetry derives only secondarily from the brilliant clarity of the universe he describes; primarily it is the product of a complicated idea about the unity of outer and inner experience, the extent to which man's exploration of himself illuminates for him the world he lives in and the God he serves, and to which contemplation of God or of the world reflects back on his knowledge of himself.

It is true that in all three cases the range of ideas expressed or implied is limited; it may be added that one feels — least in Smart, most perhaps in Thomson — that these are poets of limited, if often unified, sensibility. They do not, like Donne, explore ideas; they simply possess them, or are possessed by them. Even Gray, who had the reputation in his own time of being the most learned man in Europe, does not display in his poetry any intellectual sophistication, any capacity to deal with or incorporate new ideas. And the limitation in the number of things these poets think about corresponds to a limitation in the number of things about which they feel profoundly. Within these limitations their achievement is impressive: not merely didactic or sentimental verse, not merely imitation of established models or the romantic outpourings of a madman, but poetry both disciplined and expressive; feeling informed by and merged with thought.

In the task of expression for these poets, imagery — both that of metaphor and that of description — plays a central role. It may, as for Gray, be used to establish patterns of conflict; or, as for Smart, to delineate a world of exotic yet familiar beauty. Its functions are, as I have tried to demonstrate, various and complex. The "visual" and the "visionary," as these words have been used here, afford a key to the modes of emphasis in the poetry described. But for all these poets, the achieved image is a unifying instrument of subtlety and power, expressing meanings often more profound and intricate than those professed, making the poetry of the middle and late eighteenth century at its best as fully worthy of extended critical attention as much that preceded and followed it.

Notes

Index

Notes

Chapter One. VISION AND MEANING:
An Introduction to the Problem

1. For treatment of various aspects of the connection between sight and aesthetic theory, see M. H. Abrams, *The Mirror and the Lamp: Romantic Theory and the Critical Tradition* (New York: Norton, 1958); Jean Hagstrum, *The Sister Arts: The Tradition of Literary Pictorialism and English Poetry from Dryden to Gray* (Chicago: University of Chicago Press, 1958); Kenneth MacLean, *John Locke and English Literature of the Eighteenth Century* (New Haven: Yale University Press, 1936); Gordon McKenzie, *Critical Responsiveness: A Study of the Psychological Current in Later Eighteenth-Century Criticism* (Berkeley: University of California Press, 1949); Ernest Lee Tuveson, *The Imagination As a Means of Grace: Locke and the Aesthetics of Romanticism* (Berkeley: University of California Press, 1960); A. S. P. Woodhouse, "The Poetry of Collins Reconsidered," *From Sensibility to Romanticism,* ed. F. W. Hilles and Harold Bloom (New York: Oxford University Press, 1965), pp. 93–137. Marjorie Nicolson, in *Newton Demands the Muse* (Princeton: Princeton University Press, 1946), documents the importance for poetry of Newton's theories of vision. In the light of the work that has been done already, I shall suggest only sketchily the extent of the various critical utterances about sight as it relates to poetic theory and practice.

2. Tuveson, *Imagination As a Means of Grace,* pp. 72–73.

3. In Abrams, *The Mirror and the Lamp,* passim.

4. Blair adds that the inferior sort of writer is vague in his descriptions: "we apprehend the object described very indistinctly. Whereas, a true Poet makes us imagine that we see it before our eyes; he catches the distinguishing features; he gives it the colours of life and reality; he places it in such a light, that a Painter could copy after him." Both quotations come from *Lectures on Rhetoric and Belles Lettres,* 2 vols. (Dublin, 1783), II, 371.

5. Richard Hurd, *Letters on Chivalry and Romance, with the Third Elizabethan Dialogue,* ed. Edith J. Morley (London: Henry Frowde, 1911), p. 138; pp. 135–136.

6. For Joseph Warton's statement of this view see above, pp. 14–15.

7. Robert Andrews, "A Hint to British Poets," *Eidyllia* (Edinburgh, 1757), p. 4; quoted by Ralph Cohen, *The Art of Discrimination: Thomson's* The Seasons *and the Language of Criticism* (Berkeley: University of California Press, 1964), p. 164.

8. "There is nothing like our ideas existing in the bodies themselves. They are, in the bodies we denominate from them, only a power to produce those sensations in us." *An Essay Concerning Human Understanding,* ed. Alexander Campbell Fraser, 2 vols. (Oxford, 1894), I, 173.

9. Ibid., I, 203.

10. *Spectator* #62 (11 May 1711); *The Spectator*, with introduction and notes by George A. Aitken, 8 vols. (London, 1898), I, 320.

11. "Our sight is the most perfect and most delightful of all our senses. . . . It is this sense which furnishes the imagination with its ideas; so that by the pleasures of the imagination or fancy (which I shall use promiscuously) I here mean such as arise from visible objects, either when we have them actually in our view, or when we call up their ideas into our minds. . . . We cannot indeed have a single image in the fancy that did not make its first entrance through the sight; but we have the power of retaining, altering and compounding those images which we have once received into all the varieties of picture and vision that are most agreeable to the imagination." *Spectator* #411 (21 June 1712); VI, 72-73. Although Addison here closely paraphrases Locke, he does not directly compare the pleasures of the imagination to those of the judgment, so does not suggest that they are inferior. The *value* of close imaginative approximations of actuality, as opposed to the more fantastic creations of the fancy, yet remained to be discussed.

12. "Words, when well chosen, have so great a force in them, that a description often gives us more lively ideas than the sight of things themselves. . . . As we look on any object our idea of it is, perhaps, made up of two or three simple ideas; but when the poet represents it, he may either give us a more complex idea of it, or only raise in us such ideas as are most apt to affect the imagination." *Spectator* #416 (27 June 1712); VI, 100-101.

13. The view that the poet was an almost divine creator was current in the sixteenth century. George Puttenham's comparison of the poet to God is well-known: "A Poet is as much to say as a maker . . . Such as (by way of resemblance and reuerently) we may say of God: who without any truell to his diuine imagination, made all the world of nought, nor also by any paterne or mould as the Platonicks with their Idees do phantastically suppose. Euen so the very Poet makes and contriues out of his owne braine both the verse and matter of his poeme, and not by any foreine copie or example." Puttenham goes on to point out that the poet may also be justly termed an imitator, "because he can express the true and liuely of euery thing is set before him, and which he taketh in hand to describe," but there is no doubt which of his functions is more important. See *The Art of English Poesie* (London, 1589), p. 1. J. C. Scaliger makes a similar point, emphasizing the superiority of poetry to those arts which involve merely accurate representation. Poetry, he says, is all-inclusive, "excelling those other arts, that while they . . . represent things just as they are, in some sense like a speaking picture, the poet depicts quite another sort of nature, and a variety of fortunes; in fact, by so doing, he transforms himself almost into a second deity." See Marvin T. Herrick, "The Place of Rhetoric in Poetic Theory," *The Quarterly Journal of Speech*, XXXIV (1948), 5. Francis Bacon points out that the special function of poetry is to remake the world closer to the heart's desire: "POESIE is a part of Learning in measure of words for the most part restrained: but in all other points extremely licensed: and doth truly referre to the Imagination: which beeing not tyed to the Lawes of Matter; may at pleasure ioyne that which Nature hath seuered: & seuer that which Nature hath ioyned. . . . The vse of this FAINED HISTORIE, hath

beene to giue some shadowe of satisfaction to the minde of Man in those points, wherein the Nature of things doth denie it, the world being in proportion inferiour to the soule: by reason whereof there is agreeable to the spirit of Man, a more ample Greatnesse, a more exact Goodnesse; and a more absolute varietie than can bee found in the Nature of things." See *Of the Proficience and Aduancement of Learning, Diuine and Humane* (London, 1605), Bk. II, fol. 17v.

These sixteenth- and seventeenth-century statements rest on the assumption that the "enlarging" vision, creator of a sort of super-reality more closely related to the supernatural than to the natural, is vital poetic equipment; the vision which simply provides a record of reality is, from this point of view, far less significant. Such assumptions did not disappear in the eighteenth century, although they might coexist with apparently contradictory ones. Professor Abrams explains how the idea of pleasure as the proper purpose of poetry involved awareness of the need to go beyond imitation. The result was that figurative language achieved great importance as a poetic device. "Certain kinds of deviation from literal language came to be treated, not as ornaments, or veiled reflections of truth, but as instances of the poetic creation of another world, peopled with its own manner of non-empirical beings." *Mirror and the Lamp*, p. 288.

14. *Spectator* #421 (3 July 1712); VI, 122.

15. *Spectator* #418 (30 June 1712); VI, 110.

16. Edmund Burke, "Introduction on Taste," *A Philosophical Enquiry into the Origin of Our Ideas of the Sublime and Beautiful*, ed. J. T. Boulton (London: Routledge and Kegan Paul, 1958), p. 16.

17. William Duff, *An Essay on Original Genius* (London, 1767), p. 6.

18. Later Duff defines explicitly the role of the *poet's* imagination: "A Poet . . . who is possessed of original Genius, feels in the strongest manner every impression made upon the mind, by the influence of external objects on the sense, or by reflection on those ideas which are treasured up in the repository of the memory, and is consequently qualified to express the vivacity and strength of his own feelings. If we suppose a person endued with this quality to describe real objects and scenes, such as are either immediately present to his senses, or recent in his remembrance; he will paint them in such vivid colours, and with so many picturesque circumstances, as to convey the same lively and fervid ideas to the mind of the Reader, which possessed and filled the imagination of the Author. If we suppose him to describe unreal objects or scenes, such as exist not in nature, but may be supposed to exist, he will present to us a succession of them equally various and wonderful, the mere creation of his own fancy; and by the strength of his representation, will give to an illusion all the force and efficacy of a reality." Pp. 159–160.

19. Bishop Lowth, for example, points out that the poet who is moved by an experience or an appearance necessarily transforms it in describing it. "The mind, with whatever passion it be agitated, remains fixed upon the object that excited it; and while it is earnest to display it, is not satisfied with a plain and exact description; but adopts one agreeable to its own sensations, splendid or gloomy, jocund or unpleasant. For the passions are naturally inclined to amplification; they wonderfully magnify and exaggerate whatever

dwells upon the mind, and labour to express it in animated, bold, and magnificent terms." Robert Lowth, *Lectures on the Sacred Poetry of the Hebrews*, tr. G. Gregory, 2 vols. (London, 1787), I, 309. (First published, in Latin, 1753).

20. "A Retrospect," *Literary Essays of Ezra Pound*, ed. T. S. Eliot (London: Faber and Faber, 1954), p. 4.

21. Thomas Sprat, *The History of the Royal-Society of London, for the Improving of Natural Knowledge* (London, 1667), p. 112.

22. "Ever since the Fall of ADAM, Men's Thoughts have been so low and grovelling, that they are unattentive to moral Truths; and can scarce conceive any thing but what affects their Senses. In this consists the Degeneracy of human Nature. People grow soon weary of Contemplation: Intellectual Idea's do not strike their Imagination: so that we must use sensible and familiar Images to support their Attention, and convey abstracted Truths to their Minds." François de Salignac de la Mothe Fénelon, *Dialogues Concerning Eloquence*, tr. William Stevenson (London, 1722), p. 80. John Dennis offered a slightly different justification for poetic emphasis on visual imagery, maintaining that the sense of sight "is a sence that the Poet ought chiefly to entertain; because it contributes more than any other to the exciting of strong Passion." *The Advancement and Reformation of Modern Poetry* (London, 1701), p. 186.

23. Samuel Taylor Coleridge, *Biographia Literaria; or Biographical Sketches of My Literary Life and Opinions*, 2 vols. (London, 1817), 17–18.

24. Hobbes's Answer to Davenant's Preface to "Gondibert," *Critical Essays of the Seventeenth Century*, ed. J. E. Spingarn, 3 vols. (Oxford: Oxford University Press, 1908–09), II, 59.

Chapter Two. JAMES THOMSON: *The Dominance of Meaning*

1. *Spectator* #414 (25 June 1712); *The Spectator*, with introduction and notes by George A. Aitken, 8 vols. (London, 1898), I, 320.

2. Preface to "Winter" (1726), *The Complete Poetical Works of James Thomson*, ed. J. Logie Robertson (London: Oxford University Press, 1961), pp. 240–241.

3. The history of attitudes toward *The Seasons* has recently been valuably documented by Ralph Cohen in *The Art of Discrimination: Thomson's* The Seasons *and the Language of Criticism* (Berkeley: University of California Press, 1964).

4. John Aikin, *An Essay on the Application of Natural History to Poetry* (Warrington, 1777), p. 57.

5. François de Salignac de la Mothe Fénelon, *Dialogues Concerning Eloquence*, tr. William Stevenson (London, 1722), p. 129.

6. John Scott, *Critical Essays on Some of the Poems of Several English Poets* (London, 1785), p. 315.

7. Warton, *An Essay on the Genius and Writings of Pope*, I, 3rd ed. (London, 1772), 47. [First ed. 1756.]

8. James Thomson, *The Seasons*, with "A Critical Essay on The Seasons" by Robert Heron [John Pinkerton] (Perth, 1793), p. 9.

9. John Holmes, *The Art of Rhetoric Made Easy*, 2nd ed. (London, 1755), p. 55. [First ed. 1739.]

10. See William Hazlitt, *Lectures on the English Poets* (London, 1818), pp. 171–172; Léon Morel, *James Thomson: Sa Vie et Ses Oeuvres* (Paris, 1895), p. 313.

11. Pinkerton, "A Critical Essay," p. 39.

12. W. Lamplough Doughty, "The Place of James Thomson in the Poetry of Nature," *The London Quarterly and Holborn Review*, CLXXIV (1949), 156; A. S. P. Woodhouse, "Collins and the Creative Imagination," *Studies in English by Members of University College, Toronto* (Toronto: University of Toronto Press, 1931), p. 84.

13. To George Dodington, 24 October 1730, *James Thomson (1700–1748) Letters and Documents*, ed. Alan Dugald McKillop (Lawrence, Kansas: University of Kansas Press, 1958), pp. 73–74.

14. Martin Price, *To the Palace of Wisdom: Studies in Order and Energy from Dryden to Blake* (Garden City: Doubleday, 1964), p. 356.

15. Josephine Miles, *Renaissance, Eighteenth-Century and Modern Language in English Poetry* (Berkeley: University of California Press, 1960), p. 22.

16. Reuben Brower, *The Fields of Light: An Experiment in Critical Reading* (New York: Oxford University Press, 1962), p. 37.

17. Morel, *James Thomson*, p. 321.

18. W. K. Wimsatt, "The Structure of Romantic Nature Imagery," *The Age of Johnson: Essays Presented to Chauncey Brewster Tinker* (New Haven: Yale University Press, 1949), p. 298.

19. Mark Akenside, *The Pleasures of Imagination* (London, 1744), Book I, ll. 446–475; pp. 34–35.

20. Ibid., Book I, ll. 503–504; p. 37.

21. Ibid., Book II, ll. 84–135; pp. 50–53.

22. Hagstrum, *The Sister Arts: The Tradition of Literary Pictorialism and English Poetry from Dryden to Gray* (Chicago: University of Chicago Press, 1958), p. 256.

23. Samuel Johnson, *Lives of the English Poets*, ed. George Birkbeck Hill, 3 vols. (Oxford: Oxford University Press, 1905), III, 300.

24. Warton, *On the Genius and Writings of Pope*, I, 42.

25. Aikin, *Letters to a Young Lady on a Course of English Poetry* (London, 1804), p. 169.

26. Scott, *Critical Essays*, p. 338.

27. From an edition of *The Seasons* published by John Sharpe (1816), pp. ix–x; quoted by Alan Dugald McKillop, *The Background of Thomson's "Seasons"* (Minneapolis: University of Minnesota press, 1942), p. 6.

28. See John Arthos, *The Language of Natural Description in Eighteenth-Century Poetry* (Ann Arbor: University of Michigan Press, 1949); Raymond Dexter Havens, *The Influence of Milton on English Poetry* (Cambridge: Harvard University Press, 1922); David Nichol Smith, *Some Observations on Eighteenth Century Poetry*, 2nd. ed. (Toronto: University of Toronto Press, 1960).

29. Percival Stockdale, *Lectures on the Truly Eminent English Poets*, 2 vols. (London, 1807), II, 114–115.

30. Quoted in Havens, *Influence of Milton*, p. 587.
31. *Influence of Milton*, p. 136.
32. See Arthos, *Language of Natural Description*, pp. 393–396.
33. McKillop, *Background of Thomson's "Seasons,"* pp. 86–88.
34. See *Background of Thomson's "Seasons,"* pp. 60–61.
35. See Arthos, *Language of Natural Description*, pp. 130–131, for the scientific associations of *crystal*.
36. Perhaps the skill with which Thomson handles this hackneyed device of setting up questions simply to supply predetermined answers can best be demonstrated by contrast with his own practice in an instance where he handles it with notably less skill. Ever since Dr. Johnson confessed that he couldn't finish *Liberty*, the poem has been generally considered unreadable; it would be difficult to argue against this view. Part III contains a long speech by the Greeks composed entirely of rhetorical questions:

> Ye guardian gods of Greece! and are we free?
> Was it not madness deemed the very thought?
> And is it true? How did we purchase chains?
> At what a dire expense of kindred blood?
> And are they now dissolved? And scarce one drop
> For the fair first of blessings have we paid? . . .
> Lives there on earth, almost to Greece unknown,
> A people so magnanimous to quit
> Their native soil, traverse the stormy deep,
> And by their blood and treasure, spent for us,
> Redeem our states, our liberties, and laws!
> There does! there does! Oh Saviour Titus! Rome!
>
> (III, 301–306, 312–317)

So artificial a rhetorical device extended to these lengths is inadequate to express genuine feeling. The final answer is hardly more inappropriate than the questions that have preceded it. This passage is typical of *Liberty* in its reliance on abstractions. In contrast, the rhetoric of *The Seasons* is usually meaningful; it fulfills well-defined purposes and participates in making complex statements.

37. Galileo Galilei, *Dialogue on the Great World Systems*, in the Salusbury translation, abridged text edition, ed. Giorgio de Santillana (Chicago: University of Chicago Press, n. d.), p. 45.

Chapter Three. JAMES THOMSON: *The Retreat from Vision*

1. James Thomson, *The Castle of Indolence and Other Poems*, ed. McKillop (Lawrence, Kansas: University of Kansas Press, 1961), p. 21.
2. Morel, *James Thomson: Sa Vie et Ses Oeuvres* (Paris, 1895), p. 620.
3. *The Castle of Indolence*, ed. McKillop, p. 18.
4. Josephine Miles, *Wordsworth and the Vocabulary of Emotion* (Berkeley: University of California Press, 1942), p. 85.

Chapter Four. WILLIAM COLLINS: *The Controlling Image*

1. Letter of 27 December 1746, *Correspondence of Thomas Gray*, ed.

Paget Toynbee and Leonard Whibley, 3 vols. (Oxford: Oxford University Press, 1935), I, 261.

2. *The Poetical Works of William Collins*, with a prefatory essay by Mrs. Laetitia Barbauld (London, 1797), p. xlviii.

3. Marcel Delamare, "L'Originalité de Collins," *Revue Anglo-Américaine* IX (1932), 17.

4. Of course it can be — and has been — argued that the nature of poetry is the subject of all Collins's odes. (See A. D. McKillop, "The Romanticism of William Collins," *Studies in Philology*, XX (1923), 1–16; S. Musgrove, "The Theme of Collins's Odes," *Notes and Queries*, CLXXXV (1943), 214–217, 253–255.) Even by this view, however, the "Ode on the Poetical Character" is central, for it defines more explicitly than any other poem Collins's notion of poetic inspiration and possibility.

5. Woodhouse, "Collins and the Creative Imagination," *Studies in English by Members of University College, Toronto* (Toronto, 1931), pp. 59–130.

6. Norman Maclean, "From Action to Image: Theories of the Lyric in the Eighteenth Century," *Critics and Criticism, Ancient and Modern*, ed. R. S. Crane (Chicago: University of Chicago Press, 1952), pp. 408–460.

7. This view is exemplified by the quotation from Fénelon (above, p. 224, n. 22) beginning, "Ever since the Fall of ADAM, Men's Thoughts have been so low and grovelling that they are unattentive to moral Truths; and can scarce conceive any thing but what affects their Senses."

8. Warton, *An Essay on the Genius and Writings of Pope*, II (London, 1872), 222–223.

9. François de Salignac de la Mothe Fénelon, *Dialogues Concerning Eloquence*, tr. William Stevenson (London, 1722), p. 80.

10. Henry Home, Lord Kames, *Elements of Criticism*, 6th ed., 2 vols. (Edinburgh, 1785), II, 351. [First edition 1762.]

11. Edmund Burke, *A Philosophical Enquiry into the Origin of Our Ideas of the Sublime and Beautiful*, ed. J. T. Boulton (London: Routledge and Kegan Paul, 1958), p. 170.

12. *The Works of Oliver Goldsmith*, ed. Peter Cunningham, 4 vols. (London, 1854), IV, 277.

13. Barbauld, *Poetical Works of Collins*, p. xxiii.

14. A. S. P. Woodhouse argues (and some earlier critics share his view) that the "rich-hair'd Youth of Morn" is the sun, its "subject Life," "all the living things dependent on its rays" ("The Poetry of Collins Reconsidered," *From Sensibility to Romanticism*, ed. Frederick W. Hilles and Harold Bloom (New York: Oxford University Press, 1965), pp. 103–104.) The figure of Apollo, of course, merges the sun with the god of poetry; it is not incompatible with Professor Woodhouse's identification, but it seems richer.

15. Miles, *Renaissance, Eighteenth-Century, and Modern Language in English Poetry* (Berkeley: University of California Press, 1960), p. 8.

16. H. W. Garrod, *Collins* (Oxford: Oxford University Press, 1928), passim.

17. *The Poems of William Collins*, ed. Edmund Blunden (London: Frederick Etchells and Hugh MacDonald, 1929), p. 37.

18. William Hazlitt, *Lectures on the English Poets*, Chapter V, quoted by Garrod, *Collins*, p. 122.

19. Oliver Sigworth, *William Collins* (New York: Twayne Publishers, Inc., 1965), p. 102. The attribution of "vividness" to the description of Pity's temple seems unaccountable, since the only physical detail Collins offers is the temple's "southern site."

20. Woodhouse, "Poetry of Collins Reconsidered," p. 122.

21. John Locke, *An Essay Concerning Human Understanding*, ed. Alexander Campbell Fraser, 2 vols. (Oxford, 1894), I, 191.

22. *Spectator* #411 (21 June 1712); *The Spectator*, with introduction and notes by George A. Aitken, 8 vols. (London, 1898), VI, 72–73.

23. Wylie Sypher, "The *Morceau de Fantaisie* in Verse: A New Approach to Collins," *University of Toronto Quarterly* XV (1945), 69.

24. "Collins," *Lives of the English Poets*, ed. George Birkbeck Hill, 3 vols. (Oxford: Oxford University Press, 1905), II, 337.

25. Coleridge, *Biographia Literaria* (London: J. M. Dent & Sons Ltd., 1952), p. 147.

26. He also recognizes, however, that such "allegorical moral beings" as Collins characteristically describes are "inevitably more shadowy than personified natural detail," and that "Collins never clogs his visual passages with an excessive amount of sensuous and iconic detail." See Hagstrum, *The Sister Arts: The Tradition of Literary Pictorialism and English Poetry from Dryden to Gray* (Chicago: University of Chicago Press, 1958), pp. 272, 275–276.

27. Woodhouse, "Poetry of Collins Reconsidered," p. 123.

28. Preface to *Persian Eclogues, The Poems of Gray and Collins*, ed. Austin Lane Poole (London: Oxford University Press, 1961), p. 211.

Chapter Five. THOMAS GRAY: *Action and Image*

1. Coleridge, *Biographia Literaria*, 2 vols. (London, 1817), I, 20.

2. Letter to Mason, 9 November 1758, *Correspondence of Thomas Gray*, ed Paget Toynbee and Leonard Whibley, 3 vols. (Oxford: Oxford University Press, 1935), II, 593.

3. F. Doherty, "The Two Voices of Gray," *Essays in Criticism*, XIII (1963), 222–230.

4. A. R. Humphreys, "A Classical Education and Eighteenth-Century Poetry," *Scrutiny*, VIII (1939), 204.

5. P. F. Vernon, "The Structure of Gray's Early Poems," *Essays in Criticism*, XV (1965), 382.

6. Bertrand H. Bronson has commented on the similarity of the two descriptions, using it to support his interpretation that "the poet himself" is the subject of both the ode and the elegy. See "On A Special Decorum in Gray's Elegy," *From Sensibility to Romanticism*, ed. Frederick W. Hilles and Harold Bloom (New York: Oxford University Press, 1965), p. 175.

7. Lord David Cecil, "The Poetry of Thomas Gray," *Proceedings of the British Academy*, XXXI (1945), 51.

8. Geoffrey Tillotson, "More About Poetic Diction," *Augustan Studies* (London: The Athlone Press, 1961), p. 88. F. Doherty comments, "we

are being given an opposition between the 'poetic' presentation of morning and the personal, felt grief" ("The Two Voices of Gray," *Essays in Criticism,* XIII (1963), 227.)

9. Duncan C. Tovey, ed., *Gray and His Friends* (Cambridge, 1890), pp. 97–98. Another version of the text, with different, and less accurate, punctuation, is printed in William Mason's edition of *The Poems of Mr. Gray* (York, 1775). Both texts are taken from Gray's Common Place Books.

10. Mr. Doherty provides an interesting discussion of the language of this line in "The Two Voices of Gray," p. 229.

11. Sir Leslie Stephen, "Gray and His School," *Hours in a Library* (London, 1892), III, 118–119.

12. Johnson, "Gray," *Lives of the English Poets,* ed. George Birkbeck Hill, 3 vols. (Oxford: Oxford University Press, 1905), II, 435.

13. Warton, *An Essay on the Genius and Writings of Pope,* II (London, 1782), 42.

14. *Monthly Review,* XVII (1757); in *The Works of Oliver Goldsmith,* ed. Peter Cunningham, 4 vols. (London, 1854), IV, 317.

15. *Quarterly Review,* XCIV (1853), 1–48.

16. Johnson, *Lives of the Poets,* III, 440.

17. Roger Martin, *Essai sur Thomas Gray* (London and Paris: Oxford University Press and Les Presses Universitaires de France, 1934), p. 448.

18. 13 January 1758, *Correspondence,* II, 551.

19. 8 January 1759, *Correspondence,* II, 608.

20. Maclean, "From Action to Image: Theories of the Lyric in the Eighteenth Century," *Critics and Criticism, Ancient and Modern,* ed. R. S. Crane (Chicago: University of Chicago Press, 1952), p. 408.

21. "On Poetry, As Distinguished from Other Writing," *British Magazine,* 1761–1763; doubtfully attributed to Goldsmith and printed in his *Works,* III, 309–310.

22. Ian Jack, "Gray's Elegy Reconsidered," *From Sensibility to Romanticism,* p. 162.

23. Doherty, "The Two Voices of Gray," *e.g.* pp. 223–224.

24. 11 June 1757, *Correspondence,* II, 504.

25. Quoted by Martin, *Essai sur Gray,* p. 457.

26. George N. Shuster, *The English Ode from Milton to Keats* (New York: Columbia University Press, 1940), p. 211.

27. Hagstrum, *The Sister Arts: The Tradition of Literary Pictorialism and English Poetry from Dryden to Gray* (Chicago: University of Chicago Press, 1958), p. 302.

28. Martin, *Essai sur Gray,* p. 350.

29. Price, *To the Palace of Wisdom: Studies in Order and Energy from Dryden to Blake* (Garden City: Doubleday, 1964), p. 342.

30. The note was copied by Mason from Gray's pocket-book; it is printed in *The Poems of Gray and Collins,* ed. Austin Lane Poole (London: Oxford University Press, 1961), p. 142.

31. F. W. Bateson, *English Poetry: A Critical Introduction* (London: Longmans, Green, 1950), pp. 181–193.

32. Cleanth Brooks, "Gray's Storied Urn," *The Well-Wrought Urn:*

Studies in the Structure of Poetry (New York: Harcourt, Brace [A Harvest Book], n. d.), pp. 105–123. [First published 1947.]

33. Hagstrum, *The Sister Arts*, p. 301.

34. See Brooks, passim.

35. Brooks suggests that it becomes, "in association with Science, a kind of wisdom which allows him to see through the vanities which delude the Proud." (*Well-Wrought Urn*, p. 120.) Bertrand Bronson adds that this melancholy, equivalent to Milton's *"divinest* Melancholy," "is the coryphaea of Music, Philosophy, Melpomene, Divinity, and Wisdom." ("On A Special Decorum in Gray's Elegy," *From Sensibility to Romanticism*, p. 173.)

36. Frank Brady, "Gray's Elegy: Structure and Meaning," *From Sensibility to Romanticism*, p. 185.

Chapter Six. CHRISTOPHER SMART:
The Mystique of Vision (*I*)

1. *Jubilate Agno* B₁, 30. Throughout my discussion of Smart I have followed the line numbering and quoted from the edition of *Jubilate Agno* edited by W. H. Bond (Cambridge, Mass.: Harvard University Press, 1954).

2. Letter to Gray, 28 June 1763, *Correspondence of Thomas Gray*, ed. Paget Toynbee and Leonard Whibley, 3 vols. (Oxford: Oxford University Press, 1935), II, 802.

3. Letter written in July, 1763, quoted in Edward G. Ainsworth and Charles F. Noyes, *Christopher Smart, A Biographical and Critical Study*, University of Missouri Studies, XVIII, No. 4 (Columbia, Mo., 1943), 107.

4. Notice of *A Song to David*, *The Critical Review* XV (1763), 324.

5. Review of Robert Browning, *Parleyings with Certain People of Importance in Their Day*, *The Athenaeum* (Feb. 19, 1887), p. 248.

6. Review of *A Song to David*, *The Saturday Review*, LXXXI (1896), 606.

7. Gordon McKenzie, *Critical Responsiveness: A Study of the Psychological Current in Later Eighteenth-Century Criticism* (Berkeley: University of California Press, 1949), p. 7.

8. Robert Lowth, *Lectures on the Sacred Poetry of the Hebrews*, tr. G. Gregory, 2 vols. (London, 1787), I, 71.

9. Samuel H. Monk, *The Sublime: A Study of Critical Theories in XVIII-Century England* (Ann Arbor: University of Michigan Press, 1960), p. 14.

10. John Dennis, *The Advancement and Reformation of Modern Poetry* (London, 1701), p. 46.

11. #125 (17 June 1756); *The Connoisseur*, 3rd ed., 4 vols. (London, 1757), IV, 160.

12. Henry Home, Lord Kames, *Elements of Criticism*, 3 vols. (Edinburgh, 1762), II, 24.

13. Hugh Blair, *Lectures on Rhetoric and Belles Lettres*, 2 vols. (Dublin, 1783), I, 72.

14. Ibid., I, 364–365.

15. Laurence Binyon, *The Case of Christopher Smart*, English Association Pamphlet No. 90 (1934), p. 8.

16. See John Middleton Murry, "On the Madness of Christopher Smart," *Discoveries* (London: W. Collins Sons, 1924), pp. 183–184; Binyon, *The Case of Christopher Smart*, p. 6; Raymond D. Havens, "The Structure of Smart's *Song to David*," *Review of English Studies*, XIV (1938), 182.

17. Quoted by Ainsworth and Noyes, pp. 116–117.

18. "Il 'Canto a Davide' di Christopher Smart," *Studi Britannici* (Torino, 1931); quoted by Robert Brittain, ed., *Poems* by Christopher Smart (Princeton: Princeton University Press, 1950), p. 296.

19. Brittain edition, p. 300.

20. See *Jubilate Agno*, ed. Bond, footnotes pp. 30, 31.

21. One source for the identification was Patrick Delany, *An Historical Account of the Life and Reign of David, King of Israel*. See Robert E. Brittain, "Christopher Smart and Dr. Delany," *Times Literary Supplement* (March 7, 1936), p. 204.

22. Havens, "The Structure of Smart's *Song to David*," p. 178.

23. Cyril Falls, "Christopher Smart," *The Critic's Armoury* (London: Richard Cobden-Sanderson, 1924), p. 118.

24. K. A. McKenzie, *Christopher Smart, Sa Vie et Ses Oeuvres* (Paris: Les Presses Universitaires de France, 1925), p. 122.

25. Preface to Smart's translation of Horace, quoted by Binyon, p. 12.

26. Daniel Webb, *Remarks on the Beauties of Poetry* (London, 1762), p. 76.

27. Lowth, *Lectures on Sacred Poetry*, I, 111.

28. William Duff, *An Essay on Original Genius* (London, 1767), p. 147.

29. Owen Barfield, *Poetic Diction: A Study in Meaning* (London: Faber and Faber, 1952), p. 152.

Chapter Seven. CHRISTOPHER SMART:
The Mystique of Vision (II)

1. Arthur Sherbo, "The Dating and Order of the Fragments of Christopher Smart's *Jubilate Agno*," *Harvard Library Bulletin*, X (1956), 205.

2. William H. Bond, "Christopher Smart's *Jubilate Agno*," *Harvard Library Bulletin*, IV (1950), 46.

3. Donald Greene, "Smart, Berkeley, The Scientists and the Poets," *Journal of the History of Ideas*, XIV (1953), 351.

4. Ibid., p. 339.

5. Sherbo, "The Probable Time of Composition of Christopher Smart's *Song to David, Psalms*, and *Hymns and Spiritual Songs*," *JEGP*, LV (1956), 41–58.

6. K. A. McKenzie, *Christopher Smart, Sa Vie et Ses Oeuvres* (Paris: Les Presses Universitaires de France, 1925), p. 98.

7. Edward G. Ainsworth and Charles E. Noyes, *Christopher Smart, A Biographical and Critical Study*, University of Missouri Studies XVIII, No. 4 (1943), 110.

8. See Karina Williamson, "Christopher Smart's *Hymns and Spiritual Songs*," *Philological Quarterly*, XXXVIII (1959), 413.

9. Ibid., p. 424.

10. John Middleton Murry, "On the Madness of Christopher Smart," *Discoveries* (London: W. Collins Sons, 1924), p. 185.

Chapter Eight. WILLIAM COWPER: *The Heightened Perception*

1. Lodwick Hartley, "The Worm and the Thorn: A Study of Cowper's *Olney Hymns,"* The Journal of Religion, XXIX (1949), 224.

2. Kenneth MacLean, "William Cowper," *The Age of Johnson: Essays Presented to Chauncey Brewster Tinker* (New Haven: Yale University Press, 1949) p. 260.

3. Maurice Quinlan, "Cowper's Imagery," *JEGP*, XLVII (1948), 285.

4. See Quinlan, "Cowper's Imagery," pp. 276–285; Hartley, "The Worm and the Thorn," pp. 220–229.

5. Norman Nicholson, *William Cowper*, Writers and their Work No. 121 (London: Longmans, Green, 1960), p. 16.

6. Hugh Fausset, *William Cowper* (London: Jonathan Cape, 1928), p. 79.

7. Johnson, *Lives of the English Poets,* ed. George Birkbeck Hill, 3 vols. (Oxford: Oxford University Press, 1905), I, 45.

8. Ibid., I, 20.

9. Fausset, *William Cowper,* p. 35.

10. 27 November 1784; *The Correspondence of William Cowper,* ed. Thomas Wright, 4 vols. (London: Hodder and Stoughton, 1904), II, 272.

11. 10 October 1784; *Correspondence,* II, 251.

12. 17 December 1781; *Correspondence,* I, 411.

13. 19 March 1784; *Correspondence,* II, 176–177.

14. To the Rev. William Unwin, 17 January 1782; *Correspondence,* I, 430.

15. Donald Davie, "The Critical Principles of William Cowper," *The Cambridge Journal,* VII (1953), 182.

16. To the Rev. William Unwin, 20 October 1784; *Correspondence,* II 257.

17. To John Johnson, 28 February 1790; *Correspondence,* III, 439.

18. François de Salignac de la Mothe Fénelon, *Dialogues Concerning Eloquence,* tr. William Stevenson (London, 1722), p. 252.

19. Henry Home, Lord Kames, *Elements of Criticism,* 6th ed., 2 vols. (Edinburgh, 1785), II, 19.

20. Hugh Blair, *Lectures on Rhetoric and Belles Lettres,* 2 vols. (London, 1783), I, 185.

21. Ibid., I, 217–218.

22. No date [1784]; *Correspondence,* II, 287.

23. Daniel Webb, *Remarks on the Beauties of Poetry* (London, 1762), p. 56.

24. 10 October 1784; *Correspondence,* II, 252–253.

25. *Scene* is one of the nouns Josephine Miles finds occurring ten times in a hundred lines of *The Task.* The only other of Cowper's favorite nouns directly associated with visual perception is *eye.* More characteristic are abstract or generalized terms: *art, beauty, god, life, nature, world.* Cowper's typical verbs include both *see* and *seem.* His vocabulary, as statistically re-

corded, seems closer to Johnson's poetic vocabulary than to that of any of his other contemporaries. See Josephine Miles, *Renaissance, Eighteenth-Century, and Modern Language in English Poetry* (Berkeley: University of California Press, 1960), p. 23.

26. 30 October 1784; *Correspondence*, II, 258–259.

27. Davie, "The Critical Principles of William Cowper," p. 182.

28. James A. Roy, *Cowper and His Poetry* (London: George G. Harrap, [1914]), p. 84.

29. Leon Boucher, *William Cowper, Sa Correspondance et ses Poésies* (Paris, 1874), p. 186.

30. Walter Bagehot, "William Cowper," *Estimates of Some Englishmen and Scotchmen* (London, 1858), p. 89.

31. Hugh Fausset, *William Cowper*, p. 235.

32. *Monthly Review*, LXVII (October, 1782), 265; quoted in Maurice J. Quinlan, *William Cowper, A Critical Life* (Minneapolis: University of Minnesota Press, 1953), p. 117.

33. John Aikin, *Letters to a Young Lady on a Course of English Poetry* (London, 1804), p. 292.

34. W. P. Ker, *Form and Style in Poetry* (London: Macmillan, 1928), p. 170.

35. Thomas Quayle, *Poetic Diction* (London: Methuen, 1924), p. 49.

36. Coleridge, *Biographia Literaria; or Biographical Sketches of My Literary Life and Opinions*, 2 vols. (London, 1817), I, 22.

37. Warton, "Three Essays on Pastoral, Didactic, and Epic Poetry," in *The Works of Virgil*, 3rd ed., 4 vols. (London, 1778), I, 401. [First edition 1753.]

38. John Constable, *Reflections Upon Accuracy of Style*, 2nd ed. (London, 1738), p. 59. [First edition 1731.]

39. Blair, *Lectures on Rhetoric*, I, 390.

Chapter Nine. THE ACHIEVED IMAGE

1. The Twickenham Edition of *An Essay on Criticism* reminds the reader of the extent to which Thomas Hobbes, for example, identified *wit* and *fancy*, using *wit* early in his career to designate a faculty including both fancy and judgment, but later employing it as an apparent synonym for *fancy*. See Alexander Pope, *Pastoral Poetry and An Essay on Criticism*, ed. E. Audra and Aubrey Williams (New Haven: Yale University Press, 1961), p. 216.

2. Ibid., p. 218.

3. Merle E. Brown, "On William Collins' 'Ode to Evening,'" *Essays in Criticism*, XI (1961), 136–153.

4. Yvor Winters, *In Defense of Reason* (Denver: Alan Swallow, n. d.), pp. 450–451.

5. Donald Greene, "'Logical Structure' in Eighteenth-Century Poetry," *Philological Quarterly*, XXXI (1952), 315–336.

6. T. S. Eliot, "The Metaphysical Poets," *Selected Essays* (London: Faber and Faber, 1953), p. 287.

7. Greene, "'Logical Structure' in Eighteenth-Century Poetry," pp. 335–336.

Index

Abrams, Meyer, 5, 10; quoted 223 n. 13

Addison, Joseph, quoted 7-8, 13, 222 nn. 11-12

Aikin, John, quoted 14, 29-30

Ainsworth, Edward, and Charles Noyes, quoted 156

Akenside, Mark, 23, 25, 182; quoted 23

Andrews, Robert, quoted 6

Armstrong, Dr. John, 59

Arthos, John, 33

Auden, W. H., quoted 216

Bacon, Francis, quoted 222-223 n. 13

Bagehot, Walter, quoted 195

Barbauld, Laetitia, quoted 66, 69, 74

Barfield, Owen, quoted 139

Bateson, F. W., 115

Blair, Hugh, 135; quoted 5, 122-123, 175-176, 203, 221 n. 4

Blake, William, 140, 152

Blunden, Edmund, quoted 72

Bond, W. H., 140, 146; quoted 141

Boucher, Leon, quoted 195

Brady, Frank, quoted 116

Brittain, Robert, 124

Bronson, Bertrand, quoted 230 n. 35

Brooks, Cleanth, 115; quoted 230 n. 35

Brower, Reuben, quoted 21

Brown, Merle E., 211

Browning, Robert, 120

Burke, Edmund, 5, 30, 68; quoted 8

Cecil, Lord David, 95

Cleveland, John, quoted 171

Coleridge, Samuel Taylor, 11, 73, 90; quoted 10, 82, 200

Collins, William, 1, 12, 66-89, 208-212, 213, 215, 216; diction, 72-74; fancy and judgment, 208-212; importance of imagery in, 5, 66-71, 74, 76; interest in nature of poetry, 66-74, 118, 119; personifications in, 74, 83, 85-88, 131, 134; works: "The Manners," 87; quoted 87;

"Ode on the Poetical Character," 66-74, 76, 77, 81, 210-211; quoted 67, 69, 70, 72, 73, 74, 210; "Ode on the Popular Superstitions of the Highlands of Scotland," 78-82, 211-212; quoted 78, 79, 80, 81; "Ode to Evening," 87, 211, 212, 215; "Ode to Fear," 74, 75-78, 80, 209-210, 211, 212; quoted 75, 76, 77, 86, 209; "Ode to a Lady on the Death of Colonel Ross," 87-88; quoted 88; "Ode to Peace," 87; "Ode to Pity," 74-75, 208; quoted 74, 208; "Ode to Simplicity," 87, 108, 210; quoted 87, 210; "Ode, Written in the Beginning of the Year 1746," 87-88, 211, 212; quoted 88; "The Passions," 212; *Persian Eclogues*, 84-86; quoted 84, 85; "Verses to Sir Thomas Hanmer," 83; "When Phoebe form'd a wanton smile," 83-84; quoted 83-84

Constable, John, quoted 203

Cowper, William, 1, 2-4, 12, 118, 165-206, 215, 216, 217; attitude toward art, 189-190; attitude toward civilization, 183-185, 186; attitude toward nature, 179-183, 186, 188-190, 192-194, 204-206; belief in didactic function of poetry, 173-174; diction, 195-206; interest in technique, 174-176; relation of faith and perception for, 173, 205-206; works: "The Castaway," 12; letters, quoted 173, 174-175, 176, 177, 185; *Memoir*, 193-194; *Olney Hymns*, 165-173, 202; quoted 166, 167-168, 170, 171, 172; "Table-Talk," 173-174; quoted 174, 176, 177; *The Task*, 1, 2, 3, 177, 178-206, 216

Davie, Donald, 90; quoted 175, 194

Delamare, Marcel, quoted 66

Dennis, John, 207; quoted 122

Doherty, F., 90, 91, 95, 104, 108; quoted 101

Index

Donne, John, 171, 215, 216, 217
Duff, William, 10; quoted 8, 136, 223 n. 18

Eliot, T. S., quoted 215

Fausset, Hugh, quoted 170, 173
Fénelon, François de Salignac, quoted 9–10, 14, 68, 175, 224 n. 22

Galilei, Galileo, quoted 38
Garrod, H. W., 72
Goldsmith, Oliver, quoted 68, 104
Gray, Thomas, 1, 9, 12, 71, 81, 90–118, 119, 213, 215, 216, 217; antithesis and conflict in, 110–113, 114–118; diction, 90–91, 150; importance of syntax in, 106–108, 110, 112; opposing patterns of artifice in, 91–103; personifications in, 100–101, 105, 109–110, 113, 131; works: "The Bard," 110–112; quoted 110–111; "Elegy Written in a Country Church-Yard," 103, 105, 115–117, 118; quoted 92, 97, 116; "The Fatal Sisters," 113; letters, quoted 66, 104, 111; "Ode for Music," quoted 113; "Ode on a Distant Prospect of Eton College," 91, 98–103, 117, 118; quoted 99, 109; "Ode on the Pleasures Arising from Vicissitude," quoted 114; "Ode on the Spring," 91–95, 97, 101, 117, 118; quoted 93; "On Lord Holland's Seat," 117; "Progress of Poesy," 103–110, 114; quoted 103, 106, 107, 109, 110; "Sketch of his Own Character," quoted 117; "Sonnet on the Death of Richard West," 91, 95–98, 101, 117, 118; quoted 96; "The Triumphs of Owen," quoted 112
Greene, Donald, 214–215, 216; quoted 143

Hagstrum, Jean, 83; quoted 25, 112, 115, 228 n. 26
Hartley, Lodwick, quoted 165
Havens, R. D., 128; quoted 32
Hazlitt, William, quoted 72
Hobbes, Thomas, quoted 11
Holmes, John, quoted 15
Home, Douglas, 78, 79
Horace, 129
Humphreys, A. R., 90; quoted 91

Hurd, Richard, quoted 5

Jack, Ian, quoted 105
Johnson, Joseph, 176
Johnson, Samuel, 11, 58; works: *Dictionary*, 1; quoted 2, 17, 18; *Lives of Poets*, quoted 29, 82, 98, 104, 171; "Vanity of Human Wishes," quoted 102

Kames, Henry Home, Lord, quoted 68, 122, 175
Keats, John, 152
Kilmer, Joyce, 1

Leavis, F. R., 90
Lloyd, Robert, quoted 122
Locke, John, 2, 6, 7, 189–190; quoted 6, 7, 77, 221 n. 8
Lowth, Bishop Robert, 10, 136; quoted 121, 135, 223–224 n. 19
Lyttelton, George, Lord, 50

Maclean, Norman, 67, 104; quoted 105
Martin, Roger, quoted 104, 113–114
Mason, William, 104; quoted 120
McKenzie, Gordon, quoted 121
McKenzie, K. A., quoted 156
McKillop, A. D., 33, 52, 54, 62; quoted 46, 48
MacLean, Kenneth, quoted 165
Miles, Josephine, 19, 71; quoted 54
Milton, John, quoted 31–32, 53; and Collins, 69, 73, 211; and Cowper, 196; and Gray, 90, 105, 107, 116; and Thomson, 31–34, 45, 52–53
Morel, Léon, quoted 22, 46
Murry, John Middleton, quoted 161

Newton, John, 173, 174, 185
Nicholson, Norman, quoted 169
Noyes, Charles, and Edward Ainsworth, quoted 156

Olivero, Federico, 125; quoted 124

Pindar, 72, 104, 105, 107
Pinkerton, John, quoted 15
Pope, Alexander, 11, 49, 90, 110, 132, 156, 189, 207–208, 210, 216; quoted 37, 207
Pound, Ezra, 11; quoted 9
Price, Martin, quoted 17, 114
Puttenham, George, quoted 222 n. 13

Index